Action for the '80s:

A Political, Professional, and Public Program for Foreign Language Education

Edited by June K. Phillips

In conjunction with the American Council on the Teaching of Foreign Languages

NATIONAL TEXTBOOK COMPANY • Lincolnwood, Illinois U.S.A.

1985 Printing

Contents

Foreword

It has been the pleasure of this editor to have participated in the last four volumes of the ACTFL Foreign Language Education Series. Many unsung people, particularly those at ACTFL headquarters, at National Textbook Company, and the many outside readers who were willing to take the time to evaluate manuscripts, have contributed to each volume. The Advisory Committee for this volume deserves mention for its participation in thematic and author choices. Members were Jack Darcey, Dorothy Huss, Dale Lange, Cathy Linder, Synn Sandstedt, Renate Schulz, Harry Tuttle, and Ed Scebold. A special thanks to Peter A. Eddy, Center for Applied Linguistics, for his service to the authors and the editor.

Introduction

Action or inaction: An editorial opinion

June K. Phillips
Indiana University of Pennsylvania

Those moments in the history of a profession when it is ready for growth and change occur rarely. This decade marks such a time. Yet it was not so very long ago, during the post-Sputnik era, that attention was lavished on mathematics, science, and foreign language. That time was glorious while it lasted, and our discipline benefited from new programs, materials, inservice grants, language laboratories, administrative and public support, and money. Enrollments grew, curriculum expanded into elementary and junior high schools, faculty were hired. But by the end of the decade, both the interest that had been generated and the enrollments that had increased plummeted.

Amazingly enough, another chance to attract some attention has come. This time, a new decade begins with the burst of interest that has accompanied the existence of a President's Commission on Foreign Language and International Studies and the issuing of its report, *Strength Through Wisdom*. The recommendations of this group have been studied, criticized, quoted; they have even provided the impetus for some follow-up in professional and governmental circles. But what about the lessons of history? If the 1980s are to have a more lasting effect than the 1960s did, some fundamental differences in the means and ends of proposed change must be assured. It will take a coalition of classroom teachers, supervisory personnel, teacher trainers, researchers, and the

June K. Phillips (Ph.D., The Ohio State University) is Professor of Foreign Languages at Indiana University of Pennsylvania where she teaches French, ESL, methods, and supervises student teachers. She has taught on the secondary level, has conducted individualized classes, has developed materials, and has given numerous workshops for teacher inservice programs. She has written *Petits contes sympathiques* and *Contes sympathiques* and her articles have appeared in *Foreign Language Annals* and the ACTFL Foreign Language Education Series, for which she has served as editor for volumes 9 through 12. She was the recipient of the IUP Distinguished Faculty Award for Research for 1979-1980. She is currently on the Board of Directors of the Northeast Conference on the Teaching of Foreign Languages and the Executive Council of the Pennsylvania State Modern Language Association; affiliations include ACTFL, PSMLA, APSCUF, AFT, AAUP, and the CCCC of the NCTE.

1

elected and appointed professional leadership to turn promises into reality. The last time around, programs collapsed of their own weight when outside support was withdrawn, or they expired of the inflexible structure of a prescribed methodology as new research, new students, and new goals arrived. Successful revitalization demands that an understanding of the decision-making process and a commitment to continuing professional growth be primary and that a particular method or technique be investigated and seen as temporary—good until something better is found.

An Individual Choice: To Act or Not to Act

Testimony at the commission hearings has been given, and the evidence weighed. "Talk" about global education, language study for all students, public awareness, professional cooperation, government and legislative support has generated volumes of prose. Unless we get beyond the talking stage and act, all the groundwork that has been laid is for naught. And the choice for action or inaction belongs not to the politicians, the public, or the administrators; it is a professional choice, the responsibility of individual language teachers. The literature on educational change supports the idea that effective change requires teacher participation at all stages, from planning through implementation. Neither governmental mandates nor public pressure can have the effect in the classroom (and therefore in the profession) that the teacher can. Outside support is needed, of course, but teachers involved with students in a compatible foreign language experience hold the power to affect, for the better, the course of language instruction in the next decades.

The authors of this volume of the ACTFL Foreign Language Education Series have taken an action-oriented approach to their topics. The information reported provides not only a theoretical background where warranted, but also proposes concrete steps to be taken in the political, public, and professional arenas. Our individual commitment on each of these levels is essential; while we may feel more comfortable in one, action for the eighties requires that we take some tentative steps into each.

After having read the chapters, the foreign language teacher should be ready to translate words into deeds. One example of active participation might be to draw up a personal list of resolutions for the year and for the decade ahead. (Perhaps the first resolution would be to do better than most of us do with our annual New Year's list.) An agenda for individual action drawn from the contents of this volume might be as follows:

Politically, as a foreign language educator, I resolve to
- study the candidates at all levels vis-a-vis their positions on educational, international, and foreign-language-related issues.
- develop a correspondence with my legislative representatives, both state and federal.

- respond to ACTFL Alert Network and the political arms of other educational organizations when they request action on specific issues.
- invite a local politician to observe a foreign language program in my school.
- attend political meetings and raise the bilingual, English-as-a-second-language and foreign language issues.
- keep a resource file of articles dealing with foreign language events and programs; be ready to use these articles when language concerns are voiced in local or state forums.

If each foreign language teacher were to participate in some part of the political process, the collective involvement would be massive and consequently influential. Although we may never be a multilingual majority, we need not remain a silent minority.

Publicly, as a foreign language educator, I resolve to
- work with colleagues to set up a public relations agenda for the school district or institution.
- plan a public awareness campaign through systematic faculty and administrative contacts.
- report to local media on people and events with a foreign language news value.
- work on a foreign language program to take to civic groups.
- look at the activities of community groups in order to identify ways that they might contribute to the foreign language program.
- plan early for Foreign Language Week with students, faculty, and parents.

In the public relations realm, a team approach is most effective and that team should include teachers from other disciplines, administrators, students, and parents.

Professionally, as a foreign language educator, I resolve to
- study at least one new curricular option to see how it works, how it might be adapted or adopted in my situation (e.g., global education, immersion, communicative competency, career programs).
- evaluate text/materials and adapt those judged to be weak so that they meet established goals and needs (e.g., more communicative exercises and tests; stronger cultural component).
- make at least one interdisciplinary contact and develop it into a mini-unit.
- read at least two journal articles per month to keep abreast of new ideas, trends, research.
- dig into the research on a selected topic and use it to evaluate what I am doing in the classroom.
- experiment with at least one "new" procedure, adapt and revise it, evaluate it, decide how it fits into my program.
- join and be active in local, state, regional, and national foreign language organizations. (Dividing the cost into a cents-per-week figure shows such memberships to be relatively inexpensive.)

- attend and participate in regional inservice programs as well as state and national meetings.
- set up a round table with peers in which problems, materials, and success stories can be shared.

Particularly on the professional level, there is no excuse for inaction. Averting boredom and burn-out is partially within our control. We do have a great deal of freedom behind the classroom door; there are multiple ways of reaching, via variable content and approach, those goals that may be imposed. Even rigid objectives, such as "being able to use the present subjunctive," are amenable to using content outside the text (e.g. locating examples of *wishes* in magazine interviews, expressing personal fears and uncertainties) and to alternative approaches (e.g., communicative, affective, functional/notional). If we fail to live up to professional responsibilities, all efforts to garner legislative and community support are futile. We have been guilty of false advertising in the past, and if we are not careful we shall be so again. Some priorities include

- talk about global education *vs.* teaching of linguistic form and encyclopedic culture.
- promise of communication skills *vs.* teaching and testing of grammar.
- definition of grammar as a tool, a means to an end *vs.* discrete point tests of rules out of context.
- rationales based on crosscultural understanding *vs.* materials that perpetuate stereotypes.
- encouraging students to try above all to communicate *vs.* correcting in red pen linguistic detail that does not impede communication.
- inviting all students to take a foreign language *vs.* failing those who do not meet the academic standards of the minority we have traditionally served.
- claiming to teach four skills and culture *vs.* tests and texts that require almost exclusively written, and some spoken, responses.

Finally, it is our task to practice what we have been preaching and what we have professed to the President's Commission. Similarly, the authors of this volume provide knowledge and suggestions for action; it is for us to perform and to implement.

In the first chapter, the ACTFL staff reports on the aftermath of the President's Commission recommendations. The staff has put a communications network in place, made overtures to the private sector, and initiated professional discussion.

Vicki Galloway offers a comprehensive look at public relations and emphasizes the need for an overall plan. She then proposes step-by-step procedures for reaching various people within and outside the schools.

Becky Owens initiates us into the world of politics and lobbies. She shows how legislation is enacted and what our individual roles in that process are. A description of the newly established Washington Liaison Office is given by Johanna Mendelson, the new director of this JNCL endeavor.

Norman Abramowitz and Henry Ferguson explore the interdisciplinary cooperation, present and projected, engendered by the foreign language/ international education connection that resulted from the President's Commission purview. They also specify avenues for continued cooperation among various segments of the educational establishment.

Gail Guntermann calls for the setting of realistic, achievable outcomes for the various levels of foreign language programs. After reviewing the purposes of language learning in terms of recent developments, she describes a group of outcomes in the areas of skills and culture that can be used as a basis for experiment and evaluation.

Lorraine Strasheim focuses on the middle school curriculum as a good place to implement global education in the foreign language program. Materials are sampled so that the teacher can begin to broaden the audience and scope of the foreign language course.

Dorothy Goodman and Glynis Scott describe the Washington International School. It is important that all foreign language people become knowledgeable about this kind of school, recommended by the President's Commission and designed to produce proficient foreign language students and international baccalaureates.

Charles Hancock analyzes both competency-based and humanistic models for teacher education. He then makes a proposal for a model that incorporates the aspects of all designs that meet the needs of individual preservice students.

H. H. Stern and James Cummins survey the current state of research in language acquisition and language learning and synthesize it into some models of the process. Problems are identified and directions for future research are proposed. Most important, results and implications from the extensive Canadian programs are made accessible to educators in the United States.

Wayne Martin informs the foreign language audience about the role National Assessment plays in many other subject areas. As we enter the 1980s, the data resulting from such an evaluation should serve the profession well in defining goals and determining levels of proficiency achieved.

Realistic resolve followed by resolute action will equip us with the knowledge and flexibility to meet the challenges of the future. Language learning is bound to become increasingly important on this globe; consequently language teaching will not cease to exist, even though its form may change drastically. Professional and personal responsibility should propel us to absorb the technological and psychological discoveries in second-language learning and teaching so that we thrive on "future shock" and are not defeated by it. An illustration of the role we play in foreign language instruction is given by Carl Sagan, the popular scientist, in his book, *The Dragons of Eden: Speculations on the Evolution of Human Intelligence* (NY: Ballantine Books [Random House], 1978, p. 222.):

It by no means follows that computers will in the immediate future exhibit human creativity, subtlety, sensitivity or wisdom. A classic and probably apocryphal illustration is in the field of machine translation of human languages; a language—say, English—is input and the text is output in another language—say, Chinese. After the completion of an advanced translation program. . . a U.S. senator was proudly taken through a demonstration of the computer system. The senator was asked to produce an English phrase for translation and promptly suggested, "Out of sight, out of mind." The machine dutifully whirred and winked and generated a piece of paper on which were printed a few Chinese characters. But the senator could not read Chinese. So, to complete the test, the program was run in reverse, the Chinese characters input and the English phrase output. The visitors crowded around the new piece of paper, which to their initial puzzlement read: "Invisible idiot."

ACTFL's 1980 agenda: Intention to action

C. Edward Scebold, Sandra B. Hammond,
Dorothy V. Huss, and Cathy Linder
ACTFL Staff

Preparing this overview of developments in language education made us uneasy, our uneasiness growing from the realization that, despite great changes in the field, much remains the same. In fact, our ability as professionals to deal with problems is diminished both by greater knowledge of the problems and by the myriad ways in which we seek to solve them. *The New York Times* of

C. Edward Scebold (M.A., University of Nebraska) is Executive Director of the American Council on the Teaching of Foreign Languages (ACTFL). Prior to taking this position, he taught Spanish on the junior high school level. He has also served as Consultant in Foreign Languages in the Nebraska State Department of Education. His professional affiliations include AATF, AATSP, the New York State Association of Foreign Language Teachers, and the Association for Supervision and Curriculum Development.

Sandra B. Hammond (M.A., University of Louisville) is a project coordinator at ACTFL for the Survey of Successful Secondary School Foreign Language Programs and of the current fundraising project in which ACTFL is engaged. She also is the project director for the Survey of Foreign Language Enrollments in Public Secondary Schools, Fall 1978, an evaluation of the status of foreign language enrollments in the country. She has coauthored the sourcebook, *Prescriptions for Success*, a critical survey of fifty successful language programs around the country, and has written the statistical report, *Survey of Foreign Language Enrollments in the Public Secondary Schools, Fall 1978*.

Dorothy V. Huss (M.A., University of Maryland) is Assistant Director of ACTFL. She has taught French at the elementary, secondary, and university levels. She has also held positions with the Office of Bilingual Education, U.S. Office of Education, and Global Perspectives in Education, Inc. Currently she is coordinating ACTFL's legislative program and directing the operation of the Alert Network.

Cathy Linder (M.S., Queens College) is editor of *Foreign Language Annals*. Her articles have appeared in the Northeast Conference *Reports* and the ACTFL *Foreign Language Education Series*. She is editor and coauthor of the handbook *Oral Communication Testing* and has contributed ancillary materials to the *Spanish for Mastery* textbooks, authored by Rebecca and Jean-Paul Valette. She has given workshops on testing and has served as cochairperson of the AATF Testing Commission. Her professional affiliations include ACTFL, AATF, and NYSAFLT.

July 15, 1980, carried a column by Fred M. Hechinger titled "About Education" in which he announces, "poll shows teachers dissatisfied."

This article, coupled with our awareness of what many teachers must experience during inservice workshops, raised a sensitive issue. Hechinger comments: "Teachers are unhappy about the old-style programs in which their bosses brought in some big name expert who gave his 'solutions' to their problems and then went on his way.

"Teachers don't want theory; they want training that will pay off in the classroom. Most of all, they do not want remedies imposed by colleges, often the very ones which failed to give them practical preparation for their jobs in the first place.

"Long-term educational observers know that teachers in the past three decades have been buffeted by constantly changing ideological whims. In the 1950s, school reformers created programs which they arrogantly called 'teacher-proof,' meaning that they would work even with the most mediocre teachers.

"In the rebellious 1960s, neo-progressives 'invented' devices such as the open classroom and child-dominated schools, where each pupil presumably proceeded at his or her own pace, with individual guidance from the teacher. Principals, eager to be 'with it,' often imposed the new methods on teachers whether or not they were capable of, or willing to, function under the new rules."

As the message of the article began to sink in, so did the realization that our perception of what foreign language educators need has been significantly shaken and altered during the recent months. It has become increasingly obvious that the "answers" often failed to address the questions.

It is obvious that teachers need support and assistance rather than another methodology or gimmick that will demand the development of new curricula. It is obvious that our concern must be the classroom rather than broad national programs that fail to touch individuals, students, schools, and communities.

Since the creation of the President's Commission on Foreign Language and International Studies, a renewed sense of urgency and optimism has surged through those who are immersed in language eduation, both in the classroom and in supportive areas. ACTFL, as a national association concerned with the future for the language-teaching profession, has initiated a number of new projects, several of which relate directly to the Commission or have resulted from discussions and work that took place during the Commission's period of activity.

Our profession is moving again. Equally important, there is a significant difference in the direction in which we are going. There is far greater emphasis on finding ways to support and to work more closely with individual teachers, helping them build their programs and assisting them with the crucial task of mobilizing the support of school and community leaders who determine the fate of their programs. Although ACTFL's projects and activities have always been fully discussed and debated, in the past intuition guided us more often than did design.

It is time to formalize a plan for the profession. First, we have the momentum that has resulted from the combination of international and national events. The message of the President's Commission report, *Strength Through Wisdom,* has been repeatedly reinforced as the media reveal almost hourly new crises in the political and economic arena. Second, there is evidence that the other language-related associations have neither the vision, the energy, nor the tenacity required to mobilize. The work must therefore be undertaken by those who are developing some sense of what the future might be. More important, perhaps we have identified ACTFL's proper role: that of an organization that should bridge the gap between professions and foster interdisciplinary connections. In initiating these activities, there is no threat to other organizations; on the contrary, the potential exists for reducing factionalism and focusing our collective energies on strengthening the impact foreign language and international studies might have on the lives and attitudes of Americans.

ACTFL has an agenda for the year 1980—and it is developing an agenda for the entire decade. In preparing for the coming decade, the ACTFL leadership—the officers, Executive Council, and staff—have concentrated on specific projects that have been identified as urgent. Dale L. Lange's first "Message from the President" appeared in the February, 1980, issue of *Foreign Language Annals.* He stated: "For 1980, two major priorities have already been determined: the establishment of a Washington Liaison Office and development of an Alert Network." Within three months both objectives were accomplished: the office was functioning and the new Alert Network had been tested for the first time. During the February meeting of the ACTFL Executive Council, a third priority was added: to find new projects and to reduce, if not eliminate, ACTFL's debt to itself through membership recruitment and corporate fund-raising. Five months later, $8,000 had been raised through corporate contributions from two corporate sponsors of ACTFL, and several proposals had been submitted to major foundations. Two proposals had tentative approval for funding to begin in the fall of 1980. A special membership recruitment program was piloted; it produced more than 600 membership renewals and new members. The second phase of the recruitment effort began in September, 1980. ACTFL is now preparing a proposal for a major public policy project, which aims to promote public recognition of the relationship between language and society, to identify issues that relate to the design of curricula to meet society's needs, and to establish a task force for designing and developing responsive programs at all levels of education.

In an attempt to consolidate information and opinions and formulate a cohesive statement of policy for the 1980s, a National Conference on Professional Priorities was planned for November of 1980 and participants were invited to write position papers on research, curriculum, materials, global education and foreign languages, teacher preparation and inservice education, and professional unity. These position papers were presented for additional reaction and refinement during the ACTFL/AATG Joint Annual Meeting in Boston in November, 1980. The final product is a combined statement of the needs and priorities in each of these areas.

For evidence of the movement from intention to action, let us look at the progress of some of the items on ACTFL's agenda for the 1980s.

ACTFL Alert Network

To acquire constituents in preparation for anticipated legislative initiatives, ACTFL organized an Alert Network for the language profession in January, 1980. Three levels of this Network are currently in place, with key individuals responsible for directing communications with regional, state, and local units; organization by congressional district is under way. Efforts are being made to bring members of the business community and local government officials, as well as educators involved in international studies, into what is essentially a network of language professionals. The Alert network enjoyed some early successes:

- The Alert Network was activated in early February. Twelve telephone calls from the central office to regional coordinators resulted, within ten days, in over eight hundred letters to Congressman Paul Simon.
- The Alert Network enthusiastically supported Congressman Panetta's Foreign Language and International Studies Incentive Act, which proposes to provide funds to students in institutions of higher education who broaden their program of studies to include foreign language and international studies.
- Strong positions were taken by the Network on the placing of foreign language programs within the new Department of Education and toward increasing appropriations for international education within that department. ACTFL is pleased with the position of international education in the new department and with those chosen as Assistant Secretary and Deputy Assistant Secretary for this area.
- The outlook for fiscal 1981 appropriations is optimistic.

The political arena can also introduce us to rewarding contacts from other areas. With those who exercise leadership in their own communities and districts, we can cooperatively make needed change and innovation in both curriculum and in public awareness.

The effectiveness of the Network as a disseminator of information must not be underestimated. Many sources have stressed that ACTFL is the only existing communications system for organizing grass-roots support for foreign language/international studies initiatives. Information is reaching interested constituents through this network: for example, practical information on Foreign Language Week activities and ways to launch a foreign language public awareness campaign within local schools or communities has been provided.

As the Network reaches out and grows, a constituency in favor of foreign language/international studies is taking shape, and ACTFL's role and impact are increasing. Foreign language education is developing links with the real world. No longer a passive member of the academic community, it has an active voice in all the national and international issues that warrant its expertise. The language community must forge a position on refugee policy, bilingual education, and mental health—all areas deliberately avoided in the past. The foreign language community is and should be involved in the current political, economic, diplomatic, and defense issues.

Business contacts solicited and fostered through the Network at both the national and grass-roots levels can be of assistance in myriad ways, including soliciting legislative support, promoting foreign language/international studies within the business community and the community at large (and so contributing to our national public awareness), providing direct funding for projects related to foreign language/international studies, and leading us to other sources of funding for projects.

Fund-raising project

In order to finance new initiatives, support current ACTFL activities, and eliminate the association's debt, a fund-raising project has been designed with the assistance of a consulting firm. The Corporate Associate program is soliciting corporate sponsors who are willing to be of continuing assistance in funding ACTFL operational expenses. Numerous proposals requesting support for specific projects related to ACTFL priorities are being submitted to major foundations.

To date, two corporations have agreed to become corporate sponsors of ACTFL: Harcourt Brace Jovanovich, Inc. and National Textbook Company. The basic intent of soliciting business involvement is to lend support to foreign language education and to assist the association with its projects.

Among the proposals submitted to foundations are one for general support and another for assistance in operating and expanding the ACTFL Alert Network.

As a result of the fund-raising project, we have uncovered numerous allies in the corporate world. This forced us to examine the potential for broadening the Alert Network to include those outside education who are supportive of our concerns. Media promotion of foreign language and international studies was an appealing possiblity, but the question of cost-effectiveness and longevity had to be examined. The long-term exposure and promotion needed is not affordable, and we will not quickly or easily find sponsors to underwrite such campaigns. Furthermore, it is not likely that promotion of this type will have any lasting effect on public attitudes.

Up to this point we have failed to take advantage of the natural alliances that exist in each of our communities: the ethnic groups, the multilingual and multicultural citizens who support much of what we consider important.

The work we have undertaken in encouraging business and community involvement has resulted in a proposal design (and search for appropriate funding) for a project that would focus on how the foreign language teaching profession can more successfully interrelate language education and other major issues: immigration and refugee policy, bilingual education, health care, and geriatrics. The more closely we examine these issues, the more convinced we are that language is a central factor in our ability—or inability—to provide for the welfare and needs of our citizens. The issues are inseparable, and particularly so as America becomes even more pluralistic and as languages such as Spanish and various Asian tongues become increasingly dominant at all levels of business, educational, and political life.

The proposed project is a three-year program that would survey, in specific geographic areas, the business community, government employees, uniformed workers, and other segments of the work force to determine precisely their practical need for knowledge of foreign languages. Information gathered through this survey would be used within the target community to develop educational programs.

A project of this type must be long-range; no attempt to assess public attitudes, to discuss educational issues as they relate to concerns of society, and to reshape curricula to conform to reality can be accomplished quickly. But such interrelationships must be realized if we hope to have lasting impact.

Our continuing exploration and development

The response from foreign language educators has been gratifying. Those participating in the Alert Network have found it to be a mechanism for receiving as well as giving information. We are all working together toward a set of common objectives, and communication is more open.

Any attempt by ACTFL to articulate objectives and priorities for professional activities must increasingly emphasize practicality and relevance to the classroom teacher. We can no longer afford to talk past one another. We can no longer afford to complain about one another's failures. The time has come to plan for the future, using the lessons of the past.

This does not imply complacency or a sanguine attitude about the past decade. The facts remain: less than 20 percent of the total secondary school population is studying *any* foreign language at a given time. Attrition rates continue to be unacceptably high after the first year of language study.

The needs of society in the 1980s demand that foreign language educators design curricula that include the 80 percent of students in our public secondary schools who are not studying languages. This need not threaten current programs or teachers. Developing proficiency in a second language is a clearly defensible goal for students at all levels of education as is their acquisition of cultural insights and an international perspective. At present, not all students are interested in language proficiency per se, nor do they see the desirability and practicality of the study of literature, whether in English or in a foreign language. However, these same students must be able to function and to communicate effectively in today's world. Knowledge and understanding of global relationships plays an increasingly important role in the lives of all Americans; and second languages, cultures, and international studies are essential to this knowledge and understanding. So organizations such as ACTFL must work with teachers, teacher educators, and administrators in designing programs intended not to supplant or replace existing ones but rather to address the full range of student needs.

Since ACTFL has launched the fund-raising project, solicited support for legislative initiatives, and established connections outside foreign language education, the response of those who have been contacted has been both surprising and encouraging. Many other concerned individuals and groups have not yet been approached. The lesson learned: Moral, physical, and financial support are available if we ask. Many care about quality education and will be supportive if they understand that their participation is wanted and needed.

We must continue to explore ways to relate language education to the pressing issues of society in the 1980s. Many U.S. citizens are unable to find proper health and psychiatric care due to a lack of trained personnel who can communicate with them and understand their problems. Refugee policy is inextricably connected with concerns about language and culture. But more important, the political and economic role of the United States in the world increasingly depends on a citizenry that is both aware and able to deal effectively with complex international issues.

In the past, these significant issues have only infrequently found their way into the discussions of our professional concerns and priorities. Yet it is obvious that language educators must begin to attack these problems and search, with our colleagues, for solutions befitting the humanistic claims that we make for our discipline. To do otherwise is to perpetuate an unacceptable status quo.

2

Public relations: Making an impact

Vicki B. Galloway

South Carolina State Department of Education

The foreign language teacher reading books on salesmanship casts an accurate reflection of the times. Words such as *publicity, promotion, advertising,* and *public relations* now flow as freely within the foreign language profession as they have for years in business circles. Marketing foreign languages as products has become a national priority.

In its final report of recommendations to the president, the President's Commission on Foreign Language and International Studies expressed an urgent need: to inform the American public of the role that other languages and cultures play in their lives. Consequently, the Commission has charged the national professional societies engaged in the teaching of foreign languages with mounting a vigorous campaign to educate the nation to the critical need to learn other languages and customs.

Just where does the job of educating the public start? Who is responsible for this enormous task? The answer to both questions is the individual foreign language teacher. National success in winning public acceptance of foreign language education will depend in large measure on the combined efforts of teachers at the local levels. It is there that national opinions are born.

Vicki B. Galloway (Ph.D., University of South Carolina) is a State Consultant on Modern Foreign Languages for the South Carolina State Department of Education. She has taught languages at secondary and university levels, coordinated first- and second-year Spanish courses at the university level, conducted summer workshops for language teachers, developed career exploration units, classroom activity guides, secondary course guidelines, and teaching materials for middle school, secondary, and university levels. She holds certification as a secondary teacher of Spanish and French and as a secondary principal. She has published in *The Modern Language Journal.* Her professional affiliations include ACTFL, AATSP, NCSSFL, ASCD.

This chapter will deal with the grass-roots public relations campaign, first in terms of program planning to bridge the gap between where we are and where we want to be; and second in terms of the means by which these efforts may be directed toward specific audiences, both internally (within the educational system) and externally (to other groups). It is based on the premise that effective public relations begins at home.

Public relations: Who needs it?

Ted Schwarz (36) tells the story of Fenster Freebush who built a better mousetrap. It came in three finishes and seventeen decorator colors and could lure a mouse hiding anywhere within a five-mile radius. It played stereo music and when it was not otherwise occupied, could be used as a combination beer cooler and fondue pot for parties. Freebush had 1,000 of these units constructed and then waited for the world to beat a path to his door. Nobody came.

Freebush had a unique product, but he probably learned his sales techniques from the foreign language profession. Our business boasts of a product that will broaden horizons, heighten cultural awareness, promote international understanding and sensitivity, sharpen perceptions of the world, develop mental discipline, and establish harmony and world peace. But if our product is so great, why is no one buying? Possibly because good products do not sell themselves.

Foreign language educators are new and reluctant clients of public relations. We are still experiencing a bit of righteous indignation from that unjust and brutal blow to the university foreign language requirement. We surround ourselves with people who think the way we do, and in faculty lounges, at meetings, wherever foreign language teachers gather, we secretly commiserate. It is us against *them*—the principals who schedule students out of our classes, the guidance counselors who advise students to take physics instead of foreign language, the parents with their "back-to-basics" philosophy, the students themselves who are just not "serious" anymore. We complain to ourselves and bemoan the fate of the misunderstood, the neglected, the deprived.

The foreign language profession has been accused of being apolitical and academic (Born, 2)—too proud to change, too stubborn to yield to the student of today, too busy to influence attitudes, too sheltered to know how. We sit back and wait for the language requirement to be reinstated—or at least for somebody to do something. We're still waiting.

A basic principle of salesmanship is that when sales are down, business redesigns and refines both the product and the marketing techniques. If foreign language education is to flourish, a new, improved product must be marketed by means of a planned, comprehensive public relations program in which every foreign language teacher is involved.

Planning for good public relations

To ensure that key people are being systematically exposed to various activities relating to foreign language programs, a great deal of cooperative teacher planning is necessary. Indeed, it is the planning that distinguishes the public relations from sporadic efforts to publicize or promote. Participation in district- or school-wide planning should be the responsibility of every foreign language teacher at every level of instruction. It is a job that will demand a great deal of visual acuity, requiring as it does our taking a searching look inward to determine where we are, a wide look around to determine where we want to go, and a long, long look ahead to determine how we're going to get there.

Step 1: Where are we?

An essential step in planning for productive public relations is product analysis—an assessment of beliefs, policies, and practices, an inventory of strengths and resources, an examination of existing contradictions. At the same time, we must take stock of our "image"—the program in relation to its universe—to discover the general climate of public attitudes and expectations. This includes an effort to discover any specific misunderstandings or exaggerated beliefs that may be creating unfavorable attitudes. An analysis of the present situation demands that we see ourselves as others see us.

Public relations has been defined as "doing good and getting credit for it" (Koestler, 20, p.4). The product must be good—vague or unrealistic program objectives will thwart the best promotional efforts. Common goals and learner outcomes for the study of a particular language must be well articulated between levels of advancement and must have the endorsement of all teachers in a given district.

Our claims must also be honest. Cutlip and Center (5, p.6) point out that "sound relationships with the public over time are compounded of performance that satisfies the public as well as communication of that satisfactory performance." Many of our claims are too subtle or abstract to have appeal, too lofty to have credibility in this cynical age. Can we promise fluency, can we offer a money-back guarantee of exciting, fun-filled hours? Do we really broaden horizons? Robinson (33, p.135) states that: "Foreign language educators around the world have long claimed that the study of foreign language gives students the key to understanding people from another culture. Unfortunately, this claim has rarely been reflected in specific instructional and evaluational practices of the foreign language classroom and the value of foreign language study for this objective . . . has been questioned, if not attacked, around the world." The public will not be fooled. The promise-them-anything-but-give-them-grammar approach may make the first sale, but a sound relationship with client publics will demand our being open and candid about the program and its limitations. The biggest public relations problem we have is the fact that we do not inform the public.

A local survey of community expectations conducted by Lazarus (22) indicated that the public expects more than just basic language instruction and favors the implementation of courses offering additional services or topics. The satisfying of such expectations will require the development of courses more interdisciplinary in nature, more in touch with student interests, more in step with the times, and more accommodating of various constituencies. There is no limit to the variety of course options available. The past has taught us that mere maintenance of the status quo is not enough. We cannot allow ourselves to become either complacent in our attitude or narrow in our program appeal. It would seem that rather than offering one product under multicolored labels, we should present a true multiplicity of foreign language experiences that meet the needs of a number of different customers. Lippmann (25) feels that the words that best describe the successful foreign language department of the future are *service* and *diversity*. Public relations is directed toward growth and expansion, not only in sales but in the product itself. Yet concern for marketable innovation must not result in the proliferation of shallow, meaningless courses that do not offer authentic foreign language experiences. It is crucial that programs meet a recognized need, solve a recognized problem, help meet an articulated goal of the buyer publics.

Who are the potential "buyers" of foreign language learning? It is a common mistake to think of the public as monolithic; yet, random promotional efforts directed to the masses are rarely successful. Each community is made up of many diverse and overlapping segments. Parents, for example, may also be business leaders or members of civic, religious, or service groups. These various publics within the general public must be identified and their special interests, concerns, and needs charted. Lazarus (22) has developed a polling device for collecting information on public attitudes and expectations:

Community Expectations of the Foreign Language Program
Answer *Yes* or *No* to the Following Questions

1 Every school should offer each student in grades 7–12 the opportunity to study a foreign language.
2 Students should study a foreign language until they can speak it fluently.
3 Foreign language study aids students in learning good communication skills in English.
4 Foreign language study for adults and those traveling abroad should be made available by the public schools.
5 Foreign language study is a luxury which is unnecessary in a time of tight budgets.
6 Foreign language instruction should emphasize the history and culture of other countries as much as language and literature.

> 7 Foreign languages should be offered in elementary schools.
> 8 A student's grade in foreign language is as important as his or her grade in English or Mathematics.
> 9 Studying a foreign language should help a student get a job or select a career.
> 10 Schools should offer Latin as well as Spanish, French, German, and other modern languages.
> 11 Schools should spend more money to improve foreign language programs.
> 12 Have you ever studied a language other than English?
> 13 Do you speak any language other than English?

The actual power structure, not some vague concept of the "public" should determine our focus. This means that we must know intimately the community and its components and be able to reach the influential, the leaders, the decision makers. The more precisely these audiences can be identified, the more ways of reaching and influencing them can be discovered. The place to start is with the identification of key policy and decision makers within our own power structures—the internal audiences. From these immediate publics, attention should move outward to special interest publics—the external audiences.

All communications regarding the foreign language program must accommodate the specific characteristics, needs, and interests of the target audience. It is essential to know their educational levels and occupations, their beliefs and attitudes, their group loyalties, their concerns and goals, and their disposition regarding the foreign language product. The Professional Selling Skills II training program from Xerox Learning Systems (31) identifies four types of customer attitudes that may be encountered:

- *acceptance:* the buyer agrees and has no negative feelings toward the product
- *skepticism:* the buyer is interested in the benefit but doubts that the product can provide it
- *indifference:* the buyer demonstrates a lack of interest due to no perceived need for the product
- *objection:* the buyer displays opposition to the product.

Lesly (23) further categorizes the general public regarding its interest in education and concludes that at least 65 percent are either isolated, uninterested, or disaffected. Therefore, the first and most monumental task is that of educating the public about the role of education in meeting future world needs. While Scebold (35) feels that the average American must be made aware of the realities of international interdependence, gaining public acceptance of this sophisticated concept will require strong, united efforts. As Cantril (3) points out, another characteristic of the public is that it does not anticipate crises, it only reacts to them.

Monsees (28, p.73) counsels that those outwardly opposed to the teaching and learning of foreign language represent not challenge, but futility. There is a segment of the population that will remain unreachable in spite of our efforts and "to expend energies and resources in an attempt to reach those who adamantly refuse to listen is inexcusably wasteful. Simply write them off." Performance may be seriously impaired if time is wasted trying to sell to people who are poor prospects. The "get-a-bigger-hammer" philosophy simply doesn't apply here.

An analysis of our present state, then, will include a realistic appraisal of our product and its image, the identification of our many and varied buying publics and a thorough and continuous assessment of the interests and attitudes of these potential clients.

Step 2: Where are we going?

A recent survey of foreign language educators (Eddy, 10) revealed that most teachers are directing energies toward public awareness activities, the majority through forms such as foreign language festivals, film showings, dramatic performances, and bulletin board exhibits. Only 10 percent of high school teachers surveyed performed no such promotional activities. Our programs seem to be getting publicity. But is that enough? There is a big gap between visibility and appreciation.

Publicity used as an information tool is just one part of the total package called public relations. While publicity may support awareness or capture recognition, a good public relations program will go many steps beyond. It will also 1) tell us what certain individuals or groups of people think of us, 2) help us determine what must be done to gain the good will of others, 3) plan ways to win good will, 4) carry on activities designed to win it, and 5) continuously evaluate and adjust efforts to maintain an optimum level of effectiveness.

Public relations is not spasmodic but rather continuous, permanent, and progressive. It is not an annual foreign language festival, a scrapbook bulging with press clippings, a spot on the local news, or an engaging bulletin board display. It is not *one* of these, but it may be all of these and more if they are conducted with a specific purpose in mind. Hatfield (15) advises against measuring only promotional efforts, and suggests placing more emphasis on effectiveness. That is, instead of concentrating on the *number* of activities performed during the year, we should decide how effective these activities have been as public relations devices. They may reach many people, but do they reach the right people, and to what extent do they influence attitudes, behavior, or policies? Random or one-shot efforts do not change attitudes or behavior. Every activity of a public relations program must be directed toward a specific objective; each strategy is part of an overall plan. Seeking publicity but ignoring purpose or effectiveness is not effective public relations.

A determination of where we are going requires our identifying our mission in terms of general and specific objectives geared to target publics. What changes in the status quo are sought? Objectives must be not only attainable and realistic, they must be potentially measurable in terms of progress toward identified goals.

Step 3: How are we going to get there?

The final and often the most consuming task is to develop strategies for reaching objectives. This development requires the thorough delineation of responsibilities among teachers, with emphasis on the timing of events, the variety of communication channels utilized, and the use of media. Such measures assure pervasiveness without duplication of effort.

Before anything can be accomplished, the foreign language teacher must have a clear idea of what foreign language education is and how it contributes to the development of every individual. The teacher as salesperson must know the values and benefits of the foreign language product. Getting the ear of the listener and not having a message to deliver is a wasted exercise. The buyer will have little trust in salespersons who cannot answer questions about the benefits of their product. We must immerse ourselves in facts, read the professional literature, and be on the lookout for supportive research. We must also learn to listen, not only to what others say but to what we say to others. It is important to avoid inconsistencies and weaknesses in our actions and arguments.

The state foreign language association can play a vital role in keeping teachers informed. Ludwig (27) sees as one of the primary functions of the state organization the stimulating of professional growth through training programs such as workshops, colloquia, symposia, regional meetings, and publications. The association should also serve as a collector and distributor of supportive research. Committee research and state-wide surveys may be done through the organization's publications, and the results of such studies shared with the membership.

Finally, in order to be effective we must first create in potential customers the recognition of a need and then indicate how our product can fill that need.

Making the internal connection

Foreign language teachers have, throughout the past decade, considered themselves proud stepchildren of the school system. We must admit that we have allowed ourselves to acquire a rather unattractive image. Lavergneau (21, p.289) feels that too often foreign language teachers are looked upon as "frustrated egomaniacs who flit about flaunting their bilingual talents." These are harsh words, yet this concept has been perpetuated by our self-imposed isolation. If foreign language study is to be accepted not as a curricular appendage but as a relevant and fundamental element of contemporary education, our elitist enclaves must be disbanded to allow our involvement in the total school program. We have been quick to spot adversaries but unfailingly slow to recognize potential friends.

The Faculty. The most effective means of winning support for the foreign language cause is working with colleagues in other areas. Foreign language teachers may even discover that there is already quite a bit of support for their subject within the school faculty. Rather than operate alone, we must solicit the cooperation of those in other disciplines by planning courses that are more interdisciplinary. Such cooperation and teacher exchange can be as extensive as imagination and energies will permit.

Eykyn and Dowds (11) report a great deal of student enthusiasm generated in advanced-level classes by the inclusion of interdisciplinary mini-units that call for teacher and class exchanges as well as interaction in such areas as art, music, debate, social studies, and word origin.

Flynn (12) offers a sampling of ways in which foreign language teachers can become involved in the total school program:

- Exchange presentations on the metric systems with the math department.
- Offer video-taped mini-culture dialogs or presentations to social studies classes.
- Teach folk dances, appropriate terms, and historical implications to physical education classes. Present classes in foreign games and sports.
- Arrange for a social studies student and foreign language student to spend a weekend at the home of a foreign person in the area, perhaps to help with babysitting or housekeeping. Have them make a dual presentation to the social studies and foreign language classes on their language and cultural experiences.
- Encourage teachers in other areas to let you and your students share any oral or written reports on a country where your target language is used.
- Publish a booklet from the foreign language department listing services available to the rest of the school. Include students in the preparation of the list.
- Set up a career center in the libary with the help of the librarian. Solicit the help of the guidance counselor.
- Sponsor a logo contest. Make a presentation to an art, a foreign language, and an English class on signs and symbols of language. Have students create their own logos.
- Study foreign-built automobiles and hold a model car contest with art and auto mechanics classes. Make labels and instructions in the foreign language.
- Teach cross-cultural gestures to groups of students in language arts, drama, and social studies. Teach foreign expressions that accompany them.
- Present a lesson on cognates to the English class.
- Conduct a discussion of cross-cultural understanding through body language with the social studies, language arts, and drama departments.
- Help students in the various arts construct a cultural mosaic based on past and present experiences.
- To demonstrate culture shock to students about to take a trip to a foreign country, work with the drama department to recreate a culture. Include

in the presentation a cultural event that evolves around food, clothes, music, interpersonal relationships, language. Invite other students and get reactions.

- Use mini-culture dialogs or original dialogs to create some street theatre. Present it in the halls or lunch room.

In this new decade, a decade of emerging global awareness and focus on world interdependence, we can no longer afford the luxury of isolation. The word "global" must be interpreted in the broadest sense of the word, as Strasheim states (38, p.33):

> It is difficult to believe that teachers who cannot accept curricular interdependence will be able to prepare students for world interdependence, whatever their chosen disciplines . . . If the microcosm of interdisciplinary and multidisciplinary collaboration—of curricular interdependence—is beyond our grasp, then the macrocosm is doomed.

The Guidance Counselor. Perhaps the most maligned of our colleagues in the educational system are the guidance counselors. We have only a vague idea of their job. We know, for example, that the guidance office is the place where all those forms originate; the counselors interrupt our classes for three days of testing every year; they must be the ones advising our students not to take foreign languages. We also have assorted ideas about what the guidance counselors *should* be doing: they should be acquainting students with career opportunities requiring foreign language skills; they should be informing students about college foreign language requirements; they should be encouraging students to study more than two years of a foreign language; they should be making our job a little easier.

The guidance counselor can be an influential and amiable partner if language teachers are willing to dismantle the age-old barriers. Loew (26) suggests several ways that the language teacher can build a healthy working relationship with the guidance office:

- Take time to explain the language program--its goals, its problems.
- Write interesting and appealing course descriptions.
- Send to parents letters cosigned by both counselor and foreign language teacher encouraging foreign language study and including a rationale directed to children with different interests and goals.
- Invite the counselor to your classroom and department meetings.
- Offer to place all transfer students by personal interview.
- Write your praise of the counselor to the principal. Send a carbon to the guidance office.
- Keep abreast of good language programs at institutions in the state.
- Inform guidance of placement policies, exemption credit, objectives of local universities.
- Provide the latest, most accurate career information.
- Know facts about why foreign language should by studied.

- Keep track of graduating students to discover ways they have found their language study useful.

Williams (43) reports that some of the questions most commonly asked by guidance counselors about foreign language are the following:

- *Which language should students be advised to take?* Teachers may wish to assist guidance in this by explaining the criteria for student language selection—such as possible career choices, geographical location, proposed travel, ethnic background, and so on.
- *Is it better to take four years of one language or two years of two languages?* Teachers may wish to explain the pros and cons of these options.
- *Which language is easier?* It is important that the point be made that no one language is easier than any other, that learning any language challenges many skills and abilities but that the study of one language may facilitate the learning of additional languages.

The Administrator. A survey of secondary school superintendents conducted by DeFilippis (7) reveals an area in which a great deal of our energy must be concentrated. When asked to state apparent causes for the present decline in foreign language enrollments, superintendents cited reasons such as irrelevance, lack of information, inappropriate teaching methods, elitist attitudes, degree of difficulty, and inescapable dullness. Such comments represent a serious indictment of past, and perhaps even existing, classroom practices and program goals. They should not, however, be surprising, for we have actually done very little to change or refine our image. Of superintendents surveyed, over 90 percent had themselves studied language in high school, yet only 40 percent had chosen to continue language study at the college level. Most of these administrators are products of a language era of conjugation, diagrams, and memorization. They recall less-than-pleasurable experiences with language study as students, and as administrators they saw good dollars go down the drain as the language labs of the 1960s collected dust, cobwebs, and graffitti in the 1970s. Many still view foreign language study as an exercise in drudgery or, what may be worse, as frivolity—"cute," fun, and on a par with needlework, disco dancing, cake decorating, and plant communication.

Our bosses may be misinformed or totally uninformed; yet they are not totally opposed to foreign language study. As buyers of our foreign language programs, they would likely fall in the categories of *skeptical* ("foreign language can by mastered in ninety days of intensive instruction—why should it be required in elementary school, high school or college?") or *indifferent* (50 percent of those surveyed believed that the lack of foreign language skills was *not* detrimental to the national interest).

Administrators represent a challenge we cannot afford to ignore, for they are the decision-makers who wield the power to make change. We will have to demonstrate to them that we can fulfill our claims by presenting concrete, reliable evidence on the values of foreign language study in contemporary society. That evidence does exist. Hancock (14) provides a summary of the abundant available research on the effects of second language study on the cognitive and affective development of students.

Awareness of the evidence to support our claims must be followed by our communicating this evidence effectively. The National School Public Relations Association in 1970 polled school administrators and state boards to determine the most difficult communication problem facing the districts. Most frequently cited was the difficulty of communicating with the teachers. Therefore, what may appear to be a lack of support for foreign language is more likely simply a lack of knowledge about our programs. No one but the foreign language teacher can remedy this situation. While inviting the principal to visit classes, to attend or participate at conferences, or to read news clippings and journal articles are all excellent ways of furnishing information, it is the rare principal who will have the time or inclination to oblige us. Administrators' Guides can help acquaint principals with the basic information on good foreign language education—its needs, problems, strengths, instructional methods —but they are not effective if they are never read. Dissemination does not equal communication.

Hatfield (16) offers several useful hints for improved communication with principals:

- *Clarify priorities.* Don't waste the principal's time with vague proposals.
- *Know their operational style.* Is the principal a reader who will want written documentation, a listener who will want to discuss, or a looker, who will react best to charts, diagrams, or graphs?
- *How do they make decisions?* If the principal wants more time, don't push for an immediate decision. Skill in negotiating includes knowing when to stop.
- *Use their point of view.* How does foreign language fit within the school program? Where does it match the school philosophy and objectives? What are administrative concerns and problems and how can your program help solve them?
- *Give them your crystal ball.* Don't be guilty of the "it's obvious to me, why can't you see it?" syndrome.
- *Don't hide problems.* We are often reluctant to expose problems for fear of placing our programs in a bad light. Evasion postpones solution.
- *Use their timepiece.* If limited time is available, state your case briefly.
- *Do your homework.* Make sure you have a firm foundation of facts for the points you wish to make.
- *Present solutions, not problems.* Don't leave principals to form their own conclusions. More opinion change is brought about if conclusions are explicitly stated. People do not buy ideas divorced from action. What will your proposal involve as far as personnel, time, cost, and so forth.?
- *What is your image?* Principals will be more apt to support change if they know the activities will be carried out successfully.

- *Speak their language.* Jargon, when used in the appropriate circles, speeds up communication; when aimed at laymen it causes confusion and resentment.
- *Be a part of the total school program.* In voicing our concerns only when something is not right within the foreign language program rather than addressing concerns of the educational program in general, we separate ourselves from the mainstream of education.

Crucial to winning support is the ability to uncover areas of mutual concern, areas that will enable us to make the powerful benefits-needs connection. In South Carolina, for example, in a series of statewide listening sessions conducted by the state superintendent (Williams, 42), the improvement of school-community relations was ranked as the primary concern nine out of ten times by superintendents, board members, principals, teachers, and parents. A principal concerned with school-community relations may be interested in and supportive of a foreign language program carrying components such as adult foreign language instruction, community festivals, and teacher and student services to the community. Vital connections can also be made between the concern about basic skills and the research in the area of cognitive development of second-language learners as well as between career education and evidence of the requirement in many jobs for foreign language as an ancillary skill.

The Students. At present, and across the country, we are witnessing an approximate 50 percent loss of students between the first and second levels of language study, to say nothing of the more advanced levels. Programs are simply not comforming either to student expectations or to teacher claims. In a survey of reasons for student attrition, Papalia (30) discovered that students left foreign language study because 1) they had completed the language requirement, 2) they felt the second and third levels were too difficult, 3) they had been advised against continuing, 4) they had opted for another subject, 5) they had lost interest in language study, or 6) they disliked the teacher. The same study presents contrasting teacher beliefs about the reasons for students' leaving the program. Those teachers surveyed attributed the high attrition to 1) minimal or nonexistent college requirements, 2) guidance counselors not recommending language study, 3) the current emphasis on science and math, 4) students' exaggerated beliefs about their expertise after limited contact with the language, 5) lack of student preparation for the following level, 6) lack of interest, and 7) the tendency of pupils to elect easy courses. The results of these surveys would indicate that teachers are concentrating on the externals, which are beyond their control, and perhaps overlooking the real causes of student attrition, those factors over which they do exert control. Quite frankly, student are turned off by the programs they experience.

The potential language student is a most important public. All promotional efforts outside the classroom will be ineffectual if the program is not relevant to student needs, that is, if the program is not rewarding by creating a sense of accomplishment, challenging of talents and abilities, and manageable in its content.

There is a great deal of merit to the idea that by eliminating some of the superfluous content of present textbooks and suppressing the urge to "cover" all chapters, more meaningful informational and affective communication can take place within the classroom. It is certainly not without reason that the majority of students feel that the second and third years of language study are just too difficult. In most cases, the second year of language study has become, literally, the "tense" year. Perhaps convinced that students will not of their own volition opt for a third year of language study, we feel compelled to force all fourteen verb tenses down their throats in the hope that some of the material will be digested. Our motives are, to say the least, questionable. Selling students on the idea of communication and then offering crash courses in verb forms does little more than confuse and alienate all but the most grammar-hungry students. From the first day and constantly throughout the course of the language experience, students should feel they are using the language, albeit in limited fashion, to communicate about things that have bearing on reality.

Teitelbaum (39) counsels us to talk relevance, not intellectualism, when dealing with today's student. Varela-Ibarra (41) advises that we fall in step with students, get to know them—eat in the cafeteria, listen in the halls, read the school newspaper, and note events that students sponsor—and so become aware of their interests. This information should be carried into the classroom, where the language is used as a true communicating vehicle to deal with topics of concern to the student.

Whereas students should be urged to continue language study beyond the first year, it is inadvisable to pressure for a commitment by informing them that effective communication demands extensive language study. Teitelbaum (39), for one, feels that the concept of sequence for proficiency is inappropriate and out of step with a generation seeking instant gratification:

> We have not fashioned a society of long range plans. Our sales pitch is geared to instant wealth, instant smile, instant coffee, instant success, instant life. Never tell your reluctant consumer how long he has to use your brand name in order to gain its benefits. Don't push for a two year commitment. (p.5)

Various incentive can be offered students to urge them to continue language study. Programs for foreign travel, funded in part through monies raised by foreign language clubs, can be an attractive and persuasive element of the program. Personal letters of commendation and encouragement written to students in the target language from the district foreign language coordinator can also be influential (Lavergneau, 21).

Students can be made a part of the act by assisting in public relations strategies. Eykyn and Dowds (11) have pupils both talk to their brothers, sisters, and neighbors about their foreign language experiences and also present assembly programs at the middle school level to spur interest in language study in entering freshmen. Toussaint (40) reports of a "cadet program" in which students receive credit toward graduation for teaching in the elementary schools.

Griffin (13) enlists student support in the production of a slide and sound "portrait" of the foreign language program for presentation to the PTA, board members, and other students. In the completed program, each language has a ten-minute segment divided into three parts: in-class activities, out-of-class activities, and student comments. This final "comments" portion of the program is designed to disabuse the audience of the idea that language programs are "frills." The educational objectives of the school are projected on the screen and as viewers read them they listen to students commenting on how these objectives are met through foreign language study.

Public relations indeed begin in the classroom, and the pupil's role as intermediary is an important one. Many of the attitudes held by the general public have been transmitted from pupil to parent to public via the community grapevine. Students are our most powerful and persuasive allies.

Making the connections externally

The Parents. All too frequently, communication between teacher and parent is limited to those cases in which something is wrong. Parents, therefore, tend to be more aware of weaknesses than of strengths within the school system. As they are with other publics, many negative or indifferent attitudes are grounded in misunderstanding or lack of information.

Winning parental support demands that we learn to look at things from parents' point of view—that we try to think, feel, and react as they will. The wise foreign language teacher will atend PTA meetings, become active in parent organizations, listen to the concerns expressed, and plan how the features of the foreign language program can be communicated in response to these concerns.

School and classroom visits, letters, and foreign language mini-courses for adults can be extremely effective devices for educating parents to foreign language concerns, goals, and teaching methods. Adkins, et.al. (1) propose a foreign language night to acquaint parents with the program. Administrators and prospective students are also invited. Darcey and Brown (6) invite parents of French students to a *petit déjeuner* and offer beginning French classes (for one hour a week after school for six weeks) to interested parents. Inviting parents of present foreign language students to visit foreign language classes serves to explain program goals, methods, materials, and the facilities used to meet these goals. Hill (17) sends letters containing interesting facts about the importance of foreign language study for college and careers to parents of prospective foreign language students.

Parents want to hear that their children are doing well, yet all too often correspondence with them regarding their children takes the form of performance criticism. Darcey and Brown (6) report of a communication technique designed for parents of elementary school children: Illustrated "Happy grams" written in the target language and bearing the child's name and recent accomplishment are sent to parents of students who have worked or tried especially hard.

Parents have the right to know what their children are studying and why, as well as how their needs are considered when we are designing new programs. The unsupportive parent is usually the uninformed one, and the teacher who fails to maintain open channels with frequent, frank communication is ignoring one of the most important and influential of publics.

The Community. A national survey of community leaders' attitudes toward education conducted by the U.S. Office of Education (Carter, 4) revealed the following voter opinions:

- Schools are considered good in general but are criticized in particular areas: "frills," too much play, curriculum, discipline.
- The most important task of the schools is to teach the fundamentals: reading, writing, spelling, arithmetic, speaking; and to instill loyalty to the United States.
- The least important tasks of the schools are to teach about the local region, to afford enjoyment of cultural activities, and to provide industrial arts education.
- About half of the voters show no evidence of any participation in school affairs and no interest in such participation.

These findings would suggest that some examination not only of our message but of our delivery systems is necessary. If the sole means of obtaining public visibility for programs is via such channels as fairs and festivals, one must consider just how these are being perceived by the target publics. Are they seen as amusing but trifling activities that serve only to reinforce the idea that foreign language study is a frill? If so, our endeavors are defeating our purpose.

The most effective appeals are those directed not to the public in general, but to special-interest groups within the community. Americans are basically joiners with a penchant for forming groups. Most of these groups are united under common goals or issues. Gaining support for foreign language programs will require moving outside of the profession to become aware of the myriad possibilities for offering services and illustrating the needs-benefits connection. Consider the following publics:

- Taxpayer groups
- Business Organizations (Chamber of Commerce, Association of Better Business Bureaus, National Association of Manufacturers)
- Religious Organizations

- Fraternal/Service (Masons, Elks, Civitan, Shriners, Odd Fellows, Rotary, Kiwanis, Knights of Columbus, Lions, Moose, Optimist)
- Veterans (AMVETS, American Legion, VFW, Disabled American Veterans)
- Senior Citizens
- Youth Organizations (Boy Scouts, Girl Scouts, YWCA, YMCA)
- Women's Groups (General Federation of Women's Clubs, League of Women Voters, AAUW)
- Cultural/Literary
- Educational (American Association of School Administrators, AAUP, American Council on Education, National Congress of Parents and Teachers, NEA, AFT, National Association of Secondary School Principals).

Levy (24) has devised a questionnaire for obtaining information from organizations about their need for services that may be offered to them through the foreign language program. Included in the questionnaire are places where the respondent can describe organizational objectives and services, special ongoing projects that might require foreign language expertise, and statements of agency needs. Organizations are also surveyed on their willingness to donate services and participate in some areas of the foreign language program.

Lavergneau (21) reports a great deal of success in reaching out to the various community bodies: every Rotary Club, Lions Club, and so forth has a commitment to international service, service generally directed to foreign countries. In a New Jersey community, the Rotary Club became a firm supporter of the local foreign language program. The international chairman asked a group of local high school students to deliver his greeting to Quito, Ecuador, along with the Rotary flag. Upon their return, the students presented a program for the members of their home Rotary Club. Each chapter of the Women's Club of America also has an international chairwoman whose help may be solicited in planning cooperative projects within the school or programs for presentation at meetings. Local libraries hold meetings on topics of community interest. Teachers and students may present programs for them, encourage them to have records, tapes, or slides representing other cultures available for community use, and urge students and families to use these resources.

In Alabama, a local high school teacher and her German Club (Dill, 8) contacted the city government officials and asked if they would like the club to devise a crest for the city. A competition to design a coat-of-arms was open to students; two hundred entries were submitted, and all were featured in the newspaper. The city's official stationery now bears that crest.

In Hawaii, the state foreign language organization, HALT, calls attention to the large number of cultural groups within the population of that state. HALT sponsors a "Family Portrait" event in which those persons currently living in Hawaii but born in another country gather to form a composite of the Hawaiian citizenry (Wollstein, 44).

Howard (18) tells of volunteer public-service work done for such agencies as the Salvation Army, UNICEF, and Goodwill in the name of the local foreign language club. Other successful practices have involved making lists of native resource persons available to hospitals, courts, and public health facilities, and offering language and culture mini-courses to groups such as journalists, police, and fire departments.

Monsees (28) provides a comprehensive outline for the organization of community advocacy groups that can help to tell the foreign language story. Such support organizations are composed not only of foreign language educators, but of community leaders who might have an interest in the promotion of some aspect of the language-culture experience—socialites, local celebrities, leaders in the arts and international business. Such advocates are able not only to serve as disinterested and unbiased spokespersons but also to contribute their special skills and talents in management, public relations, organizational development, and government. Such advocacy groups can become the foreign language leaders in the community, they can serve as the source of information on foreign language; in short, they can become our friends in power. (See Chapter 4 for other ideas on community cooperation.)

A survey conducted by the University of Michigan Survey Research Center (Eddy, 9) under the auspices of the President's Commission reveals encouraging information about public attitudes toward foreign language study:

- 45 percent of those surveyed indicated that they would like to study a foreign language.
- 84 percent of parents with children sixteen or younger said they would encourage their children to study a foreign language in school, primarily to increase their awareness and powers of communication.
- Over 75 percent of the respondents wanted foreign languages offered in elementary schools.
- 92 percent wanted languages offered in junior high and high school and 47 percent believed that languages should be required.
- 38 percent favored a language requirement for admission to colleges and universities and 40 percent favored such a requirement for college graduation.

In one community, Lazarus (22) found the public overwhelmingly in favor of foreign language programs as long as foreign language study presents no threat to other areas of the curriculum. The public is in favor of expansion, but not if that expansion is perceived as too innovative, too costly, or too threatening for any other reason.

Public concerns and expectations will vary from one community to the next and among special-interest groups within a community. It must not automatically be assumed that the public in general is opposed to foreign language study, as such pessimism may serve only to drive us back into our corner. Where strong opposition is encountered, perhaps it is futile to attempt to combat it; but where indifference is found, it must be fought, for it is based largely on ignorance; where acceptance exists, we must take advantage of it.

Developing PR strategies

What we say to audiences is important. How and when we say it is equally important. A basic element of public relations is pervasiveness. When an issue appears to be all around people, they tend to accept its importance and assume that it is "the thing to do." To be effective, public relations must be as versatile; it must use as many channels as available talents and resources will permit. However, several factors should be considered when selecting the proper channel for the message. These are 1) appropriateness of medium for target public, 2) cost of preparation, 3) facility of preparation, and 4) effectiveness.

The list that follows summarizes some of the most commonly used communicative vehicles. It is by no means exhaustive. In discovering inexpensive and effective delivery systems, one is limited only by imagination. But a word of caution is necessary. Before undertaking any of the following, make sure you follow appropriate channels and obtain clearance from the administration or district informational services staff. In many areas, there are restrictions regarding individual publicity efforts.

Foreign Language Festivals/Days/Weeks

This is one of the most popular and potentially effective tools for gaining program visibility, ethnic awareness, and community involvement. It can provide an outlet for displaying student talents and fostering a sense of achievement through competitions and awards; it can also create important interdisciplinary links among the visual and performing arts, athletics, and classes in history and culture. Events may be local, regional, or statewide; they may be sponsored by schools, universities, language organizations, or departments of education. Popular activities include parades, proclamations, public forums and town meetings, career exploration, international cookery, displays and exhibits, fund-raising booths, demonstrations, mini-courses, and student competitions in the areas of visual arts and crafts, music, song, dance, fashion, essays, poetry recitation, drama, word games, extemporaneous speaking, cultural and historical knowledge, metrics, puppetry, film making, and sports and games. The ACTFL Foreign Language Week Packet, available from the ACTFL materials center, offers some excellent suggestions, as do Keyes and Larsen (19) and Wood and Badanes (45).

Community involvement and assistance in planning and conducting activities and judging competitions should be encouraged. The media should be notified prior to the event and invited to attend or participate. Local banks and merchants may be contacted and asked to display greetings in the foreign language in windows or on marquees.

Newspapers

The News Release. The basic way to tell your story through the media is the news release, a complete, clear, and concise account of an event or program prepared for use by print and broadcast media. A release should be written in plain, direct language and must always be accurate. The story must be timely and contain solid news value. Always type your release double-spaced on bond paper. Copies should be mimeographed or photocopied—never send carbons. Type your name, school address, phone number, and date in the upper left corner of the first page. use an appropriate heading, such as "For Immediate Release," "For Release at Will," "For Release Upon Receipt," "For Release July 27." Leave a one-inch blank above the story and margins of about one inch at the sides of the paper for editing. Type *more* at the bottom of each page except the last, and *30* or # at the end of the story. Number each page after the first.

In the text, use full names, titles, and identifications of persons, institutions, and organizations on first reference. Never write "our school." Avoid expressing opinions. If editorializing is needed, use a quotation. Avoid a dull lead (the opening paragraph that summarizes the information in the rest of the article). Be sure your story answers the questions: Who? What? When? Where? How? Why? If you deliver your story in person, do so before 9:00 A.M. or after 1:00 P.M. Aim for the Monday paper, if possible; Sunday is traditionally a slow day for news.

Letters to the Editor. This is perhaps the most overlooked channel for conveying information, yet readership surveys indicate that it is one of the most thoroughly read sections of a newspaper. While the news release allows only for the reporting of newsworthy events, the editor's column is for expressions of opinion. Direct appeals to the reader's emotion and logic can be made here. Limit letters to 250 words or less. Correct all grammar, spelling, punctuation. Poorly written letters will reach the trash can, not the reader.

Fillers. These are brief items of one or two paragraphs used by newspapers to fill out columns when other stories leave gaps. Local items are usually welcomed. Human interest fillers are especially popular.

Press Clippings. Don't just paste them in a scrapbook and put them on the shelf. Send them, display them, or better yet, use them to promote additional publicity. Instead of filing that article on the President's Commission, seek opinions on it from influential citizens from various sectors of the community; conduct interviews, record comments, and develop these into a feature story.

A handy guide for the preparation of news items is *The Publicity Handbook,* available from the Consumer Service Department, Sperry Hutchinson Co., 330 Madison Ave., New York, NY 10017 (25¢).

Television

Know your stations and their programs. Watch local shows so that you are informed when you call the station. Request appointments with program and news directors. Never mail public service announcements to a TV station (see paragraph following), asking in your letter that they be aired. Approach the station in person. Know exactly what message you hope to deliver. Do not, for example, tell the program director only that you would like to talk about foreign language education. There are several areas that deliver information: specials, segments, personality spots, news items, editorials. Before seeking air coverage, ask yourself: What is my message? Who should receive it (keep in mind the different kinds of viewers watching at different times of the day)? Which of the various types of programs will get my message across? Approach the program director with specific suggestions for coverage. The booklet *If You Want Air Time* is available from Director of Public Affairs, WOKR TV, 4225 W. Henrietta Rd., Rochester, NY 14623.

Radio Spots

Television and radio stations must devote a certain amount of free air time to Public Service Announcements (PSAs) for worthwhile nonprofit organizations; however, many groups compete for this limited program space. Make sure your "spot" is interesting. PSAs that offer service or solicit support have greater appeal to broadcasters. Remember the limitations of this medium. Use simple but descriptive words that form pictures, thus giving dimension and color. The radio audience is largest between 6:00 and 10:00 A.M. and 4:00 and 6:00 P.M., so the message should be sufficiently stimulating and thought-provoking to occupy the mind of the person sitting wearily in rush hour traffic. A sixty-second spot announcement is equal to 150 words; 20 seconds equals 50 words; 10 seconds equals 25 words. If you are recording your PSA, *timing must be exact.* The trend is toward 10- and 20-second spots. Use reel-to-reel tape. If you are submitting written material, send several copies and make sure they are all legible.

Surveys/Questionnaires

Let your information work for you. Use surveys and reports to answer critics or call attention to a problem.

Letters. Letters to parents, community groups, or businesses should reflect your knowledge of their specific concerns. Make sure the opening paragraph creates a good impression. Demonstrate to them that you have done some research and are aware of their needs. Also, avoid *Dear Sir/Madam, Dear parent,* or *your son/daughter.* Use names.

Phone Calls. Eykyn and Dowds (11) suggest that when registration forms come in for eighth-grade students, ask permission to see these forms. Go over them and check for students who could have taken foreign language but did not. Write down their phone numbers and call them. Although they cannot change their schedules, they might be willing to fill their study halls. But remember that telephoning can be risky. Letters can be thrown away if people aren't interested; phone calls demand immediate response, and many people consider them an intrusion.

Other attention-getters

Signs, Posters, Bulletin Boards. Located outside the foreign language classroom, these may all be great attention-getters. Enlist the cooperation of the art department or select talented students to produce an appropriate display. Focus on one theme. Keep it simple and thought provoking. Ask the viewer to do something. The title is the focal point; make it short and catchy. A Christmas tree made of construction paper and bearing the words *Feliz Navidad* will do little to capture anyone's attention.

Within the school, signs and labels in the target language may arouse students' curiosity and help create the impression that learning another language is the thing to do. And posters need not be confined to the school grounds; local businesses might be willing to display them in their windows.

Buttons and Bumper Stickers. These items, bearing catchy slogans or phrases in the foreign tongue, can be either handmade or commercially provided. They can be sold by language clubs at school and during festivals.

Metered Messages. Slogans or brief messages can be sent on metered mail in the space ordinarily marked by the canceling machines. Ask companies and agencies using postage meters to use a "cut" carrying the foreign language message. A cut may be purchased from the manufacturer of the meters for $20. Contact a company or write Pitney Bowes, Inc., 69 Walnut St., Stamford, CT 06904.

Brochures. Your foreign language department should have a brochure explaining its program and purpose, outlining benefits, and listing special activities. When designing a brochure, keep your audience in mind. Will the brochure be directed to parents, administrators, students? Keep the layout simple and functional. Do not use a design that impedes rather than enhances the message. Long blocks of text, small print, and single spacing will repel the reader. Break up long copy with subheads, information in boxes, bullets, boldface type, and illustrations; but always use these with restraint. A useful publication called

"Making Your Own Foreign Language Brochure" written by Lorraine A. Strasheim is available from the ACTFL Materials Center.

Demonstrations. Arrange to teach a sample class in a large store window or in a central area of a shopping mall. This will bring your program to many people who would not otherwise have the opportunity to see a foreign language class in action. Encourage media coverage.

Classes. Within the community, offer short courses especially suited to the needs of target publics such as police officers, business leaders, journalists. Courses in preparation for travel abroad can be made available to interested citizens.

Outdoor Advertising. This must be succinct, able to tell the story at a glance. Discuss format and availability with a member of the Outdoor Advertisers Association of America, Inc. Contact their headquarters (24 W. Erie St., Chicago, IL 60610) for the name of a person in your area. Never post your own advertising outdoors in any location without first obtaining clearance.

Presentations and Assemblies. Programs presented to students, PTA, civic groups, school boards, and so forth may take any conceivable format and include audio-visual materials or live performances. These programs are usually more successful when students are the chief performers. Printed material distributed to the audience is a plus. If audio-visual equipment is used, make sure it is functioning properly; always have an alternate plan.

Publications. Handbooks, manuals, newsletters, professional journals, and school newspapers are effective devices for carrying the foreign language message. Make sure that such publications reach the hands of those outside the foreign language circle. Professional journals not devoted exclusively to foreign language, such as the *Bulletin of the National Association of Secondary School Principals,* are extremely effective vehicles for reaching influential publics. Other possibilities include church bulletins, company house organs, small neighborhood weeklies, and newsletters of various clubs and organizations.

Speakers' Bureaus. Enlist the support of the speech department to build a student speakers' bureau that can carry your message to community groups. To build a speakers bureau 1) develop a file of research data on the subject; 2) prepare written material for distribution; 3) develop a list of speakers and subjects related to foreign language and appropriate for various audiences; 4) list all pertinent data about student speakers for publicity purposes; 5) set up a speakers' training program; 6) devise some catchy titles; 7) compile a list of organizations to which speakers will be offered and contact these; 8) promptly fill all requests; and 9) follow through for audience reaction.

Also request that speakers from civic organizations address foreign language groups. In planning their presentations, these speakers will have to learn all about the group they are addressing. In becoming informed, they may also become sufficiently involved to serve as powerful advocates of future endeavors.

The State Foreign Language Organization. This group can serve as a research and distribution headquarters for public relations efforts. Surveys conducted by the association can both collect information about the public and create public awareness when survey results are published.

Seagrave (37) reports of public awareness generated by an awards program administered by one state association. Local, regional, and state awards are given in recognition of outstanding teacher and student performance, for excellent foreign language programs (these awards presented to school boards), for public service (these awards presented to an individual or organization not connected with the teaching of a foreign language but nonetheless making a contribution to language education), for culture through the arts (these awards presented to a teacher of another subject in whose classroom foreign language and culture are also important), and administrative support (these awards to a specialist in another area who has been especially supportive of foreign languages).

Thank You. One of the most essential factors of good public relations is the expression of appreciation for assistance, support, or opportunities provided by individuals or organizations. Express promptly in writing your gratitude to the news media, club, organization, or business that has helped to further your promotional effort.

Timing PR activities

Although one event may be memorable or one article persuasive, it takes a series of diverse efforts all directed toward a single goal to win lasting public attention. Roman and Maas (34) state that two elements are essential for a successful campaign. These are frequency and continuity; people forget within half a day 60 percent of what they have been exposed to. The more often our message is repeated, the more likely it is that it will be retained. Experts in public relations recommend "pulsing" promotional efforts—providing continuous advertising plus periodic "bursts." For example, a promotional burst prior to fall registration or following parents' receipt of test scores can increase the impact of the continuing campaign. Carefully timed strategies can help to give credence to and engender support for the foreign language cause. Maintaining a calendar of school and community events and charting our efforts to correspond to these will assure that our efforts are reaching the publics at the best possible times. Figure 1 presents a sample short-term plan for accomplishing this. The far right column states the needs and concerns of selected target audiences; the left column shows where our program features can link up with these concerns. The monthly divisions indicate continuous and pulsed activities and outline specific responsibilities of the students and of five foreign language faculty members.

School Year 1980-1981

Benefits/ Features of FL Program	Sept. (Orientation) **	Oct.	Nov.	Dec.	Jan.	Feb. (Pre-registration) **	March	April (Test Scores Out) **	May	Concerns of Publics Principal	Parents	Students
Research on second lang. learning & cognitive development	5: Prepare Brochure; 3: Speak to Lions Club; 2: Prepare PSA (radio)	6: Student presentation to Rotary; 1: Display in public library	4: Arrange for TV "spot"	1, 6: Presentation to church group	3, 5: Presentation to women's group	1: Plan parent tea; 2: Assembly middle school; 4: Letters to parents		1: Speak to PTA; 2: Presentation to Sch. Board; 3: Brochure to parents; 4: Let.-ed.		Basic Skills	Basic Skills	
			6: Students to elementary schools (Nov–Dec)									
Program visibility/ Community service/ involvement	6: Prepare slogans, signs for display; 1: Survey community needs	Send lists of services to community agencies	FL Intensive week-end 1, 2, 3, 4, 5, 6	6: FL Club service to Goodwill, etc.	1, 2, 6: Demonstration in shopping mall		4: Contact news media for FL Day; 1: News release; 3, 6: Bulletin Boards	FL Day/WK Festival 1, 2: Contact local businesses; 3, 5: Coordinate media efforts	1, 2: Mini course to parents; 6: Press clippings for feature story	School/Community Relations	School/Community Relations	
	1, 2, 3, 4, 5 Offer Adult Classes (Sept–Oct)				1, 2, 3, 4, 5 Offer Adult Classes (Jan–Feb)							
Evidence of demand for FL as ancillary skill in careers	3: Speak to guidance— deliver info on careers; 4: Prepare press fillers	6: Student article in school newspaper; 5: Letter to editor	6: Presentation to Boy Scouts	Business reps speak to classes on FL importance	4: Letter to editor; 1, 2: Career display-library; 5: Flyer on career info	Distribute career info; 6: Careers bulletin board	5: Short course to area business-people or public		Assembly-high school; 5: Contact business for metered messages	Career Education	Career Education	Job Opportunities
		1, 2, 3, 4, 5, 6 In-class career exploration (Oct–Dec)										

Key: 1, 2, 3, 4, 5 – Teachers; 6 – Students

Figure 1. Sample Short-term PR Plan

A United effort

Our future depends on our ability to communicate with the public and among ourselves. At present, our greatest handicap is our inability to work among ourselves in concert. Each level, each language, maintains a separate identity and views the others as different entities entirely. High school teachers blame middle school teachers and are in turn blamed by university professors for failing to prepare students adequately for their level of language study. French teachers resent Spanish teachers who resent German teachers for "stealing" their students.

The 1977–1978 report of the MLA Task Force on Institutional Language Policy (32) cites this present lack of articulation as a most serious and pressing problem. The report recommends the formation of statewide language articulation programs led by committees composed of teachers and administrators at all levels of education and served by the state foreign language supervisors acting as consultants. The report further states that elementary, secondary, community college, and university faculty from institutions located close to one another should meet regularly throughout the year to identify problems of articulation.

Planning for public acceptance and support of foreign language requires a profession united behind common goals. While loyalties to a particular language or level of instruction are admirable, we must remember that we are not in high school Spanish or college French—we are in the foreign language business and we are all in it together. Indeed, until we are able to accept this and to communicate with one another, we are not ready for public relations.

Conclusion

A well-planned, effective public relations program must pass the test of the seven Ps:

1 *Product.* Is there a flexible foreign language program that can grow to meet changing needs?
2 *Public.* Have we conducted an investigation to identify and study a variety of target audiences?
3 *Purpose.* Is our mission clear? Have immediate and long-term objectives been established?
4 *Professionalism.* Are we, as teachers, well informed, knowledgeable salespersons?
5 *Persuasion.* Are we able to match the benefits of the foreign language product with the needs of the publics?
6 *Pervasiveness.* Have we made use of a variety of properly timed strategies to accomplish our objectives?
7 *Participation.* Is ours a continuous, coordinated, and united effort with clearly defined responsibilities? Have we the stamina to follow through on our ideas?

Our campaign must begin now, for establishing a productive and healthy relationship with the public takes time. With knowledge, imagination, and a spirit of cooperation, we can not only create awareness but change prevailing attitudes. Public relations is not just a good idea—it is our responsibility.

References, Public relations: Making an impact

1 Adkins, Jeannette, et.al. *Communication Leads to Understanding.* [Paper presented at the ACTFL Preconference Workshop on Public Relations, Atlanta, November 1979.]

2 Born, Warren C., ed. "New Publics," 119-56 in *New Contents, New Teachers, New Publics.* Reports of the Working Committees of the Northeast Conference on the Teaching of Foreign Languages. Middlebury, VT: Northeast Conference, 1978. [EDRS: ED 165 444.]

3 Cantril, Hadley. *Gauging Public Opinion.* Princeton, NJ:Princeton University Press, 1947.

4 Carter, Richard I. *Voters and Their Schools.* Stanford, CA:Stanford University Institute for Communications Research, 1960.

5 Cutlip, Scott M., and Allen H. Center. *Effective Public Relations.* Englewood Cliffs, NJ:Prentice-Hall, 1952.

6 Darcey, John M., and Christine Brown. "Caught in a Web?" [Paper presented at the ACTFL Preconference Workshop on Public Relations, Atlanta, November 1979.]

7 DeFilippis, Dominick. "Views of Secondary Superintendents on Foreign Language Study: A Support Constraint Analysis." *Foreign Language Annals* 12(1979):139-44.

8 Dill, Alice as related by John Howard. Personal Communication, 1980. [Letter.]

9 Eddy, Peter A. "Attitudes Toward Foreign Language Study and Requirements in American Schools and Colleges: Results of a National Survey." *ADFL Bulletin* 11:2(1979):4-9.

10 _____ "Present Status of Foreign Language Teaching: A Northeast Conference Survey," 43-45 in Thomas H. Geno, ed., *Our Profes-*sion: *Present Status and Future Directions.* Northeast Conference Reports. Middlebury, VT: Northeast Conference, 1980.

11 Eykyn, Lollie, and Karen Dowds. [Public Relations Workshop sponsored by Columbia College, Columbia, SC, April 1979.]

12 Flynn, Mary B. "Fifty Ways to Infiltrate the System: How to Make Foreign Language Part of the Total School Program." Arlington, VA: Arlington Public Schools, n.d. [Mimeo.]

13 Griffin, Robert J. "Your Foreign Language Program: Telling It—and Showing It—Like It Is." *Foreign Language Annals* 11(1978):43-48.

14 Hancock, Charles R. "Second Language Study and Intellectual Development." *Foreign Language Annals* 10(1977):75-79.

15 Hatfield, Thomas A. "Publicity, Publications and Promotion: Making the Most of What We Have." *Art Education: The Journal of the National Art Education Association* 32:5(1979):14-18.

16 _____ "The Administrator As Resource: How to Win Friends and Influence Principals." *Art Teacher: A Magazine of the National Art Education Association* 19:3(1979):10-12.

17 Hill, Lucinda. Personal Communication, 1979. [Letter.]

18 Howard, John. Personal Communication, 1980. [Letter.]

19 Keyes, Marilyn, and Roger Larsen. "Boosting Enrollment Through a Departmental Activity: Foreign Language Week." *Foreign Language Annals* 11(1978):61-63.

20 Koestler, Frances A. *Planning and Setting Objectives.* New York:National Communication Council for Human Services, 1977.

21 Lavergneau, Rene L. "Involving the Community in Spanish Programs." *Hispania* 57(1974):287-91.

22 Lazarus, Francis M. "Community Expectations and the Foreign Language Program." *Modern Language Journal* 63(1979):182-87.

23 Lesly, Philip. *Lesly's Public Relations Handbook.* Englewood Cliffs, NJ:Prentice-Hall, 1976.

24 Levy, Stephen L. "Using Community Resources in Foreign Language Teaching." Brooklyn, NY, 1975. [EDRS:ED 102 878]

25 Lippmann, Jane N. "Rationale for Language Study," 37-69 in Gilbert A. Jarvis,ed., *The Challenge of Communication.* ACTFL Foreign Language Education Series, Volume 6. Skokie, IL:National Textbook Company, 1974.

26 Loew, Helene, "Working Together: Guidance Counselors and Foreign Language Teachers." *Foreign Language Annals* 11(1978):367-74.

27 Ludwig, Robert J. *Leadership in Foreign Language Education: Developing the State Foreign Language Association.* New York:MLA/ERIC Clearing House on Language and Linguistics, 1972.

28 Monsees, Anita. *Building Community Support for Foreign Languages.* New York:Northeast Conference on the Teaching of Foreign Languages and American Council on the Teaching of Foreign Languages, 1980. [Available from ACTFL Materials Center]

29 _____ "Public Awareness: How Can Associations and Institutions Use Public Relations Skills?" 71-89 in Gilbert A. Jarvis, ed., *The Challenge of Communication.* ACTFL Foreign Language Education Series, Volume 6. Skokie, IL: National Textbook Company, 1974.

30 Papalia, Anthony. "A Study of Attrition in Foreign Language Enrollments at Four Suburban Public Schools." *Foreign Language Annals* 4(1970):62-67.

31 *Professional Selling Skills II.* Greenwich, CT:Xerox Learning Systems, 1976.

32 "Report of the Task Force on Institutional Language Policy." New York:Modern Language Association, 1978.

33 Robinson, Gail L. "The Magic Carpet Ride to Another Culture Syndrome: An International Perspective." *Foreign Language Annals* 11 (1978):135-46.

34 Roman, Kenneth, and Jane Maas. *How To Advertise.* New York:St. Martins Press, 1976.

35 Scebold, C. Edward. "An ACTFL Position Paper: Foreign Language and International Education in the Twenty-first Century." *Foreign Language Annals* 12(1979):27-28.

36 Schwarz, Ted. *The Successful Promoter.* Chicago:Henry Regnery Company, 1976.

37 Seagrave, Maryalice D. "Everyone Loves a Winner." *Foreign Language Annals* 11(1978):49-52.

38 Strasheim, Lorraine A. "An Issue on the Horizon: The Role of Foreign Language in Global Education." *Foreign Language Annals* 12(1979): 29-34.

39 Teitelbaum, Sidney L. "The Selling of Foreign Languages." [Paper presented at the Colloquium of the New York State Association of Foreign Language Teachers, Albany, 1972.] [EDRS:ED 063 846.]

40 Toussaint, Gerard. Personal Communication, 1980.

41 Varela-Ibarra, José L. "Selling Languages." *Foreign Language Annals* 8(1975):111-13.

42 Williams, Charlie G. "Reaching for New Heights." [Results of statewide listening sessions in South Carolina, 1979.]

43 Williams, John. Personal Communication, 1979.

44 Wollstein, John D. Personal Communication, 1980. [Letter.]

45 Wood, Paul W. And Leslie Badanes. "Student Motivation: Try a Foreign Language Day!" *Foreign Language Annals* 11(1978):53-59.

3

Public policy:
The Washington connection

Becky Howard Owens
American Council on Education

Introduction

The political landscape in the nation's capital is dotted with all manner of organizations, coalitions, and individuals, all vying for influence over actions taken by the federal government. Each day marks the arrival of new groups on the scene, groups that appear to be a cross between contestants on *Let's Make A Deal* and pilgrims to Lourdes. A telling index is that in these and earlier troubled times, the construction industry flourishes in Washington while other markets stagnate.

Despite the existence of groups such as Common Cause, the League of Women Voters, and the American Friends Service Committee, the term *lobbyist* still conjures up the image of a cigar-smoking, slightly sinister perverter of the public will. This characterization has been kept alive by conscientious journalists who have sought, in the best muckraking tradition, to safeguard the integrity of the process that determines public policy. And the stereotype is indeed based on fact. As Woodrow Wilson was quick to point out, "suppose you go to Washington and try to get at your government. You will always find that while you are politely listened to, the men who are really consulted are the men who have the biggest stake—the big bankers, the big manufacturers, the big masters of commerce . . . The government of the

Becky Owens is director of the Office of International Education Policy and Associate Director of the Division of International Education Relations at the American Council on Education. She has been with ACE since 1973, formerly serving as Associate Director of its International Education Project. Prior to that time, she was on the Committee on the Future of International Studies as well as the staff of Senator Thomas F. Eagleton. She serves on the government regulations advisory committee of the National Association of Foreign Student Affairs, the federal relations committee of the International Studies Association, and on the Board of Trustees of the International Development Conference.

United States at present is a foster child of special interests" (Green et al., 4, p. 29).

These images die hard; but if there ever was truth in the Will Rogers quip, "Congress is the best money can buy," such is no longer the case. Sweeping changes have been brought about by new legislation governing campaign contributions and organized lobbies. As new interest groups are formed and the ranks of their membership swell to embrace a substantial portion of the population, old stereotypes gradually are giving way to a new style of legislative and policy involvement.

Pressure groups, whatever one chooses to call them, are deeply rooted in the American political heritage. They have both a statutory and a social basis. On the statutory level is the First Amendment's guarantee of free speech and the people's right to petition their government. As a social phenomenon, interest groups are considered to be inherent in the American psyche. Reference to this is made in Essay Number 10 of *The Federalist*, in which James Madison observes that "liberty is to faction what air is to fire. . . ." Alexis de Tocqueville (3) commented extensively on this peculiarly American tendency to promote—through organized groups—an extraordinary array of causes:

> As soon as several of the inhabitants of the United States have taken up an opinion or a feeling which they wish to promote in the world, they look out for mutual assistance; and as soon as they have found one another out, they combine. From that moment, they are no longer isolated men, but a power seen from afar, whose actions serve for an example and whose language is listened to. The first time I heard in the United States that a hundred thousand men had bound themselves publicly to abstain from spiritous liquors, it appeared to me more like a joke than a serious engagement, and I did not at once perceive why these temperate citizens could not content themselves by drinking water by their own firesides. I at last understood that these hundred thousand Americans, alarmed by the progress of drunkenness around them, had made up their minds to patronize temperance (p. 117-18).

From childhood through adulthood, from Cub Scouts and Brownies through fraternities and sororities to the Knights of Columbus and the Daughters of the American Revolution, Americans are encouraged to congregate and cooperate with like-minded citizens. That contemporary American politics should have this dimension is an inevitability. Today's Boy Scout is tomorrow's political activitist.

Educational interest groups

The federal government has reached its role in American education by steps. Although the Constitution delegates responsibility for education to state and local governments, it retains in the federal the prerogative of influencing educational initiatives for the advancement of social objectives. The shock of Sputnik prompted the enactment in 1958 of the National Defense Education Act. Precedent was established to use schools and colleges as the means to an end: eliminating racial inequality and sexual discrimination, alleviating crime and delinquency, removing societal barriers for the handicapped, reducing poverty and unemployment, and unlocking educational opportunities for students whose native language is not English.

This federal involvement with education has in the last two decades served to expand foreign language study, area studies, and scientific research. At present, the Department of Education is spending approximately $12 billion in support of federal education activities, including some $7 billion on elementary and secondary education and $5 billion on higher education. And higher education has become a large and diverse enterprise: a $50 billion sector employing more than 600,000 instructional and research staff and 1.3 million administrative and support personnel in some 3,000 institutions enrolling more than 11 million students and serving many millions of citizens in public service programs. Federal support currently provides approximately 20 percent of total operating funds for higher education (5).

In light of the growing importance of the federal government in all levels of education, the performance of educational interest groups has in past decades been relatively weak. There are valid reasons for the low profile such groups have traditionally maintained. One is the image of the lobbyist. Educators have been understandably reluctant to be viewed as money-grubbing lobbyists. Another is the fact that it is nearly impossible to achieve a consensus among the disparate professional interest groups found on any given campus. Yet another is the assumption, based on the mentality of the 1960s, that federal assistance was either unnecessary or unobtainable, that it would come with too many strings attached or would not justify the amount of effort necessary to get it. Finally, there has been confusion about federal tax laws that place lobbying restrictions on the nonprofit sector. This last point will be discussed in more detail later in this chapter.

Whatever the reasons that had kept education interest groups from more aggressively pursuing federal policy goals, the past decade has witnessed the emergence of these groups. At both the level of higher education and that of elementary and secondary education, performance has improved dramatically. The associations of higher education have pulled together to achieve a consensus position on the 1980 Higher Education Act, which contains numerous benefits for all types of two- and four-year institutions. This is in stark contrast to 1972, when the same effort ended in a shambles. These associations both closed ranks and united with influential labor lobbies to secure overrides of several attempted vetoes on labor and HEW issues during the Nixon years. Elementary and secondary educators, through the efforts of the National Education Association, are credited with the recently established cabinet-level Department of Education—this despite their failure to enlist the support or neutralize the opposition of the American Federation of Teachers and other groups. Education interest groups have now become active and effective participants in what one observer has termed the greatest political show on earth, the Washington policy arena.

Together with a new and urgent economic need to increase federal support of education, the improved performance of the education lobby has come in direct response to Congressional expectations and pressures. Representative Edith Green, chairwoman in 1972 of the House Education and Labor subcommittee, could barely contain her displeasure with the failure of higher education to render effective support for her efforts on its behalf. Her successor and current chairman of the subcommittee, Representative William D. Ford, commented in a recent interview (7):

> The education community has matured rapidly in recent years in their ability to understand the processes by which federal policy decisions are made, but they still have a long way to go. By and large, they're learning how to count. School administrators at all levels who know how to compete before their state legislatures come in here and reveal that they don't understand the basic legislative process and how different it is from any other legislature . . . I ask how many spent ten minutes in the past year talking to a member of Congress, either where they live or where their institution is located, specifically about an education issue. Unfortunately, you see an awful lot of downcast eyes as people realize they may never have talked to a congressman except me or a member of my committee. That's not how the system functions. Educators have been surprisingly reluctant to voice their views. We don't pass legislation here by making brilliant speeches and carrying the day with impeccable logic as they do in the movies. We pass a law when a majority is able and willing to recognize that a problem affects the people they represent (p. 35).

Ford's counterpart in the Senate, Claiborne Pell, goes so far as to say that education is more important to a nation than is its health. He, too, has been critical of past efforts, referring to the building that houses the majority of higher education associations as the Dupont Circle Fudge Factory. Pell now regards the higher education lobby as "much more professional and reasonable. They recognize they have to make compromises among themselves and also take into account the views of the Congress and the administration." (7)

Whether the effectiveness of the education lobby has been helped or hindered by the number of educational associations now on the scene is an open question. As if in response to the Biblical command, "go forth and multiply," the education community has proliferated. Their numbers alone could cause another Washington interest group, Zero Population Growth, to blanch. Counting the number of groups with a fundamental impact on educational policymaking is a bit like trying to guess the number of jelly beans in a jar. In his 1975 monograph, Stephen K. Bailey fixes the number at somewhere between 250 and 300 education associations, organizations, and institutional representatives located in or near the nation's capital. His taxonomy of these groups by types of representation includes: *umbrella organizations* such as the American Council on Education; *institutional associations* like the American Association of Community and Junior Colleges; *teacher unions* like the American Association of University Professors; *professions, fields, and disciplines* such as the Music Educators National Conference; *librarians, suppliers, and technologists* like the American Library Association; *religion, race, and sex* such as the National Catholic Educational Association; *liberal/labor lobbies* like the AFL-CIO; *institutions and institutional systems* like the New York State Education Department; *administrators and boards* such as the National School Boards Association; and *miscellaneous,* which includes organizations like the National Student Lobby (Bailey, 1).

Bailey notes that, among the 250 to 300 education groups identified, only a handful of 20, or so, were acknowledged by Congressional and administration education specialists to have substantial policy influence. Common elements found among staff members of the dominant educational associations were college degrees (often advanced degrees in law or education); extensive professional experience in journalism, administration, or teaching; previous work experience on Capitol Hill, in the Department of Health, Education, and Welfare, or other governmental settings; and origins in "America's hinterland, not in the Northeast."

A Specific note on international education lobbies

For a variety of reasons, lobby efforts for the international education field have been episodic. The word that explains the emergence and disappearance of such groups has been *crisis*. The word is both fitting and unfortunate— fitting because *crisis* aptly describes the Washington climate at the time of Sputnik, but unfortunate because *crisis* also describes the results of the tenuous and sporadic nature of the federal commitment.

There are a number of reasons why the international education lobby did not survive and become a permanent fixture since 1958. Then and through much of the 1960s, federal support to the field was merely frosting on the cake of private foundation largess. The Ford Foundation alone contributed some $242 million, or approximately $22 million a year, to international education efforts during the 1960s. The federal government, as of fiscal 1980, has failed to spend more than $18 million in any given year for language and area studies. A second reason is the "Motherhood Factor." While widespread support for international education exists among education associations and the institutions they represent, it has been, at best, of second priority when placed among programs promising more direct financial benefit and having potentially greater impact. The maintenance of an independent lobby or of a special focus lobby within a lobby was considered too costly. A third and more complex reason has to do with the nature of the field itself. Many disconnected activities comprise the international education field. A partial list would include language training and pedagogical research, scholarly exchange, foreign area and transnational research, technical assistance programs in developing countries, advanced foreign affairs research, the education of foreign students, study-abroad programs, global education, and teacher training. Efforts to represent such diversity are fraught with difficulty, and this difficulty is compounded by disputes among the various areas.

Since its inception in 1918, the American Council on Education (ACE) has had a commitment to international education. Prior to World War II, the Council's activities in this area were limited. Following the war, they expanded significantly, embracing a constantly widening sphere of policy concerns. However, discontinuities characterize ACE's presence in this area. Offices, committees, and commissions were created in response to needs articulated by the United States academic community and were terminated as those needs were met. In the early 1960s the Council disbanded yet another of its commissions while simultaneously helping to pave the way for the creation of a new semi-autonomous agency to represent exclusively international education concerns. That agency was Education and World Affairs (EWA).

Through its coordination of higher education institutions and language and area centers, EWA was instrumental in helping to secure passage of the International Education Act of 1966. This legislation, which was unanimously passed by Congress, was never funded, for anti-Vietnam sentiment swung Congressional and Administration attention back to pressing domestic problems. If it was not the sole cause, this defeat certainly hastened EWA's departure from the Washington scene.

To compensate for the loss of EWA, the International Council for Educational Development (ICED) temporarily assumed the burden of establishing a Washington office. The office performed essential service to the field during the lean years when President Nixon was trying to cut off federal funds for language and area studies. Finally unable to maintain a Washington office, ICED pulled back to its New York base and out of the legislative realm. In its place (and with its assistance) was established an ad hoc Committee on the Future of International Studies (COFIS), supported by individual contributions from approximately 100 college and university campuses. Unlike its predecessors, COFIS was charged with a dual mandate: 1) to block the termination of federal support for language and area studies and, indeed, to restore adequate funding levels for these programs and 2) to encourage the American Council on Education to resume policy leadership for the field by establishing a permanent office.

COFIS went out of existence in the fall of 1973 when ACE initiated the office it still maintains. Throughout the past decade, international education program offices have been maintained within the office of the higher education associations. Some of these programs, such as the activities of the National Association of State Universities and Land-Grant Colleges in the area of agricultural research and technical assistance, represent the particular policy interests of their member institutions within discrete segments of international education.

Interest group behavior

Before focusing on specific opportunities to influence policy decisions, it may be useful to provide an overview of the diverse types of interest groups in Washington and the respective functions of each. Formation of a group begins with the assumption that there is a compelling reason for its existence. Forming a group requires expenditures (sometimes large ones) of time, money, energy, and countless other resources. At some point, someone must have raised and received a satisfactory answer to the question, "why Washington and not Dubuque?" A group must perform some function or functions of critical importance to its membership in order to survive, although these functions may change—temporarily or permanently—as issues dictate. Groups are rarely static. At times the group must be at liberty to deploy its resources for a variety of related and even unrelated causes while still meeting its primary responsibility for direct services to its members.

While groups may be expected to perform a range of services for their constituents in general, their most typical and essential function is the pursuit of resources and policies beneficial to the members. Organizers are more willing to risk their own capital if they see the prospect of a substantial return on their investment. Other types of functions might include the assumption of an advocacy role for a particular philosophical or ideological point of view, the creation of a favorable public image for the members of the group, or the development and dissemination of information useful to constituents or government officials. At times all these elements are collapsed into the group's unified effort to influence public policy.

The ways in which groups bring their human and financial resources to bear on the political process are as varied as the groups themselves. At the heart of the policy process are elected officials. The natural assumption is that many of these elected officials have a not unnatural interest in being reelected. And, they are certainly in no position to help an interest group if they are not returned to office. Many nonprofit organizations, among these the National Education Association, have established Political Action Committees (PACs) under a different tax code for the purpose of accumulating funds to support the campaigns of legislators who have been helpful to them. In addition to the obvious tactic of direct campaign contributions, other means of assistance can be provided. Groups with unionized memberships, including teacher unions, have the option to commit electoral support. Other groups may apply the organizational and political skills of their members to campaign efforts, provide speaking platforms during the campaign, endorse a slate of candidates, or provide substantive information on campaign issues. Again, the range of possibilities is staggering, as are the opportunities to work against candidates whose views are not compatible with the objectives of the group.

After the election, what next?

The first and most important step toward incorporating the views and pursuing the goals of a particular interest in the policy arena is the careful and consistent monitoring of an endless stream of regulations, provisions, and laws. The second step is more monitoring; the third, still more monitoring. For any effective effort to be mounted, clear, precise, and immediate interpretations of consequential actions must be provided to the members of the group. For even a narrowly focused organization, this task can be staggering. The effort will typically involve the daily scrutiny of newspapers such as *The Washington Post* and *The New York Times;* government publications including the *Federal Register* and the *Congressional Record;* and of specialized journals and tabloids containing relevant information.

Subsequent strategies will be based on information obtained from the monitoring of pertinent government activities. The group must keep abreast of developments that might harm or help its interests. If a policy initiative suggests negative consequences or spells disaster for the group, a defensive strategy is in order. Contrary to the widely held notion that interest groups attempt to promote causes, these groups spend almost as much effort trying to prevent actions. Efforts to prevent often are more effective: It is easier to get a legislator to do nothing than to do something.

Initiating activity requires a more deliberate and more carefully planned strategy. Central to the success of this effort is the cultivation of good working relationships with key staff members on essential subcommittees and in member's offices. Access often does spell success; and lack of access surely guarantees failure. Contact with these key aides or with the member provides the chance to use the most important tool available to the representative of an interest group—information. Ever-increasing demands are made on members of Congress to become technical experts on scores of issues. The lobbyist who has reliable data and substantive knowledge to contribute to a member's understanding of a given topic is an invaluable resource.

Other elements necessary to developing a strategy for initiating legislative activity include identifying a sponsor for the initiative, building support for that sponsor's effort through co-sponsorship, balancing majority and minority support, ensuring that the group's members are clearly expressing their encouragement and appreciation, and building alliances with other influential political groups that back the initiative.

Perversities of education lobbying

Interaction between the education groups on one hand and the Congress and Administration on the other is hampered by the restrictions of Section 501(c)(3) of the Internal Revenue Code. This section prohibits an organization from claiming a tax-exempt status if it is an "action" organization (that is, one that devotes a significant amount of its time and resources to dealing with the Congress).

The conditions that presently govern the relationship between education groups and the Congress are a legacy of the highly-criticized Federal Regulation of Lobbying Act of 1946. Passed in reaction to scandal, the act required paid lobbyists to register as such with the Clerk of the House and the Secretary of the Senate and to file quarterly reports with the House Clerk. In the thirty-three years during which the statute has been on the books, few lobbyists have been prosecuted.

Rather than dampen the reformist spirit in Congress, the relative weakness of the 1946 Code has served to increase the efforts of those members who want stricter controls. Nearly each new session of Congress begins by putting Tax Code reform on its docket and ends having failed to pass any new tax legislation. The most recent modification dates from the passage of the 1969 Tax Reform Act, which was intended to impose a particular restriction on the activities of tax-exempt entities, notably foundations. During the height of domestic tensions that were in part related to Vietnam, the Nixon Administration believed that these institutions emerged as all-too-outspoken liberal activitists.

Legislation introduced in 1976–1976, and 1977–1978, failed; legislation is at present pending. Each of these efforts has similar components, including a much more stringent reporting and filing requirement for nonprofit institutions, restrictions on contact with Administration officials, and some restriction on the activities of grass-roots lobbies. The regulation in effect until a new law is passed states that an organization will be regarded as attempting to influence legislation if the organization (a) contacts or urges the public to contact members of the legislative body for purposes of proposing, supporting, or opposing legislation; (b) advocates the adoption or rejection of legislation; (c) attempts to influence the outcome of a political campaign; or (d) mounts grass-roots campaigns designed to affect the opinion of the general public.

Although some tension is inevitable in education groups who must operate under some conditions, there have been few prosecutions for violations of these requirements. However, the activities of organizations covered by

501(c)(3) do tend to take on a sleight-of-hand character as these organizations seek to "influence" but not "lobby," to provide pertinent information to Congress only at the "request" of that body.

Stages of the policy process

The first step in a year-long effort to move legislation through the Congress is the preparation of an agency budget for the fiscal year. The budget office of the agency usually begins this effort by midsummer of the preceding year. Around November the agency submits a budget for each of its programs; the budget is then reviewed by the Office of Management and Budget. The OMB takes the aggregate budgets of all the federal agencies and puts them into overall alignment with the fiscal and policy priorities of the President.

In January of the new year, the President announces the broad dimensions of the budget to Congress and to the nation in his State of the Union message. About one week later, the detailed budget is formally released through a series of briefings held for interested groups by each of the federal agencies, and the budget is formally transmitted to the Congress. In Congress the relevant sub-committees receive budgets for programs under their jurisdictions and begin scheduling hearings on the budget and policy proposals.

By late February or March, hearings begin and Administration witnesses defend their budget and program submissions. These hearings, which may last a month or more, are followed by hearings for public witnesses. All interested parties who wish to support or challenge the Administration budget may ask to testify before the subcommittees at this point. During this phase, constituent mail and visits with members are extremely important. The subcommittee then undertakes the task of shaping the legislation or budget in a session known as *markup*. When the subcommittee has completed its work, the bill is forwarded to the full parent committee, which also must pass on the legislation. The subcommittee's version of the bill may be accepted, or changes may be made. Finally, the bill is sent from full committee to the floor of the House or Senate committees and subcommittees. By the time floor action has been taken by both chambers, it is usually late summer or early fall.

The final step to produce a completed law is a House-Senate conference committee that arbitrates any disputes between the House and Senate versions. Here again, it is essential that interested groups make known their preferences. When a compromise bill is arrived at, it must be returned to the House and the Senate, both of which must approve the Conference Report. Assuming satisfactory compromise has been achieved in the conference committee, this is a *pro forma* step. The legislation then must be forwarded to the President for signing. In the event of a Presidential veto, a two-thirds majority in both houses is needed to override the veto.

Opportunities for individual participation

The opportunities for citizen participation in the policy-making process are many, and these efforts can be effective. One may act alone or as a member of an interest group. The range of options for individuals participating in this process includes the following:

- Become familiar with the Congress, its procedures, its members and their ideologies and interests.
- Establish contact with key members and their staff assistants. Keep such contacts, whether written or spoken, brief and to the point.
- Present testimony before the appropriate Congressional subcommittees, or submit written testimony for the record.
- Join in the efforts of others to endorse and support legislation favorable to your area of concern.
- Communicate with Congress not only about negative actions taken but also to indicate appreciation for efforts you consider positive.
- Become a dependable source of information and data on the impact of various proposals upon the members' state or district.

After Congress: Tackling the Executive Branch _____

The policy process in Washington is designed to turn optimists into cynics faster than Chrysler can lose money. Our governing principle must be that pitfalls are many and real victories are few. Certainly, within the Executive Branch—a mélange of nonelected officials, presidential appointees, and career civil servants, as well as the president himself—there is opportunity for interference from those not sympathetic to interest group aspirations. One recent convert to cynicism remarked, "The biggest mistake I ever made was thinking I had won the victory just by getting a bill through Congress. That was only the beginning." The president may veto a bill; or, barring that extreme action, he may refuse to permit the spending of all the money Congress has designated; or the federal agency charged with carrying out the program may write ineffective or even counteractive regulations within the Congressional guidelines or simply may not enforce the provisions of the law.

The single factor that lends the most weight and importance to the activities of the Executive branch is not its size or its scope but its broad discretionary authority. Every day, options are exercised and decisions made by executive officials; these actions can shape policy either directly or indirectly. The complexity of modern society contributes to and necessitates the increase of discretionary powers by executive personnel. Even mundane operations require an increasingly high degree of technical knowledge. Since the government is involved in nearly every phase of human existence, its decision-making processes must adapt to rapidly changing conditions. In general, the slower and more deliberative method of the legislature, with its tendency to lock solidly into place laws and statutes, is ill-suited to adjust to dynamic circumstances. Indeed, Congress adds to the discretionary powers of the Executive branch through its prior consultation with agency officials to ensure the technical accuracy of pending legislation.

Gaining access to the Executive branch is not easy. Non-elected agency officials have little reason to be as responsive to pressures of interest groups as are members of the legislature. Often groups with established relationships to the Congress represent interests and issues of little interest to the president. While Executive branch officials below cabinet level tend to have little impact on members of Congress, individual members frequently may exert measurable influence on behalf of interest groups on agency decisions. Finally, lurking within the Executive branch is an agency of great importance to all interest groups but readily accessible to none: the Office of Management and Budget.

When dealing with the Executive branch, interest groups have the same objectives as those they have when dealing with the Legislative branch—advancing and protecting the group's aims. Here too, the most critical step in efforts to influence is the monitoring of its anticipated activity. Presidential directives, proposed regulations or proposed changes in regulation, agency position statements—all provide clues to impending policy decisions which must be examined.

Some tactics are similar to those used with the Congress. The President may be, and often is, sent letters by groups seeking to meet with him or gain his endorsement or support for a position. In general, this tactic is doomed unless the letters arrive in such volume that they simply cannot be ignored or delegated. However, contact with groups may be instigated by the President when he is seeking support for a new course of action.

A more likely avenue of access to the White House is through one of several advisory offices. The past two decades witnessed a burgeoning of special staff positions and offices established to serve either as gatekeepers or as conduits of interest group opinion to the president. Such positions include the special assistants to the president for aging, consumer affairs, ethnic affairs, Hispanic affairs, women's concerns, and the like. Offices include those dealing with science and technology, the environment, drug abuse, domestic policy, and economic policy. Thomas Cronin (2) states that "presidents have appointed either an aide or an office for every American dilemma."

But strategy for dealing with the Executive branch may also employ a set of approaches vastly different from those used with the Congress. An interest group may ask an agency to hold open public hearings in Washington or in the several regions, or that an agency be brought into a hearing by the Congressional committee charged with overseeing its programs. Litigation may also be used. When an interest group takes this step (for example, to enjoin an agency not to take a particular action) sympathetic members of Congress may provide added leverage by joining the suit. Still another step to spur Administration or

Congressional action is working for passage of a state law that might then also be enacted at the national level. (This happened with no-fault insurance.) Finally, getting involved during presidential campaigns with the platform committee and the leading candidates can often yield results, as it did in the 1976 quest of the National Education Association for a separate Department of Education.

Conclusion

The 1970s were a decade of explosive growth for lobbying groups in the nation's capital. To be sure, groups had a significant impact in the preceding century. However, given the more limited scope of government at that time, their influence was likewise limited. The dramatic increase in the numbers of interest groups in the second half of the twentieth century has been accompanied by a shift from the direct purchase of political influence (common in the 1800s) to more sophisticated methods of eliciting support from Congress. While the investment of substantial sums of money in congressional campaigns is still common, it is neither so blatant nor so unquestionably effective as it was in the era of Senator Boies Penrose from Pennsylvania. In the early 1900s, when addressing a group of his corporate sponsors, he said, "I believe in a division of labor. You send us to Congress; we pass laws under . . . which you make money; . . . and out of your profits you further contribute to our campaign funds to send us back again to pass more laws to enable you to make more money" (Green et al., 4, pp. 7–8).

The growth of interest groups competing for influence in the political arena has paralleled the increase in the complexity of our society, and consequently of our government. (Barring some radical reform in campaign financing practices or the adoption of stringent new tax codes to restrict the activities of interest groups, this situation is here to stay.) Of some 20,000 or more bills and resolutions introduced annually in Congress through the committee apparatus, only approximately 1,000 are reported out of committee. As the work load of Congress has swelled to embrace multifaceted problems, narrow subject-area specializations have developed among the members of Congress. This tendency has contributed to the fragmentation of interest groups, a dominant (and controversial) trend of the past two decades.

The burgeoning bureaucracy has created a second major trend in this century, a trend that is also unlikely to change. Bureaus, departments, institutes, agencies, and independent regulatory commissions were given life during the 1930s. Most of them have proven to be hardier than crabgrass and twice as difficult to eliminate. Interest group lobbying directed toward the Executive branch—a neglected and unnecessary art form until the 1900s—surely is here to stay.

It would be unwise to speculate on which of these two branches of government is more critical to an interest group. The simple answer is *both*. Neither can be slighted, for theirs is a fluid relationship with shifting spheres of power and influence. In addition, there generally is some degree of tension between the two branches that frequently may be exploited to the advantage of a particular interest. This tension is less evident with a strong president and a majority party controlling the Congress, as was the case during Lyndon Johnson's presidency. Conversely, when Congress was dominated by the opposing party, as it was during Richard Nixon's presidency, the machinery of government is paralyzed by the resulting clash of wills.

In reaction to Nixon's "imperial presidency," Congress has loomed large in the policy-making of the 1970s. Perhaps the most telling indication of this increased assertiveness is its expanded attention to foreign policy, an area dominated almost exclusively in the past by the Executive branch. The Congress initially struggled to wrest control from Nixon and Kissinger, but it has continued to strengthen its hold on foreign policy through the passage of the War Powers Act, through threats of scrapping the Panama Canal Treaty, and through failure to pass the SALT II Treaty. Yet a strong and respected president could cause the balance to shift again.

It is important to bear in mind the fluidity of the relationships among and between the Congress, the Administration, and the myriad interest groups. This force is described by Bailey (1) as the "Yin and Yang of democratic politics." It is impossible to predict the precise shape, nature, or role of interest groups in the coming years, yet few such groups in existence today exhibit the characteristics of an endangered species. In fact, they are alive and well and operating under the assumption that the squeaky wheel gets the grease. But it would also be unwise to assume that the system can absorb, or that the public will tolerate, an infinite number of such groups.

The current economic health of the nation together with pressures to balance the budget may determine the direction taken in the 1980s. Fragmentation and jealousy has been an enduring problem of varying intensity within education interest groups and within the international education elements within such groups. If cuts in Federal spending continue, this problem can only increase as groups vie for those funds that are available. The need for closer collaboration among international education groups is essential, but cooperation must evolve in a manner that enriches and benefits the various parts, preserves the integrity of diverse program interests, and ultimately advances the whole. Interested groups and individuals must work together to defend the need for making international education a higher priority on the national agenda; they must gain increased access to Congressional and Administration decision-makers; and they must, with their counterparts at state and local levels, become more sophisticated about electoral politics; above all, they must widen the network of involvement. The prospect for success in a united effort of this nature may be stronger now than at any previous point in the nation's history; the price of failure surely will be to perpetuate, in the words of Congressman Paul Simon (6), "a population increasingly insensitive to the complex problems of an increasingly interdependent world."

References, Public policy: The Washington connection

1 Bailey, Stephen K. *Education Interest Groups in the Nation's Capital.* Washington: American Council on Education, 1975.

2 Cronin, Thomas. *The State of the Presidency.* Boston: Little, Brown, 1975.

3 de Tocqueville, Alexis. *Democracy in America,* Volume II. New York: Alfred A. Knopf, Inc., 1945.

4 Green, Mark J., James M. Fallows, and David R. Zwick. *Who Runs Congress?* New York: Bantam Books, Inc. and Grossman Publishers, 1972.

5 *A Higher Education Agenda for the 96th Congress.* Washington: American Council on Education, 1979.

6 Simon, Paul. Testimony to the Subcommittee on International Operations, U.S. House of Representatives, Washington, July 1978.

7 "An Unlikely Duo: Claiborne Pell and William Ford," 33–37 in Marcy V. Massengale, ed., *Educational Record* 61:1. Washington: American Council on Education, 1980.

A case study:
The foreign language liaison

Johanna S. R. Mendelson

Joint National Committee for Languages

A Tallahassee, Florida, public interest group recently printed a T-shirt with this message:

> "I can't wait to see the day that the schools have all the money they need and the Air Force has to hold a bake sale to buy a bomber."

I have yet to see the Air Force short of funds; but the schools, and especially certain educational programs, have succumbed to Proposition 13 fever at the local level and the fiscal conservatism of the Congress at the national. Education in general and international education in particular falls low on the list of national priorities in 1980. It is a paradox of our times that precisely when the United States requires expertise in the management of global affairs, support for education designed to meet those needs has fallen to record low levels. In spite of its being made a cabinet-level agency, the Department of Education will encounter a long, hard battle to increase funding for educational programs to a realistic level after years of decreasing appropriations and the effects of severe inflation. Even more ironic is that the National Defense Education Act (the educational response to the cold war) is now more than twenty years old and faltering for lack of money. This program, more than any other, was directed at combating a serious deficiency in our knowledge of other nations; of our allies and enemies; and of foreign languages, cultures, history, politics, and economics. How did a program that is so much a part of this nation's security and its need to know and learn about the rest of the world fall into such disarray? This and many other questions about foreign language training and international education were the subjects addressed by the President's Commission on Foreign Language and International Studies, which was convened in 1978. A year of hearings, public inquiries held around the country, and special reports commissioned by this body yielded a sorry picture of

Johanna S. R. Mendelson (Ph.D., Washington University) is Director of the Washington Office of the Joint National Committee for Languages, where she develops legislative priorities, consults with legislators and their staffs and with other Washington agencies concerned with language study, international education, and related issues. She has experience in monitoring legislation and policy concerning language and area studies; she has served as co-chair of the Washington Office of the Latin American Studies Association, as assistant director and information officer for the Center for Defense Information. She is currently co-chair of the Washington Humanities Forum.

America's ignorance of things foreign, evidence of a decline in language training unparalleled in our educational history, and finally a mandate to revitalize
foreign language training and international studies to meet the challenges
America will face in the closing years of this century.

The most obvious challenge mentioned in the Commission's final report,
Strength Through Wisdom, was to increase federal funding for foreign
language training and international studies to a realistic amount—an amount
that would provide instruction to students at all educational levels and so well
distributed geographically that persons in every state could be afforded some
opportunity to learn more about the rest of the world.

Meeting this challenge was another matter. In spite of the growing number
of constituencies devoted to working for international education and foreign
language training, these groups often worked independently (and redundantly)
without a uniform program or specific goals. If the recommendations of the
President's Commission were to be more than a dead letter, some concerted
action by professionals was needed.

The Joint National Committee for Languages (JNCL), a coalition of ten
professional language associations, embarked on a Washington project in 1980
with the creation of a liaison office designed to serve the profession in several
ways: to monitor and respond to legislative initiatives growing out of the
recommendations of the President's Commission; to initiate and develop programs for legislative implementation, programs that would reflect new trends
in foreign language training and national needs; to focus attention on the
absence of national policies about foreign language needs and their link to
international education programs; and finally (and perhaps most importantly)
to ally the language profession with those professionals concerned with the
promotion of international education.

The Washington liaison office is precisely what its title implies. It is a liaison
between the federal government and the professional associations that it represents. It provides information about federal programs and legislation and
simultaneously serves as a forum for voicing professional concerns about
federal policies on foreign language training and international education.
While outlets for an exchange of information have long existed in each professional organization and at universities with programs sponsored by the American Council on Education's Division of International Education Relations, a
special outlet for voicing the mutual concerns of professional organizations—
an outlet that encompasses the interests of individual teachers, scholars, and
administrators—is unique.

The philosophy of the liaison office is based on the premise that the profession is already organized and that it now must make use of a network designed
to spread the word about issues that confront it and require a response. For
example, the American Council on the Teaching of Foreign Languages
(ACTFL) divided its national membership into twelve geographic regions, and

selected leaders to serve as recipients and disseminators of relevant information. (See *Foreign Language Annals* 13 (1980): 200–2 for details.) Other organizations, such as the Latin American Studies Association, are already broken down into regional affiliates whose leaders could become contact points in a communication chain designed to evoke response to events affecting the profession on a national level. The Washington liaison office also affords the opportunity to unite on certain issues with major national organizations like the American Federation of Teachers, the National Educational Association, and the National Council for the Social Studies. Such contacts provide a great deal of clout in efforts to promote foreign language training and programs in international education. The possibilities of these consolidated efforts are enormous, and a Washington presence—in the form of a liaison office—can inaugurate these long overdue alliances in the educational field.

Getting involved

On the political battlefield, you must affect legislation before it affects you. Learning how to use your particular interests to complement those of others can help to win powerful allies.

To affect legislation successfully requires three ingredients: timing, information, and legwork. All three are critical to the ability of a group to achieve the desired action on an issue or a piece of legislation. These three are also to be considered when a constituency responds to a Washington liaison's call for support. For example, this year the incorporation of programs heretofore known as the National Defense Education Act, Title VI; the Mutual Exchange and Education Act, Section 102b; and the International Education Act of 1966 were slated for incorporation into a new title of the Higher Education Act of 1980. This drastic revamping of all education programs dealing with foreign language training, international and citizen education, and foreign exchanges made it imperative that constituencies affected by it make suggestions on the rewriting of this new title of the Higher Education Act. *Timing* was a critical factor in making known opinions about this legislation. Work on the legislation began in the first session of the 96th Congress in the House of Representatives and continued into the second session in the Senate. The House of Representatives held hearings about the new title last spring, drafted a bill reflecting the hearing commentaries, and wrote a report on the title. This report appeared in November 1979. The information in it reflected the recent findings of the President's Commission and expressed some of the same concerns about the pressing need to continue effective programs in foreign language training and international education. Next, the House version was sent to the appropriate Senate subcommittee (*viz.,* the Senate's Arts and Humanities Subcommittee of the Labor and Human Resources Committee). There in committee the House version met the Senate version, which contained some major changes and additions. These changes reflected both the concern of educators who wanted more funds for citizens' education programs and the feeling that the private sector should play a more visible role in educating Americans about foreign trade. These new additions to the bill were adopted.

The report reflected the composite interests of various university and professional-association constituencies. It also renewed the federal commitment to education in foreign cultures and to foreign language training. These activities were so carefully monitored that at each stage of the process the liaison knew where the bill was and whether there was a need for letters of support from constituents. When this written support was needed, the ACTFL network put out a call. Timing was critical to monitoring the legislation.

It was equally urgent that *information* and letters of support for Senate initiatives be provided for Committee staff. In the case of this Senate bill, letters from corporate executives in support of business involvement in international education were extremely valuable.

Legwork, the last ingredient in the triangle, was important because of the large amount of shuffling between House and Senate that was necessary to reaching agreement on the language of the bill. Long hours of telephoning were necessary in order to sustain interest and attention. The liaison also had to anticipate problems that the legislation might encounter in conference, when members of authorizing committees of the House and Senate sit down to hammer out final language before the bill goes to the president for signing.

In addition to understanding the importance of timing, information, and legwork in lobbying, knowing some other guidelines can be helpful. First, know thy congress, and know their legislation. Know the individuals on the committees that affect your area of interest. Second, let the constituencies you represent know who the key members of Congress are. You cannot make your voice heard unless you know who is responsible for a piece of legislation and what his or her position is on a given issue. A Washington liaison can help you find out who's who, and can assist you in defining the issues and listing the pros and cons of a position. It is your responsibility, however, to back up the liaison office with letters, telephone calls, or telegrams when the need arises. And if you are a constituent of a person on one of these key committees you are doubly bound to communicate because your letter or phone call will carry even more weight.

If you are coming to Washington and you wish to see your representative, contact your liaison office. By letting your representative know how you feel, and by asking for his or her thoughts about foreign language and international studies, you gain support for this issue. Members of Congress are elected to represent *your* views, and they should listen when you discuss your feelings with them.

It is not necessary to travel to Washington and express your views in person; every representative in the House and Senate maintains local offices. Make a visit to one of these, and follow up with information if it is requested. The information will be passed on to Washington. Always be sure to let local offices know that your organization has a Washington office. This way the representative can correspond with the liaison.

Finally, it is important that, when your association asks you to send letters to a representative in support of or critical of legislation, these letters be sent immediately. As mentioned earlier, timing is the key to affecting legislation beneficial to you as an individual and as a member of your profession. Carbon or xeroxed copies of correspondence should be sent to the liaison office.

There are many things you can do locally. Use existing community forums to articulate your point of view. Civic associations, PTAs, world affairs councils, churches and synagogues all sponsor programs. The only way to call attention to an issue is to bring it to the public. By doing so you will identify yourself as a leader and will attract others who would like to become involved. These people can become valuable allies.

Another excellent way to bring issues to the attention of politicians is to let those politicians respond to your concerns about Federal policies, foreign language training, and the need for international education. If you attend political rallies or if a candidate for office appears at a local gathering, be sure to ask questions about this issue. If you do not receive a satisfactory response, follow up with a letter. Candidates for elected office should be aware of the President's Commission report; if they are not, you should tell them about it.

Remember that most politicians want to respond to the needs of their constituents. However, some of these needs conflict with others; it helps to gain visibility and develop credibility with a politician's staff so that your group has a better chance of being heard and of having your need filled.

When meeting with your representatives, state your case simply and succinctly. If you do not know the answer to a question, say so; and add that you would be happy to find out. Do promptly any follow up that you promise.

There are many ways that you can make your presence felt even in our political process. There are things you can do through membership in a professional organization that supports lobbying activities on behalf of the profession—you help indirectly by paying your dues and directly by responding to requests for letters to Congress on specific issues. The guidelines that follow are designed to help you in composing such letters.

Letters and postcards

Your representative's vote on a particular issue is strongly affected by local public opinion; yet how many times has each of us said, "I've been meaning to write to my representative, but I just can't find the time"? You need not always write a formal letter; keep a stack of postcards at hand. A postcard, if received when an issue is in committee or just before a vote, can be useful to your representative because Congressional staffers keep tallies of those for and against an issue. (To receive "Action Alerts" when key issues are before Congress, write ACTFL or JNCL.)

Where to Write

Representative _____   Senator _____
House Office Building   Senate Office Building
Washington, DC 20515   Washington, DC 20510

How to write the president

The White House provides the president with a synopsis of comments on his speeches and on other issues. Direct your comments to the president's staff. You will get a more individualized response if you ask a specific question about the president's policy or a factual question such as, "what initiatives has the White House taken to ensure that the recommendations of the President's Commission on Foreign Language and International Studies will be implemented in the next few years?" Write:

> The President
> The White House
> Washington, DC 20500

For immediate response send a wire

1 Dial Directory Assistance, (800) 555-1212, and ask for the toll-free Western Union number for your area code.
2 Dictate your message and have it charged to your phone.
3 Current costs: A "public opinion message," delivered within hours to a member of Congress, your statehouse, or the White House is available at a special reduced rate of $2.50 for up to 15 words.

4

New opportunities for interprofessional cooperation

Norman Abramowitz
Henry Ferguson
New York State Education Department

As aliens to this land and as a people of commerce, Americans have always had a foreign dimension to their lives and livelihoods. What has been diminished over the years is the sense of global perspective that should accompany this dimension.

The idea of teaching from a global perspective is as old as Ben Franklin and as American as Jeffersonian democracy. It is a combination of the Enlightenment belief in liberal education and the practical goals of vocational education and education for citizenship.

Norman Abramowitz (A.M., University of Tennessee; A.B., CCNY) is Associate in Foreign Area Studies at the New York State Education Department, Albany, New York, and a teacher of social studies. He has extensive experience both in coordinating faculty development seminars and materials development projects on the pre-collegiate level in Asian and international studies and in research and administration of grants in the field. He has served as a member of the U.S. Commissioner of Education's Task Force on Global Education and as a consultant to the National Assessment of Educational Progress of the Education Commission of the States and to UNICEF. He has co-authored articles in the publications of the Association for Supervisors and Curriculum Development and of the National Council for the Social Studies.

Henry Ferguson (Ph.D., Harvard University) is Director, Center for International Programs and Comparative Studies, New York State Education Department. He has taught South Asian Studies, Intercultural Studies, and History at Union College in New York, Trinity College in Connecticut, and Syracuse University. He was Senior Fellow in Oriental Studies at Columbia University. He was the founding Chairman, Joint Area Colleges Committee on Non-Western Studies in East Central New York, and he served as Director, Educational Resources Center, New Delhi, India. He has been president of Connecticut Book Publishers Association and of InterCulture Associates, Inc., a publishing firm. The second edition of his *Manual for Multicultural and Ethnic Studies* (1978) will be published in 1981.

Thomas Jefferson saw the teaching of history as a means of availing the young "of the experience of other times and nations; it will qualify them as judges of actions and designs of men; it will enable them to know ambition under every disguise. . ." Franklin saw the study of world history as giving opportunity to "expound on the advantage of liberty" and the "benefits arising from good laws, and from a due execution of justice. . ." (Commager, 5, p.24).

Most school children know that some of the Founding Fathers—among them John Adams and John Jay—served as ambassadors abroad. The curriculum of Franklin's Academy in Philadelphia, in stressing world history and foreign languages, reflected Franklin's foreign experiences. In 1816 the U.S. Military Academy opened its doors to foreign students. In 1840 the Library of Congress began exchanging books with foreign nations, and in 1878 a Division of Foreign Schools Systems was established at the U.S. Office of Education.

In the eighteenth and nineteenth centuries, the study of foreign languages was seen as a practical means of connecting people by teaching about their common heritage and by articulating their common fate. Knowledge of languages was also viewed as a means of facilitating commerce. And the literature of other languages, in turn, with its descriptions of different lands and peoples, was regarded as a humanizing and civilizing influence.

In the recent past, one expressed aim of American education was to understand the world at present so as to be able to deal with the world as it was to become. Forty-six years ago, the American Historical Association's "Investigation of the Social Studies in the Schools" recommended developing in Americans an informed appreciation of the cultural bonds that were developing rapidly among all nations of the world, of the increasing economic interdependence of politically separate areas and peoples, and of the emerging economic integration of the globe.

What is different now is that the ingredients of a liberal education are missing, and there is a need to convince American educators and the public at large of the desirability and usefulness of such an education for all students.

The concept of a core curriculum as a means of achieving a liberal education has given way to the pressures engendered by universal education, of an isolationist political ideology, and a misreading of "progressive" education literature.

In addition, the nomenclature of the subject matter of international studies has changed with the rise of new disciplines and the improvement of technology. The study of political economy and of geography and agronomy has given way to international economics, cultural anthropology, and ecological and environmental studies. The lines between science and social science and among the components of the social sciences themselves have become more distinct in the last century as a result of specialization, departmentalization, and the explosion of knowledge.

Barriers and fences ⸻

Although compartmentalization of learning goes at least as far back in Western history as the thirteenth century, its acceleration and institutionalization took place in America within the last century. Universities in the United States showed a remarkable liberality and fluidity in their course offerings, their requirements, and their assignment of faculty until the latter third of the nineteenth century. The experiences of major figures in American higher education in the German universities and particularly in their seminar system propelled our colleges into a departmental framework toward which the increasing complexity of knowledge and methodologies had already been moving them. As the twentieth century became even more complex and technology acquired the honorific *high*, it became manifestly impossible to persist in the myth of the Universal Man, either as an objective for educating the American collegian or as a model for the faculty member on the college campus. Departments acquired their own independent identities and quickly found ways to make those identities permanent. Fences were erected, the most obvious, of course, being the evolution of countless new and esoteric languages for each of the professions—jargons to which the uninitiated could not be party.

The structure of American education at the same time required that the person who wished to be a classroom teacher of young and adolescent children had to pass through a university program. There are very few teachers still in service who are products of the old normal school, and practically none who were able to begin to teach without the baccalaureate. This change meant that for four years the preservice teacher was exposed to the departmental and disciplinary divisions that had come to characterize the American university. Accreditation of teachers, too, came to be done according to narrower criteria than before. Thus was reproduced in the American school, particularly the high school, all of the barriers to intellectual exchange that were already hobbling the university and making its campus politics a Machiavellian nightmare. In recent years this trend has become much more obvious, and it has become clear that while such divisions may work to protect a particular group of professionals, they also work to limit or obstruct change of any kind. Each department considers itself required by the laws of survival to protect itself against intruders. Even the fellow teacher who wants to cooperate is looked upon with suspicion. Dialogue between disciplines can become impossible amid the clatter of academic machine guns and the explosion of hostile memoranda.

In addition, the task of infusing global perspective into curricula is made more difficult by the imprecision of the term *global education,* which means different things to different people. As a new term in educational circles, it suffers from the added disability of being regarded by some as a vehicle for special pleaders and political activists. The alternate term, *international education,* has its own liabilities, most of these created by its generally being used as a synonym for comparative education by those institutions of higher education.

Whatever its name, the effort to revive the study of issues of global concern and the study of languages of foreign peoples has created greater awareness of the need for reestablishing dialogue among the disciplines, especially the social sciences, and for more cooperative efforts among educational institutions to achieve common goals.

Although differing in methodology and in expected outcomes, educators seem to agree on the need to set practical educational goals in global and international studies that citizens at large can support with confidence.

Becker (2) views the issue as one concerned with basic competency in this interdependent world and as providing a means of helping to "connect rather than divide men, to make clear their common humanity and to emphasize their common fate." (p.3)

Some see global education as a means of promoting critical thinking, creating a personal value system, providing a way of developing empathy for other cultures as well as an awareness of how other nations and people affect the United States. Still others see global studies as providing "survival skills" for the United States and for the individual in this increasingly turbulent and unpredictable world. This has been the rationale behind much of the federal support of international studies over the last thirty-five years.

In 1946 President Truman saw American participation in UNESCO as a means to free the minds of all people of ignorance, prejudice, suspicion and fear and of educating them for "justice, liberty, and peace." The 1960 Presidential Commission on National Goals advised that a basic goal for each American is to achieve a sense of responsiblity as broad as his worldwide concerns and as compelling as the danger he confronts.

The final act of the Helsinki accords of 1975 committed the signatories "to encourage the study of foreign language and civilization as an important means of expanding communication among peoples."

The 1958 National Defense Education Act, which provided funds for research, instruction, materials, and student support in "critical languages" and—in later years—in foreign area studies, was, as its name implies, presented to Congress as a defense measure.

The university area centers that grew out of this funding developed interdisciplinary degree programs, provided for geographic area specialization, and encouraged students to begin the study of modern languages as a part of their course work in the social sciences. The area centers fostered the integration of the social sciences and brought diverse disciplinary approaches to bear on area problems, thereby enabling students to themselves integrate such knowledge.

Congressional funding for university area studies programs continues to this day and should be the envy of precollegiate educators despite the inflationary inroads that reduce the real dollar values of these fixed allocations.

In the 1979–1980 federal fiscal year, some $16 million is being disbursed to eighty universities and colleges under provisions of the National Defense Education Act. In addition, $6 million is reserved for research scholars, who will study abroad, and for other graduate and undergraduate fellowships and programs. By contrast, in this same year, funds for precollegiate international education are $2 million for the new Citizen Education for Cultural Understanding Program (which does not include foreign language programs) and $1.5 million for Group Projects Abroad. Most recipients of the grants are colleges and universities. An additional sum of $42 million is allocated for international cultural exchanges under programs of the U.S. International Communication Agency; these exchanges do not involve school programs for school teachers. At the time of this writing, upward revisions for 1981 appeared likely.

It is estimated that the Ford Foundation disbursed more than $300 million to universities in support of international studies programs from 1951 to the late 1960s. Three out of eight college and university scholars who studied abroad in 1973 were supported by this foundation. In 1976, 460 foundations awarded 4,000 grants, 679 of which were for international studies; all were for work above the high school level. In the same year, 800 major American corporations awarded grants of $438 million, only $6 million of which were disbursed for precollegiate educational programs. Most important, none of these funds went for programs in international education or foreign languages. We must find means of doing better.

Of the millions of dollars disbursed by the U.S. Office of Education for the upgrading of the knowledge and skills of precollegiate teachers under the NDEA program of the late 1960s, only a small percentage were allocated for subjects that may be called international or global.

Outreach from universities to schools

The foregoing discussion is not meant to suggest that university based projects have had little effect on the schools. A number of teachers of social studies and the humanities have improved their professional skills and widened their international perspectives in these programs. Some of these teachers are now forming the spearhead of a movement to secure federal and foundation support for projects developed at the school-district level rather than at universities.

A number of curriculum projects conducted by colleges and universities have been introduced in schools. A few have even survived the cutting off of outside funding for their projects. Some have published significant instructional materials. The discipline-oriented projects covered subjects such as anthropology, geography, sociology, and economics—thus occasionally providing an international or intercultural dimension. The area studies projects were perforce multidisciplinary; their aim was to develop greater understanding of the totality of a culture. A number actually did so, and many teachers have benefited from them.

One thing that encourages continuation of this trend is the requirement, instituted in 1976 and still in effect, of the U.S. Education Department that university programs in language and area studies funded under Title VI of the National Defense Education Act include "Outreach Activities" to schools or communities, and that these activities equal at least 15 percent of the total budget support of the centers.

Although these efforts have been beneficial to teaching and learning about other nations and cultures on the precollegiate level, they are seriously deficient. They are too few in number to change the content of courses of study all over the United States, and they are characterized by a "trickle down" philosophy that is not conducive to the stimulation of thought and creativity on the part of the clients for these efforts—precollegiate teachers. The efforts have also had little effect on the content of textbooks in the social studies and in literature.

The point is that teachers on the precollegiate level should not consider themselves lucky when they become partial beneficiaries of a small fraction of someone else's budget. Teachers do not need to assume a client role in the academic and funding marketplace. Much depends on confidence in their own abilities to learn from the cooperative efforts of other groups and to learn the politics of funding and of organizing.

There is precedent for this kind of activity. In New York City, school board candidates endorsed by the two largest municipal employee unions won three-fourths of the 288 seats on 32 community school boards in an election held in May of 1980.

There is also much to learn from colleges. Consortiums of colleges and universities have been formed to pool resources in area studies and critical languages and to form a solid front to secure and maintain federal and private funding of their programs. Scholarly organizations such as the Association for Asian Studies and the African Studies Association perform the same functions for their collegiate members (and virtually ignore precollegiate concerns).

An International Services Office is now funded by the American Association of Community and Junior Colleges to promote projects in this field at their member institutions. The field work of this central body and of others such as the American Association of Colleges for Teacher Education provides lessons on how institutional membership in a consortium can be mutually helpful in pursuing common goals.

Detailed information on this kind of organizing can be found in:

- *Internationalizing Community Colleges.* The American Association of Community Colleges, Washington, DC
- Frank H. Klassen and Howard B. Leavitt (eds.). *International Perspectives of Teacher Education: Innovations and Trends.* Washington, DC, The American Association of Colleges for Teacher Education, 1977.

It is important to stress that the project work of a number of university centers still forms the major portion of curriculum revision in the social studies and humanities today. Some of these projects are:

- The Social Studies Development Center and the Mid-America Program for Global Perspectives in Education at Indiana University
- The Mershon Center of Ohio State University
- The Center for Teaching International Relations at the University of Denver
- The Bay Area China Education Project of the University of California and Stanford University
- The Project Social Studies (for elementary school) of the University of Minnesota
- The Intercultural Understanding Projects at the University of Pittsburgh
- The projects on East Asian Studies Education at the University of Michigan and at Columbia University.

Many of these projects field test their work in a number of state and school districts. These affiliations provide opportunities for further cooperation in lobbying for more federal and state funding and for mutual efforts in seeking foundations' funds.

Descriptions of relevant university projects and the work of not-for-profit educational organizations in this field may be found in three reference sources:

- James M. Becker (ed.). *Schooling for a Global Age.* McGraw Hill Book Co., New York, 1979.
- Fred Czarra (ed.). "Directory of Resources: Global/International Education," *The Social Studies.* September-October 1979, Vol. 70, No. 5, Heldref Publications, Washington, DC
- *Directory of Resources in Global Education.* The Interorganizational Commission on International/Intercultural Education. C/O Ms. Jane Millar-Wood, Overseas Development Council, 1717 Massachusetts Avenue N.W., Washington, DC 20036.

The Role of non-university education projects _____

There are a number of private, non-university educational organizations whose curriculum work and inservice training programs deserve attention. One prominent independent educational organization is Global Perspectives in Education, Inc. with headquarters in New York City and regional offices elsewhere. Since 1970, GPE has labored to make global studies at the precollegiate level a coherent and cohesive field of study. It has produced an array of teaching materials and useful classroom lessons, and, through the publication of a newsletter and of the quarterly *Intercom,* has developed a clearinghouse and nationwide network of global studies programs.

One of GPE's recent projects, supported by funds from the National Endowment for the Humanities and other granting sources and entitled "Global Perspectives, A Humanistic Influence on the Curriculum," has produced useful materials for infusion into current curriculums K through 12.

Other organizations whose research and materials are expressly designed for school use include: The Asia Society; The Overseas Development Council; Service Center for Teachers of Asian Studies at Ohio University; Population Reference Bureau; Foreign Policy Association; Global Development Studies Institute; I/D/E/A and the North Central Project of the Charles Kettering Foundation; American Friends Service Committee, Inc., Philadelphia, Pennsylvania; Education Development Center, Newton, Massachusetts; Oxfam-America.

The effort to foster global and international studies in the schools through affiliation with State education departments, local school districts, teachers' organizations, and individual teachers themselves is a protean feat. To succeed in producing practical and scholarly classroom materials coupled with useful inservice and preservice teacher education programs illustrates an adaptability that higher education institutions and private educational corporations are rarely acknowledged to possess.

A number of state and local educational authorities recognize the necessity of curriculum and instructional change, and several have been strong and articulate advocates of this change. Those advocating even more fundamental changes, such as articulating the social science study of other cultures with that of language and literature and developing a coherent and articulated K–12 curriculum that will meet the needs of the next decades can learn from their example.

Some examples of progress at the state level _____

As early as 1961, the New York State Education Department hired a consultant in international education who later directed its Center for International Programs. In the mid-sixties, the social studies curriculum in the state was revised to include the study of the cultures of Latin America, the Middle East, and Eastern Europe in elementary schools as well as those of Africa and Asia in junior high schools. The syllabuses of foreign languge instruction have recently been broadened to include greater emphasis on cultural understanding. In social studies instruction on European civilization (grade 10) and American civilization (grade 11), emphasis is placed on study of the cultural and social influences that are transnational in scope. In 1976, the Board of Regents in a position paper, *Education and Global Interdependence,* directed the State Education Department to develop standards of basic knowledge about world political, social, economic, and cultural issues (6). Further, the guide recently published for teachers in modern languages stresses activities designed to demonstrate the links between culture and language.

Nebraska has published "Strategies for Communication in French, Spanish, German, English" designed to help infuse the study of culture into language learning. Other state education departments also have global programs. Guidelines for instruction in other cultures have been adopted in California, Delaware, Florida, Illinois, Kentucky, Michigan, Minnesota, New Jersey, Pennsylvania, Utah, and Wisconsin.

Evidence gathered by the 1977 Report of the Council of Chief State School Officers Committee on International Education demonstrates that an increasing number of states permit school districts to grant inservice credit or credit toward certification for activities such as teaching abroad; and they encourage local districts to sponsor teacher exchange and student study abroad.

Additional reference sources on strategies for schools wishing to start pre-collegiate programs in global studies and on origins, activities, and effects of existing programs can be found in:

- Rose Lee Hayden. *Statewide Approaches to Changes in International/ Intercultural Education.* New York State Education Department and Council for Intercultural Studies and Programs, New York City, 1975.
- *Agents of Chage: Case Studies of Organizations and Programs in International/Intercultural Education for the Schools.* Papers prepared for the Wingspread Workshop on Strategies for Change, 1976. Council for Intercultural Studies and Programs, New York City.
- *Internationalize Your School.* National Association of Independent Schools, 1977, Boston.
- *ACTFL Foreign Language Education Series.* Articles on multicultural education in Volume 8 (1976) and Volume 9 (1977).
- Norman Abramowitz, Andrew Leighton, Stephen Viederman. "Global and International Perspectives," *Improving the Human Condition: A Curricular Response to Critical Realities.* Association for Supervision and Curriculum Development, 1978 Yearbook, Washington, DC.
- H. Thomas Collins. *Global Education and the States: Some Observations, Some Programs and Some Suggestions: A Report to the Council of Chief State School Officers.* Washington, DC (n.d.).

- Robert Weatherford (ed.). *Proceedings of the Pinehurst Conference in Global Perspectives in Education for Chief State School Officers: A Report to the Council of the Chief State School Officers.*

Over the years, the leadership of the National Council for the Social Studies (NCSS) has exerted considerable effort to bring about curricular change and better instruction in foreign area studies. These efforts, involving the cooperation of diverse constituencies and groups of professionals, are described succinctly by Mehlinger (13). The NCSS can become an important vehicle for efforts to bring social studies and language teachers together to work towards common goals. The membership of NCSS extends into virtually every school district in the nation.

A number of school districts all over the nation have added elective courses in social studies, courses on the society and governments of Asian, African, and Latin American nations. The New York City Board of Education in 1980 added to its ninth-grade culture studies syllabus a unit on Latin America. It also is considering requiring one year's study of the culture of French- and Spanish-speaking nations as part of the foreign language sequence in the schools.

All of this activity is indeed heartening. However, there is a darker side. Ongoing efforts at cooperation among teachers of the social studies, English, foreign languages, and the humanities are very difficult to find. One of the principal purposes of this chapter is to highlight these efforts, to present them as a serious and constructive activity toward a more meaningful global education. The few that do exist are worthy of note. Would there were many more to report.

Foreign languages

While the teaching of foreign languages in the public schools now encompasses languages not taught a generation ago (e.g., Russian, Mandarin Chinese, Hebrew, Swedish, Polish, Swahili) the study of foreign languages in high school or below is nonetheless declining. This fact is documented by the Report of the President's Commission on Foreign Language and International Studies (17).

None of the university programs described or the organizations listed see their role as that of fostering the study of languages in conjunction with the study of cultures or—for that matter—by itself. The Commission reports that only 8 percent of American colleges and universities now require a foreign language for admission, compared to 34 percent in 1966. And only one of twenty high school language students goes beyond the second year of such study.

The reasons for this decline are many; inadequate teacher training, decreasing budgets, lack of administrative support, inadequate and dull methodologies and materials, and poor testing are listed by the Commission. Even where languages are taught, few syllabuses stress learning about the culture. According to C. Edward Scebold, Executive Director of ACTFL, among the skills stressed in language instruction, culture study ranks a weak fifth behind listening, speaking, reading, and writing (Collins, 4).

Other problems. While many of the university-based programs in international studies are models of interaction, (incorporating both "outreach" and "dissemination") few are models of school and teacher cosponsorship (exhibiting evidence) of shared administration or of jointly formulated goals and activities. Even fewer claim to provide the experiential learning that comes from original curriculum planning, foreign study, or other cultural immersion activities. In 1979, it was estimated that a total of 250 teachers studied for a period of at least six weeks under U.S. Office of Education Projects Abroad. Under the present law, these projects do not permit study for language competency. They are designed for cultural learnings, although language teachers are eligible for consideration if they demonstrate a geographic area of interest.

Experience points to the conclusion that, if the study of foreign languages and international studies is to be upgraded, teachers, administrators, and citizens in the local communities must make an effort to marshal public opinion (and the funding that follows). Otherwise, the recent Report to the President from the Commission on Foreign Language and International Studies will be merely a cry in the wilderness.

A start has been made. As early as 1977, ACTFL and NCSS entered into a collaborative effort to benefit both professions. This effort was born of the coincidence that like-minded leaders were on the same campus: presidents of both organizations happened to be on the faculty of Indiana University in Bloomington. We like to think that Anna Ochoa and Lorraine Strasheim would have collaborated even if they had lived in San Diego and Orono, Maine. But their proximity to each other and to another NCSS leader, Howard Mehlinger, made it easy to sit together and plan common strategy. Before their ideas could jell into a proposal of any kind, the President's Commission had been authorized and so formed a convenient and important focus for their efforts. Thus a "marriage of interests"--as Paul Purta of NCSS calls it--began as a casual relationship.

Ochoa and Strasheim did the bulk of the work on a Joint Resolution to the President's Commission, a resolution that was approved in Chicago by both boards. The resolution begins with the premise that preparation for life in the late twentieth and the twenty-first centuries demands global education. It goes on to state that such education is the responsibility of a multidisciplinary faculty and the total K–12 school program. The recommendations ask that a program of building public awareness, of encouraging research, of creating curriculum and instructional materials, and of fostering staff development be started in order to help bring about the results needed.

The common interests of the two groups expressed in the Resolution assumed three things. First, that foreign language learning should not be separated from the cultural and social bases out of which the languages grow. Second, that the integration of language and culture study must start as early as possible in the precollegiate sequence. Third, that such interdisciplinary collaboration is not the American norm and does not happen easily. There must be substantial reforms in teacher education and inservice training.

The collaboration has not ended. ACTFL is borrowing the leadership network idea (organized according to Congressional District) from NCSS. The two groups are exchanging mailing lists, and there is growing program-swapping at annual conventions.

The leadership of ACTFL and NCSS believe, as Purta does, that this marriage is meaningful and should be enduring. But what of the rank and file? Few teachers are sure of how to use this situation to launch cooperative curriculum endeavor at the school-district level. Yet it is at this level that the question of a permanent relationship will be resolved.

The Report of the President's Commission

The Report recommends, among other things, the formation of twenty regional centers for foreign languages and international studies, twenty to thirty summer institutes per year, incentive funding for colleges and schools for foreign language instruction, twenty international high schools (to be expanded to sixty), model K–12 programs in six states as a start, and mandated foreign language instruction in schools and colleges. All of these new actions are to be supported by an increase of $178 million dollars over the 1979 budget in federal appropriations for international and language studies in the 1981 fiscal year.

For good or ill, the report makes no recommendations on how foreign languages and international studies are to be integrated; on how curriculum methodology is to be reformed; on how local schools and colleges can work together; or on who should hold the money and the authority, assuming such is forthcoming. The report is markedly silent on how to secure such massive funding from an increasingly defense-minded Congress and an inflation-ridden public and on what to do if massive federal funding is not forthcoming.

But the national commission has already done much to alert public officials and educational leaders to the problems and to the opportunities. The title of the commission and the scope of its purview has already had the highly desirable effect of joining international studies issues with issues of foreign language learning. Partially as a response to the report, the President has raised his request for Fulbright Hays exchanges by about $4 million over last year's request.

The public itself seems to want institutional change, although not necessarily with dollar signs attached.

In April 1979, a survey on nationwide attitudes on foreign language study conducted by the University of Michigan Survey Research Center revealed what might be some surprisingly good news. (See p.31 for some data.) This report and that of Commisioner of Education Boyer's Task Force on Global Education (copies of which may be secured from the International Studies Branch of the Department of Education) may spur interest of local educational agencies in the imaginative mixing of the funds and activities of federally funded projects of various sorts in order to develop programs in international studies and language education (7).

A recent "National Longitudinal Study," prepared for the National Center for Educational Statistics, surveyed a sample of high school graduates who had been out of school four years in 1976. Fifty-nine percent expressed their view that their high school education should have been more rigorous in basic academic subjects. Almost two-thirds of the respondents felt that vocational training should have been given greater emphasis. It is our responsibility, singly and collectively, to act on this information, to articulate to the public the basic need of students to develop intercultural learning and language skills, and to persuade teachers and school administrators of the need for their active participation in the many facets of this endeavor. This must be done locally and nationally through cooperative efforts between teachers and their professional organizations. It is, however, in the local community where the battle will be won or lost. In recent years there have been a number of locally developed programs that demonstrate the success of do-it-yourself curriculum innovations.

Shoreham-Wading River Middle School on Long Island (Claudia Travers, Teacher Contact) goes beyond the usual assemblies, foreign food festivals, and foreign pen-pal activities. School-to-school exchanges of groups of eighth-grade students are encouraged. Language instruction in the language of the host is provided during these stays.

The work of the private International School in Washington, D.C. is described in detail in Chapter 7.

A public high school in Queens, New York, Hillcrest High School, (Pearl Warner, Principal), offers an almost unique program in integrating language study with culture studies. The School of International Studies is organized as a "school within a school." It involves the English, Language, and Social Studies Departments in an optional interdisciplinary program designed for students in their junior year. Four years of language instruction is coupled with an optional senior year internship in an international business or agency. Juniors at Hillcrest study the literature, politics, history, and society of the nations of Europe and of India and Japan. Seniors do likewise with the Middle East and Latin America, and they also study American government and foreign policy. Nine languages are offered: six levels of French and Spanish, four of Italian and German, and three of Hebrew, Chinese, Russian, Greek, and Latin. All this is done through modular scheduling. This program, although supported in part by a federal grant under the provision of the citizenship education section of the NDEA, is not otherwise dependent on outside funding.

Other public school examples. The City School District of Oswego, New York, has this year begun an interdisciplinary "Humanities" approach to teaching about non-western nations. This cooperative program, funded under a grant from the National Endowment for the Humanities, combines faculty members from the State University College at Oswego and from Cornell and Syracuse Universities and materials from the Asia Society and the Center for International Programs of the New York State Education Department. When completed, the project will contain a syllabus and instructional materials on the culture and literature of India, China, Southeast Asia, the Middle East, and Africa south of the Sahara.

A scattering of public and private high schools in the nation are involved in language learning through "self-instruction," using materials and techniques available from the National Association of Self-Instructional Language Programs. This program, designed for college use, is easily adaptable to pre-collegiate instruction and involves using native speakers in the community (Loew, 11). Other schools are experimenting with language-immersion techniques.

One local activity that has received national attention deserves mention. Some years ago, a small group of high school teachers of social studies and Spanish joined college faculty members in the New York City metropolitan area to form their own organization, The Association of Teachers of Latin American Studies--ATLAS (1). The group, now numbering over 300, developed many activities to upgrade such study in the schools, to enrich their own professional competence, and to encourage educational leaders to pay more attention to Latin America. Teacher-run and teacher-focused, ATLAS has gathered funds for a Group Project Abroad study tour to Mexico and for the development of a curriculum guide on Mexico and the Mexican American. Language teachers, social studies teachers, and college faculty members pooled their knowledge in writing this guide, thereby gaining valuable interdisciplinary experience. ATLAS is a growing and effective organization and remains independent of any educational agency or national professional organization.

The programs just described are by no means a comprehensive listing. They are selected examples of the variety of things that are now being done to upgrade basic education for global awareness. Some of them require outside funding, but many do not. Max Rubin, currently Chairman of New York State's Special Task Force on Schools and formerly a member of the Board of Regents, has concluded that the inaction in improving the quality of schools, is attributable more to inertia than to tight budgets. He contends that the unit for improvement or reform is not the state, not even the district, but the individual school.

Rubin's theory has ample support from research studies by the National Science Foundation (16). For example, projects dependent on outside support frequently die when that support vanishes. Unless a curriculum change is agreed to and actively supported by parents, teachers, administrators, and the school board, little long-term success can be expected.

The desire of the nation at large to go back to the "basics" might be expanded to include the study of other cultures and other languages. The Commission has indeed taken a first step toward this in bringing public attention to the matter. After the excitement of preparing and submitting testimony to the President's Commission, the profession seems to be asking "What now?" Most professionals in language and international studies are now committed personally and professionally to maintain the momentum that built up in 1978 and 1979. The leadership of twelve national educational organizations, including the national councils of most subject-oriented organizations, joined together in 1978 to circulate a statement on the essentials of education (14). Among the essentials listed is the ability to "understand other languages and cultures." To define essentials is not sufficient. "Such a definition calls for a realization that all disciplines must join together and acknowledge their interdependence." Where that energy should be directed and the ways that it may serve our common purposes are still indistinct. Other chapters in the ACTFL Series have addressed the directions and means from a national perspective.

Working within the community

The profession at the local and community level is the focus of this chapter, appropriate to what has already been called "The Decade of the Grassroots." Philosophy in the late 1970s pointed increasingly to a return to basic structures as principles were reexamined. The President's Commission did not address restructuring of American education. However, other serious examinations of the state of language and international education have addressed root causes, as has the personal testimony of one member of the President's Commission (Bullard, 3). All these examinations point with increasing strength to the need for fundamental changes in American institutions and procedures.

American education is founded on institutions of a local nature, working from a community or regional base and operating according to processes and procedures that grow out of local conditions. So to change American education is inevitably a matter of working from the bottom up rather than from the top down. Even a perfunctory glance at the history of the 1960s and 1970s will suggest that, for all the federal intervention in the form of decrees, decisions, and disbursements, the most effective and satsifying social and institutional changes were those that emerged from the local, state, or regional activities of citizens and groups. Examples of this may be found in such sensitive issues as integration of the schools and open housing: communities with the most successful programs tend to be those that created their own responses. While national leadership is clearly involved in such massive social changes, the changes that stick are those that local citizens themselves construct, with or without the help of the federal government.

What is necessary to revive and invigorate foreign language and international education work, where they receive their paychecks, and where they vote. What could be easier, then, than to work from this position of strength? national education work, where they receive their paychecks, and where they vote. What could be easier, then, than to work from this position of strength?

But the history of efforts to work from this position suggests otherwise. There is no single discipline covering international education or cultural education. There are turfs and pads over which we or others extend a proprietary interest. Nothing much can be done unless we are willing to admit others to our territory and until we are welcome in theirs. Efforts to make this happen tend to fail in practice, usually because the individual or group pushing the effort has a particular axe to grind, is ambitious or otherwise self-serving, or is too readily identified with a hitherto "hostile" camp. Attempts to hold joint conferences or conventions have a way of producing jealousies and antagonisms. There is enough evidence in the wreckage scattered across the landscape to remind us that the frontal approach to professional collaboration is often too loaded with historic rivalries. It seems appropriate to recommend casual, step-by-step approaches to professional cooperation both locally and nationally. Experience in sharing common goals and methods with others should lead us to a more wholehearted cooperation as the years pass—and so should our failures to make an impact.

There are some easy steps to take on the professional level:

Invite speakers from other, even rival, professional associations to speak to your own. It is a principle practiced to good effect in nations with a parliamentary system wherein politicians know that the best way to neutralize a critic is to bring him into Parliament where he can be exposed. Whether we need to be this Machiavellian about it may be questioned, but the need to communicate better with those who have interests closely related to our own is clear. Through knowledge of their professional objectives and principal methods, we may be able to forge common links, not only through curricular changes and alterations in the way we do things in the classroom, but in the local institutional and political arena where our fates are often decided by others. Speaking engagements—both having others into our organization and going out into theirs— will, if practiced routinely, lead to more familiarity and more possibility of interprofessional collaboration. When your organization has a meeting coming up, invite colleagues from related professional organizations to attend. You will be informing them of your professional objectives. You will have to adapt your program to meet the interests of people from outside of your profession. The argot of your group may have to be changed (not a bad thing when you think about it) and pedagogical subjects of interest only to your own profession may have to be avoided (and again, perhaps not such a bad idea), but you will be actively communicating with those who share more broadly defined goals.

Share mailing lists. See to it that your local, regional, or state association routinely shares its mailing list with related professional associations. If you are in a language association, share with the social studies people. Mailing lists are a considerable asset even though they cost substantial amounts of money to create and to maintain. Our aim is communication between professions; therefore, the sharing of mailing lists facilitates interprofessional cooperation. Remember that this sharing should be done routinely, not just on an *ad hoc* basis. The cost is very little compared with the long-range benefits. When your treasurer tells you that the extra 3.1¢ postage is too much, remind him or her that the cooperation is worth it.

Begin to share substantial benefits of association membership. Many local and regional associations have insurance plans or other fringe benefits for members of the group. Most insurance companies and other agencies will have no objections to extending these benefits to others, as long as they work in an allied and actuarially sound profession. This is also good common sense, and it should step on no one's toes. Among the benefits that might be shared are cut-rate travel costs to your national convention and cut-rate registration fees at the annual meetings of the national group.

Travel together. Language, social studies, and humanities teachers share more than a common curricular concern. They share a common fascination with other cultures and peoples. They are all inveterate travelers. An easy and logical step toward interprofessional collaboration is to design a summer travel program. Even if you want to go your own way once you have landed in another country, there are substantial benefits to booking together a charter flight or making reservations as a group. Seven hours on a plane may bring about more togetherness than the profession has enjoyed in years, and the feeling may endure when colleagues are back at faculty meetings in the fall, facing tough curricular decisions. Spending three to six weeks together in a culture in the third world might be even more beneficial. The language teacher may be able to provide assistance in communication in, for example, Niger, while the social studies teacher may be able to provide political and social briefing for the Paris-trained linguist.

Experiment with joint meetings. If you should invite persons from another profession within the field of international education, it is best not to segregate them into a workshop of their own or ask them to do a show-and-tell session for your people. It is better to embrace them as peers within a common profession, involving them in your professional work and adapting your professional exchanges to allow them to communicate.

Embark upon joint endeavors on the community level. Here we enter into a whole new area where we need practice and experience. One of the tragedies of professionalism is that it has separated us from our communities. The endeavors that we as professionals must undertake do overlap those that we as citizens should be doing.

Insist that teachers' unions develop interest in the curriculum and in the upgrading of teacher competence. These groups have matured in recent years as their fight for the right to exist has been recognized, but they still express too little concern for what the teacher does in the classroom and too little support for improving the quality of education through better classroom instruction.

Make your concerns as an individual citizen known to political leaders and attend local meetings that influence either directly or indirectly decisions on education.

Be proud of your idealism and proclaim it in terms that are both practical and understandable. At too many meetings of teachers recently we have heard, "there's no beating the system," "we don't get any support from the administration and can't get any," and "it's the people at the top who are the obstacles." There is no reason that the idea of better global education can't be expressed in reasonable terms, repeatedly. History shows that ideals are stronger than institutions and are able, with support of articulate citizens, to erode the fortresses that protect specialized interests and anachronisms.

Reaching citizens

The institutionalization of American education has made it possible to improve and enrich what is offered to students. The control given to administrators has permitted a more coherent pattern of education than otherwise would be possible. However, this institutionalization has erected barriers not only between the school and its community but between the teaching faculty and the community. We were shocked to learn recently that a number of schools in New York City flatly refused to invite parents to school assemblies featuring performances by a reputable classical music group because "it was too much trouble." We would ask how a school can hope to survive politically and socially, not to mention fiscally, in a community with which it has virtually severed its ties? The same question can be asked about the teachers. We all know that they are citizens themselves, but there has developed a sense that they must separate their activities as citizens from their professional activities. This may have its origins in a need to protect academic freedom in the classroom, but its esoteric character condemns it as out of date in the present era. Teachers are citizens. They are also professionals. As professionals, they have a contribution to make to their community. Making that contribution is an act of good citizenship.

The field of international education is one in which the line dividing the citizen from the professional is so indistinct as to be nonexistent. The community in America needs daily reminders of its place in a large, complex, and increasingly interdependent world. Citizens of each locality need repeated reminders that their decisions are often not absolute, nor should they view America's national decisions as absolute. The energy crisis is only one immediate reminder of this. Yet our sense of localism breeds an isolationism that blinds citizens to the realities of the world. World resources become more scarce; growing pollution demands global responses. New nations and fresh revolutions change the map, the world economy, and the political realities.

Teachers and scholars of language and international studies are, in fact, a reservoir of knowledge and skills available to the local community that finds itself in a confusing, complex, and confounding world. This fact is not generally apparent because we in the profession have hidden within it and have been reluctant to act both as professionals and as citizens.

We recommend a number of activities that will serve to introduce us both as professionals and as citizens to our local communities. Many of us have been engaged in these activities for years but have tended to hide our doing so under a bushel. The importance of these activities and their relevance both for the community and the classroom will be taken up later in this chapter.

Volunteer to host foreign visitors. Many communities have a member association of the National Council for International Visitors (1630 Crescent Place NW, Washington, DC 20009). The local organization receives news of international visitors coming to the community from NCIV, then arranges for volunteers to handle the details of the visit, including home stays, local transportation, and scheduling. Such activities benefit not only the foreign visitor but the hosts as well. There is nothing quite so refreshing—even if sometimes unsettling—as to have to explain to a person from another culture what it is that you do professionally. For the language teacher, the benefits of using the language are obvious. For any professional, the visibility it gives is worth the effort.

Advise immigrants. Our days of receiving the world's tattered and torn are not over. Now they come from Kampuchea and Vietnam, from South Asia and Cuba, and from the Soviet Union. All immigrants need help settling in. Most of them could use substantial tutoring or less formal assistance in understanding American values and behavior. Many of them need help in learning English. While programs exist for teaching them English, there are few programs that apply the one-on-one concept of tutoring or personal assistance. Again, here is a social need in your own local community, a need that can be richly rewarding in professional terms.

Work with foreign students and student exchanges. Many teachers of foreign languages and cultures have been active in arranging for exchanges. Class exchanges have become, if not common, at least familiar. Niskayuna High School in New York State sent forty of its students to Germany during the summer recess. In September, forty students from Germany visited their community. Involved in this exchange were the Chamber of Commerce, the school board, the school administration, and dozens of volunteers, including the host families who for the most part were parents of the American visitors to Germany. Other teachers have been involved in the AFS International/ Intercultural Scholarships, the Experiment in International Living, Rotary International, Youth for Understanding, Four-H and many other study abroad programs, working as advisors, travel leaders, host parents, and so forth. A group often neglected by elementary and secondary school teachers is the substantial group of university students in the community who have come from abroad—200,000 or more in the late 1970s. Such students often need rooms, board, and an opportunity to get to know an American family. Foreign language and international studies teachers have even more to offer than other citizens, and they can benefit professionally from such services. For information on university students, contact the National Association of Foreign Student Affairs, 1860 19th Street NW, Washington, DC 20009. Other organizations include: AFS International/Intercultural Programs, 313 E. 42nd Street, New York, NY 10011; Council on International Educational Exchange, 777 UN Plaza, New York, NY 10017; The Experiment in International Living, Brattleboro, VT 05301; Future Farmers of America, Box 15160, Alexandria, VA 22309; the branch of Rotary International in your own locality; National Four-H Council, 7100 Connecticut Avenue NW, Washington, DC 20015; School Exchanges Service, National Association of Secondary School Principals, 1904 Association Drive, Reston, VA 22091; International Christian Youth Exchange, 74 Trinity Place, New York, NY 10006; International Student Services, 291 Broadway, New York, NY 10007; Youth for Understanding, 3501 Newark Street NW, Washington, DC 20016. Information on still others may be obtained through the Council on International Educational Exchange, 205 East 42nd Street, New York, NY 10017.

Guide tours abroad. This year, many citizens will be taking foreign tours and would welcome professional guides competent in foreign languages but from the community. You might get a free trip to the country of your specialty in return for helping to assemble a group, providing orientation prior to departure, and handling the details of the travel abroad. The real payoff would be the friendships and alliances that form during the trip and last long after it.

Provide predeparture orientation. You may have to advertise to make your service known but the need for this orientation is present in almost any community, even rural ones far from our ports of entry and exit. Business travelers and managers being assigned overseas are frequently in need of predeparture orientation from a professional. Indeed, most of them are more in need of such orientation than they believe themselves to be. An aggressive marketing effort launched by language and culture teachers toward local businesses with overseas activities—and even toward small and medium-sized firms that have export potential but no present operations abroad—could pay off in contacts with the local leadership. Keep in touch with other professions, with doctors, lawyers, and so forth, who have conventions or conferences outside the country. Brief them before they go. Build up contacts so that this is a growing volunteer—or paying—activity.

Advise business on conditions abroad. Many foreign language and international studies teachers are in close touch (or know those who are) with conditions in countries of their specialty. By keeping business executives posted on overseas developments, you will not only keep evidence of your competence in front of an important local constituency, you will also improve that competence through practice. It is not difficult to obtain regular information on the economic factors that may be difficult for a business to obtain. It may prove more difficult to be a political soothsayer, but your experience in the country of your specialty probably outstrips that of anyone else in your community (except, of course, that of your peers in local schools and colleges).

Organize adult study circles. This Scandanavian concept has had little exposure within our educational institutions, but it has been practiced by those interested in foreign policy through the Great Decisions program. (Foreign Policy Association, 345 East 46th Street, New York, NY 10017.) While Great Decisions is a well organized program with easy-to-use learning and resource materials, it does not have a monopoly on all things international. Any small group of adults that joins together to study any single topic is an adult study circle. Circles on international subjects are limited only by imagination. One possibility is to organize self-instructional study groups on foreign languages. In this activity, the teacher of languages would work with interested adults to establish the group, to provide the tapes, and to instruct the native speaker of the language who would serve as tutor to the group. For more information on self-instructional language programs, contact National Association of Self-Instruction Language Programs, Center for Critical Languages, Temple University, Philadelphia, PA 19122. Over forty-eight courses are already available, not only in the "critical" languages but in the "traditional" languages as well.

Groups formed to study energy, a single foreign culture, global pollution, conflict, and various current topics would find no dearth of suitable study materials. The schools and local institutions of higher education would be more likely to help with resources if they have been convinced that by doing so they are building up a new and energetic constituency in the community. Business again offers opportunities in that it needs personnel who know the ins and outs of international trade. Language and international studies teachers can organize study groups among business people to attack these subjects in an organized fashion.

Participate actively in adult education courses at school. Many language teachers shrug their shoulders at the adult public's indifference toward language study. Instead, new approaches to language instruction should be sold to the adult education department of the district or school. How about trying courses in drama in another language? Studies (*The New York Times,* January 22, 1980) show that drama, because it uses body language, gestures, and pantomime, communicates more effectively to the new or rusty language student than does the textbook. If adult language courses are highly academic and intended to teach adults to *read* another language, they will not develop much of a following. But a course in contemporary or classical drama in another language, a course leading up to the actual performance of the play in the school auditorium may find a significant group of college educated adults turning out for it. Imaginative approaches to language study for adults who had a marginal knowledge of the language when in college or school may range from preparing tourists for trips to France or Guinea to preparing potential opera buffs for Wagner or Verdi (this latter could come complete with stereo music). There are no limits whatsoever to these activities. They will inspire registrations in the adult education program, but they will do more by building up an adult constituency that favors language instruction.

Arrange citizen forums on important issues. Many communities have public forums to which important speakers are invited, and there are countless speakers who address international topics. Active participation on the boards of committees of organizations sponsoring such programs is a proper role for language and international studies educators. If your community were to put together a regular forum on public health, there would be at least one doctor involved. We are experts, professionals in international affairs, and we ought to be making a positive contribution to related activities in the community.

Offer background to the local media. Volunteer yourself and your colleagues to provide information about cultural areas to the local newspapers, television, radio stations. University professors are often shown on the six o'clock news, but local teachers have specialized knowledge, too. A regular contact with a local news outlet is of tremendous importance for other professional purposes. Let us say that the school board is going to take a vote on cutting language courses. If you had already established a relationship with the local paper and even gotten to know a reporter, you would be able to provide important exposure of a matter of vital importance to your profession. Another way to gain visibility is to serve without fee as an advisor on the foreign country you know best. You might put together a team of social studies and language teachers, thus offering something that the college professor working alone could not match. Your school or district would also benefit from this endeavor. If your group is going abroad, offer to do an illustrated column for the local paper, a column offering fresh perspectives of another culture (not just a travelogue). Remember, when a school board member sees you on television giving expert interpretations of foreign events, that member is not likely to regard language and international studies as frills.

Help gain recognition of the activities of others. If your community has an international center or international council, encourage it to have an annual awards banquet or other event to recognize citizens who have performed outstanding international services. The mayor or governor would probably be happy to gain exposure by presenting the awards. These awards need be no more than a printed certificate. Honors given to those who have done the most for international activities in the past year will atrract attention to important international concerns. Awards might be given for activities such as international development, international youth exchange, higher education, public service, business, cultural affairs, art, and community service.

Organize a regional international council. If your community or region does not have an international council or center, then it might pay to see if one could be established. The center may then serve as a vehicle for conducting most of the activities just discussed. But do not abdicate your own professional leadership to others: stay in the forefront if you want to keep your profession alive.

Any language or other teacher with international concerns may participate in any of these twelve activities; all of them ought to be covered by the local professional community. By collaborating with professionals from other disciplines and by cooperating with language and international studies professors from local colleges, you can make clear the common purpose. One first (and obvious) act that each of us can perform is to make friends with a social studies teacher or a humanist with responsibilities for international teaching. This is so self-evident, so taken for granted, that hearing it is startling and might even sound revolutionary. Many of us would be astounded to realize that we have not been making friends with our professional associates. Yet if we are all together in a leaky lifeboat, it behooves each of us to bail. By working together with mutual trust, we may avoid the situation in which we push each other off the lifeboat in order to stay alive.

Building academic ties.

A corollary of making friends with your peers in international studies in the school or school district is getting to know the local professors of international studies. Recent studies show that international education is not doing badly at the university level (McCaughey, 12), but the entire university community is endangered by declining enrollments and inflated costs. Outreach programs from college and university centers of international studies have been in existence for several years, many of them mandated by federal guidelines. These outreach programs might better be labeled "in-grab" programs: the school people may be the pursuers instead of the pursued. As the university centers seek a new constituency for their resources, they are more receptive to overtures than ever before. The scholarly faculty may be still a bit more remote than the outreach coordinators, but it is important to lure them out into community action for international education.

Making friends with a professor is one step toward tearing down institutional walls that obstruct change in education. Curricular innovation and curricular reform both depend upon institutional changes. Politically speaking, though, an institution is never more than the people who comprise it. Thus it should be a matter of urgent priority for language and international studies professionals working in elementary and secondary schools to reach onto the college campuses to make acquaintance—and establish common cause—with the university faculty. The material resources are immense on college campuses, but the human resources are even greater. Slow and methodical but nonetheless regular efforts on the part of the school international establishment to draw into active collaboration its peers in the universities is a practical possiblity. The difference in learning objectives, backgrounds, and teaching methods between school and university people should not be allowed to obsure real similarity of interest.

Special effort must be made to embrace all experiences of foreign countries and demonstrate to the community how they have strengthened and enriched its life. There is no easy way to do this, but the first step is clearly to draw together, on an informal or even formal basis, everyone you can think of who has lived, served, studied, or traveled abroad. This group will include military personnel and missionaries; people such as Peace Corps volunteers, US AID advisers, and Fulbrighters, whose assignments may not be as readily perceived as having goals similar to those of international educators but who nonetheless share a concern for America's strength in an unsettled world. Local imagination and group interaction may lead to new and effective ways of impressing upon the community awareness of its own rich international resources--and the opportunities it may be missing in not exposing its young to those resources.

In short, the community must become the arena for interprofessional cooperation. It is there that the forces will be generated to affect state education departments, national accreditation commissions, and the federal government. The project at the Ohio State University's Mershon Center, "Columbus in the World/The World in Columbus," has shown clearly the enormous impact of local foreign policies on the development and evolution of national policies. (For information write Dr. Chadwick Alger, Director; CIW/WIC Project; Mershon Center; The Ohio State University, Columbus, OH 43210.

At the same time, social studies, humanities, and language professionals who are involved in international education should take aim at certain other targets. A strong posture in the local community, alliance with community leaders who are international minded, and a united front with professors from local colleges and universities will make the image all the more formidable.

Targets for interprofessional marksmanship

Teacher education has come a long way in recent decades, but there is not yet a sufficiently universal requirement for international, intercultural, multicultural, or pluralistic education for preservice teachers. The American Association of Colleges for Teacher Education, working under a grant from the National Institute of Education and working with the National Commission for the Accreditation of Teacher Education, evolved a multicultural component for teacher education that NCATE has, since early 1979, mandated for colleges it accredits (15). The requirement for undergraduates reads:

2.1.1 Multicultural Education

Multicultural education is preparation for the social, political and individual realities that individuals experience in culturally diverse and complex human encounters. These realities have both national and international dimensions. This preparation provides a process by which an individual develops competencies for perceiving, believing, evaluating, and behaving in differential cultural settings. Thus, multicultural education is viewed as an intervention and an ongoing assessment process to help institutions and individuals become more responsive to the human condition, individual cultural integrity, and cultural pluralism in society.

Provision should be made for instruction in multicultural education in teacher education programs. Multicultural education should receive attention in courses, seminars, directed readings, laboratory and clinical experiences, practicum, and other types of field experiences.

Multicultural education should include but not be limited to experiences which: 1) Promote analytical and evaluative abilities to confront issues such as participatory democracy, racism and sexism, and the parity of power; 2) Develop skills for values clarification including the manifest and latent transmission of values; 3) Examine the diverse cultures and the implications for developing teaching strategies; and 4) Examine linguistic variations and diverse learning styles as a basis for the development of appropriate teaching strategies.

Standard: The institution gives evidence of planning for multicultural education in its teacher education curricula including both the general and professional studies components.

While institutions for which NCATE accreditation is important will be attempting to implement this important recommendation, there are many other undergraduate departments of education and psychology that prepare teachers for certification for whom the NCATE standards are paper tigers. It behooves the new coalition of international education professionals to apply pressure to these departments and colleges to achieve substantially the same objectives. (Write Dr. Frank Klassen, AACTE, 1 Dupont Circle, Washington, DC 20036.)

Teacher competence in a second language. Related to this is the need for better cultural education for all preservice teachers. Certainly, all social studies teachers should have a language requirement in their preparation for teaching in that field. Likewise, language teachers should have substantial social and humanities background in the culture of their language before setting out to teach it. At present, according to the American Council on Education, "at most only 5% of prospective teachers take any course relating to international affairs or foreign peoples or cultures as part of their professional preparation." Even mathematics and science teachers might be expected to be alert to the rest of the world lest we prepare young people for citizenship in an isolated Fortress America; yet few, if any, teachers of math and science are required to have international or language courses in their preservice preparation. A solid phalanx of social studies, humanities, and language professionals from all levels of education would be of enormous help to the educational leaders who are trying to reverse this dangerous trend toward cultural incompetence in our schools.

Bilingual education has made remarkable headway in helping America's bilingual minorities to find a fulfilling role in our society, yet critics of it abound. The criticism that language and international studies professionals might be aiming at bilingual education is that it is the privilege of a minority while it ought also to be the birthright of the majority. Those of us in language and international studies should be joining to put pressure on the Congress and on the new Department of Education to abolish the stipulation that bilingual education go only to students whose mother tongue is not English. To master, at least orally, a second language should be the privilege of every American. We professionals must make it an obligation of the system to deliver this opportunity and privilege to all (Franchine, 9).

Model programs have received much attention from state education departments working with federal funds (Elementary and Secondary Education Act. Title IV-C). The manner in which states decide upon programs and projects for IV-C funds varies, but evidence suggests that most states are open to suggestion and even pressure from informed outsiders. Here is an area for joint effort by language and international professionals. Not only should each state's IV-C program have a slot for model programs in international education, but local school districts should be actively preparing their own model programs for the competition for funds. The requirements are stiff, but the rewards are not insubstantial. Inclusion of a school's model program in the National Diffusion Network is a highly visible feather in the cap for many districts and their teachers. The President's Commision recommended model high schools and regional centers, but it is possible to accomplish both objectives, at least in part, through existing institutions. This is also an area where bilingual education has had striking successes. It is time for international education to take its turn at bat.

Basic competencies. Although often a cover for reactionaries, the movement back to the basics is a matter of incontrovertible reality. Whatever the motives, it may well be the best friend international studies has had for a number of years. It is up to those of us who are working in the field to add to the basic competencies those that prepare students for the world as it is today and as it may be tomorrow. Unfortunately, the way basic competencies have been reinstituted in some schools and districts prepares students for a world that no longer exists. What may have been good enough for us thirty-five years ago may not fit the world of the 1980s.

The advent of the 1980s attracted soothsayers, prognosticators, and prophets in unusual numbers. Among them are our own colleagues who are into "futuring." It is an amiable and satisfying activity that offers many insights into the present and possibly the future. Unfortunately there is too much temptation to try to *predict* what the future will actually bring and not enough incentive to prepare skills for coping with *whatever* the future throws at us. The world is changing at a rate unprecedented in history. The changes are not only the obvious ones of technology and science but also of religions and cultures, families and economies. It is not only reasonable but essential that we prepare students for the unexpected.

Among the basic competencies, therefore, must be abilities to define, analyze, interpret, and respond to both challenges and opportunities. Perhaps the most obvious but most often neglected advantage to foreign language study is that the study of one language prepares a person to learn another language. Learning the gestures of nonverbal communication in France prepares one for learning the gestures of the Indian or the Chinese. Learning culture clues in the contest of one or two cultures prepares one for learning clues wherever they may emerge. And these skills of analysis and communication also prepare one to observe the behavior of someone from another culture and respond to it without misunderstanding and the conflict that often follows.

There is no question that language learning at an early age is one of the more basic skills we can give a child. Studies show that the brain's principal facilities for native language acquisition appear to atrophy at about puberty (Geschwind, 10). Language learned after that age uses different and apparently less efficient paths in the cerebral cortex. Most of us have had a chance to observe how easily children pick up another language, and we sense that they lose that language almost as quickly. However, the evidence suggests that having learned a language at an early age makes acquisition of another language much easier later on. It is all the more a shame, therefore, that the profession has generated its own internal hostilities over language learning at the elementary school level.

Let us make one major endeavor as we take our campaign for international education into the streets: Let us remind ourselves, our colleagues, our schools, and our communities that the ability to meet an unknowable future—a future in which the only thing that is certain is change itself—depends on skills of social and cultural communication learned early in life. As the language teacher helps develop these skills, the social studies teacher and the humanities teacher would be helping to develop skills in observing, understanding and reacting to other cultures as well as skills in defining the human experience in global terms. Cultural sensitivity is a set of skills that can be identified, developed, and honed to sharpness by the combined and coordinated work of social scientist, humanist, linguist.

What does all this have to do with what goes on in the classroom? We started with the supposition, based on historical premises, that there is a communication between language instructors and those who work in allied fields of international education. Our prescription for healing this serious ailment has been a modest list of community activities and professional activities which, at least on the surface, appear to have very little relevance to the classroom.

We aver, nonetheless, that it is out of such simple and matter-of-fact pieces that our profession will be restructured.

A framework to restructure the profession

Visibility for the profession. The more we moan about how badly off our profession is and how wronged we are by the neglect of language and international study, the less attractive we will appear to our peers, our school boards, and our communities. Instead of the hangdog expression of the 1970s, we need a new image. The image that some of us offered during the hearings of the President's Commission will not help the field much either: a lot of professionals came on entirely too strong for many of the cultivated academic tastes of those on the Commission and in the audiences.

What is needed is a new image in the local community. When citizens look at what is happening in the community, and they see that the leaders of the day are members of our profession, the profession will gain stature and substance. This stature has to be regularly reinforced by exposure in the public media, in public meetings, and in personal encounters. It is hard work. It takes time. It requires persistence over the course of not weeks or months but years. Those who look to a series of public service announcements on commercial and public television to reverse a social, political, and institutional trend of twenty years are not being realistic. The exposure the profession may be able to obtain in national media will be worthless without coherent and consistent work on the local level. We must work to prepare ourselves for future action. We must be visible to our fellow citizens before we will be listened to by responsive school boards or administrations.

International awareness and sensitivity in the community. We will succeed in our rebuilding campaign only insofar as our communities become more aware of their participation in a larger world and become sensitive to the dangers of isolation from global events and movements. The importance of capitalizing on international economic opportunities should be obvious, but many small and medium-sized corporations still are reluctant to enter the export market, usually because they are neither well informed about its opportunities and its perils nor possessed of skills for selling in another cultural environment. And yet the economic strength of the community depends on how well local industry uses international opportunities.

Economically, the interdependence of America and the world is made abundantly clear by the current energy situation. The international implications of pollution, global ecology, and declining natural resources should all make our citizens alert and active beginning at the local level. The need for sensitivity to the wider world is clear. An internationally sensitive and alert community will see the relevance of language and international studies to its own strength. But this connection may not be an easy one for citizens to make. There is still a good bit of scorn for the "internationalist," who is often thought to be a "one-worlder," or worse. We have to work hard to overcome images and stereotypes of a generation ago, the age of the first Cold War. We, as citizens and professionals, must slowly but methodically build community awareness of the challenges and opportunities of this global age.

Reforms in the infrastructure of international studies. The changes in teacher preparation and even teacher certification and licensing will not only benefit our profession but will change it. If we are successful in creating multicultural requirements in preservice training, we ourselves will have to respond by changes in how we seek inservice training and in how we implement the curriculum. If, for instance, we were to be wildly successful and the school faculty of 1990 were totally bilingual, we would have to evolve ways of maintaining the bilingual competence through inservice programs, through the casual use of other languages in the faculty room, and even the formal use of other languages in classrooms where language study is not itself the subject.

Such reforms will not take place without our professional involvement. We must be both the instigators and in a sense the victims of these changes. We must be aware that we cannot tamper with the infrastructures without changing our own operating methods and curricula. We are not used to military comparisons, but perhaps one is in order. If we are to fight a battle for what we believe is right, then we must be willing to suffer some losses. There are going to be some sacrifices. Some jobs may be lost. Some budgets may be cut. Some territorial lines may be redrawn. What we must have is the distant vision of the strategist rather than either the narrow outlook of the tactician or the blurred image of the soldier in the front line. We will not win in a few weeks or even a few years, but we can hope to achieve our campaign aims if we are willing to undergo some losses now in order to enjoy a victory a few years hence.

Changes in curriculum and method. Many of the casualties will be the result of changes of curriculum and methodology. The FLES battle suggested two armies at war. The issue was not whether language study was a good thing. The issue was who was to teach language and how. Let's face it: that battle was a skirmish. There will have to be more such battles, and they will be pursued despite high cost. And it may not be those who wish to revive, resuscitate, and reform language and international studies who will win.

But must we wage war among ourselves? Is there not some way that we may work together against the much more formidable enemies of ignorance and isolationism? "Global education" has been recommended as one approach. The concept is fuzzy "and it is too grandiosely abstract for most intellectual tastes" (Fisher, 8, p.6). In application it means a curricular infusion of global concepts, subject matter, materials, and even methods, not into the social studies curriculum alone but into the entire curriculum. Someone is going to have to lead the movement for this curricular reform, and some teachers are going to have to pay a high price for this kind of reform. No one, it would appear, will be left untouched.

The issue boils down to a very basic question: Are we serious in believing that international understanding starts in the schools with the encouragement of basic skills in communication and cultural analysis, that international understanding is essential to any meaningful peace in the world, and that global perspectives are necessary for human survival?

Interprofessional collaboration starts in the school, operates in the community as well as the profession, and ends up in the classroom as we seek to produce a generation prepared to face up to change and seize the opportunities that change offers.

References, New opportunities for interprofessional cooperation

1 ATLAS mailing address: P.O. Box 73, Lefferts Station, Brooklyn, NY 11225
2 Becker, James. "Perspectives of Global Education." [Unpublished, 1976]
3 Bullard, Betty M. "Personal Statement to the President's Commission on Foreign Language and International Studies," pp. 1-8 in *President's Commission on Foreign Language and Area Studies: Background Papers and Studies.* Washington, DC: U.S. Government Printing Office, 1979.

4 Collins, Thomas H. *Global Educa-tion and the States, Some Observa-tions, Some Programs and Some Suggestions. A Report to the Coun-cil of Chief State School Officers.* Washington, DC, 1978.

5 Commager, Henry Steele. "The Americanization of History," *Satur-day Review of Literature.* (Novem-ber 1, 1969):24.

6 *Education and Global Interdepen-dence: A Statement of Policy and Proposed Action by Regents of the University of the State of New York.* Albany:The State Education Depart-ment, 1976.

7 Relevant federal acts include the fol-lowing:
The Adult Education Act
Arts in Education Amendments of 1974 to Special Projects Act, Sec. 409
Basic Skills Education Amendments of 1978, Title II, Part B
Career Education Incentive Act, PL 95-207
Higher Education Act, Title I (Com-munity Service and Continuing Edu-cation)
Community Education Amendment of 1974 of The Special Projects Act, Sec. 405
Elementary and Secondary Educa-tion Act, Title I (Disadvantaged); Title IV-B—educational improve-ments, Title IX—Part I (Ethnic Heri-tage Act)
Education Amendments of 1974, Special Project Act, Sec. 402 (E.T.V. and Radio)
Title IV-C (assistance to local educa-tion agencies)
Education Amendments of 1978, Special Projects Act, Title III (en-vironmental issues)
Mutual Educational and Cultural Exchange Act, Sec. 10 2 (b) (6), PL 87-256 (study and research abroad)
National Defense Education Act, Ti-tle VI. Domestic program in inter-national and foreign language area studies by colleges and universities
National Diffusion Program, Title III, Sec. 303 and the General Provi-sion Act, Sec. 422 (a)—provides for nationwide dissemination of exem-plary education programs
Higher Education Act Title VI-B—Teacher Centers
General Education Provisions Act, Sec. 405, National Institute of Edu-cation supports research on educa-tional aspects of national priorities.

8 Fisher, Glen. *American Communi-cations in a Global Society.* 1979:6

9 Franchine, Phillip. "Chicago Taps Language Wealth." *American Edu-cation,* (May 1980):8-15.

10 Geschwind, Norman. "Language and the Brain." *Scientific American* 22:4(1972):76-83.

11 Loew, Helene Z. "Self-Instructional Language Programs for Secondary Schools." *SYSTEM* 7:1(1979).

12 McCaughey, Robert A. *The Perma-nent Revolution: An Assessment of the Current State of International Studies in American Universities, A Report to the International Division of the Ford Foundation.* New York: Ford Foundation, 1979.

13 Mehlinger, Howard D. "Social Stud-ies Educational: A Transnational Profession," in Howard D. Mehlin-ger and Jan L. Tucker, eds., *Teach-ing Social Studies in Other Nations.* National Council for the Social Studies, Bulletin 60, 1979.

14 Organizations for the Essentials of Education. These organizations are: American Alliance for Health, Phy-sical Education, Recreation and Dance; American Council on the Teaching of Foreign Langauges; As-sociation for Supervision and Cur-riculum Development; International Reading Association; Music Educa-tor's National Conference; National Art Education Association; National Association of Elementary School Principals; National Council for the Social Studies; National Council of Teachers of English; National Coun-cil of Teachers of Mathematics; Na-tional Science Teachers Association; Speech Communication Association.

15 *Standards for Accreditation of Teacher Education.* Washington, DC: National Council for Accreditation of Teacher Education (Adopted May, 1977, effective Jan. 1, 1979):4.

16 *The Status of Pre-College Science, Mathematics, and Social Science Education: 1955-1975,* Vol. III *Social Science Education.* Boulder: Social Science Educational Consortium, Inc., 1977.

17 *Strength Through Wisdom: A Critique of U.S. Capability. A Report to the President From the President's Commission on Foreign Language and International Studies.* Washington:Superintendent of Documents, 1979.

5

Learning outcomes in the language classroom

Gail Guntermann
Arizona State University

Introduction: The need for realistic minimum outcomes ___

As leading United States citizens increasingly recognize that the study of other languages and cultures can contributed to the improvement of world relations and the restoration of American political and economic influence abroad, second-language educators may look forward to growing public recognition and support. In order to bring to fruition this new hope and provide a solid foundation for continued progress, the profession must 1) reassess current offerings in the light of present and projected needs, 2) keep abreast of constantly emerging information from many related fields of study, 3) establish realistic outcomes and make them known, and 4) demonstrate that they are achievable.

This writer joins a growing number of educators and others citizens (e.g., Lafayette, 16; Congressman Leon Panetta, 27; the MLA/ACLS Task Forces, 29; and Schulz, 32) in calling for agreed-upon minimum outcomes for the basic levels of study in general academic courses. The progress made during the 1970s in devising systems for identifying and specifying performance objectives has resulted in a diversity of courses and programs. While it must be recognized that learners' goals and preferences and the specific purposes for which

Gail Guntermann (Ph.D., The Ohio State University) is Assistant Professor of Spanish and foreign language teaching methods at Arizona State University. She has taught Spanish at the high school and college levels and ESL at all levels. She has served as Language Coordinator for Peace Corps and other language training programs in Brockport, New York, and El Salvador. Her articles have appeared in *Hispania, The Modern Language Journal,* and *Foreign Language Annals.* She has conducted workshops and presented papers at local, regional, and national levels. Her affiliations include ACTFL, AATSP, TESOL, the Rocky Mountain MLA, and the Arizona Foreign Language Association, of which she is currently Executive Secretary-Treasurer.

they may ultimately use their languages vary considerably, their future inter-actions cannot be predicted with any certainty; it is time to identify a common core of fundamental knowledge, attitudes, and skills.

The first step in the planning process will be to reach a consensus on overall *goals,* which will then be defined more specifically in terms of their essential components, or learner *outcomes.* The set of outcomes for any given level of study should provide a clear picture of the learnings that students are to achieve by the end of the course and the desired levels or degrees of pro-ficiency. They should be stated in terms that can be subsequently translated into performance *objectives* for individual units and lessons.

Accomplishments of the past decade

In the 1970s the emphasis on the individual learner, as well as disillusionment with the unfulfilled promises of audiolingualism and a demand for accounta-bility, brought about a movement to state narrowly defined objectives in terms of measurable changes in learners' performance (Steiner, 35). The application of performance objectives, while resulting in more careful planning by many teachers, also contributed to the proliferation of relatively superficial, easy-to-achieve ends. The taxonomies of educational objectives (Bloom, et al., 3; Valette and Disick, 41), designed to teach students to function at all levels of the cognitive, affective, and psychomotor hierarchies, were too often ignored.

Systems of overall curriculum planning were explored in the second half of the decade. In 1975 the reports of the Northeast Conference working com-mittees (Born, 4) comprised a guidebook of procedures for goals clarification and the planning, implementation, and evaluation of teaching units built around cultural themes; in 1979 Medley (20) outlined a needs assessment pro-cedure for deriving goals and objectives of increasing specificity—from district, building, and departmental goals to objectives for each language, level, unit, and activity. The end of the 1970s saw movements to specify realistic, achiev-able goals and to determine which of the many facets of language study would receive priority. The task of specifying outcomes becomes ever more complex since influential factors from many areas—national, local, and individual needs, and information from linguistics, psycholinguistics, neurolinguistics, sociolinguistics, intercultural communication, and foreign language education —can be expected to grow and change in the 1980s. These influences must be considered in the process of assessing educational priorities and seeking real-istic means to meet them.

In this chapter, major influencing factors will be reviewed in order to identify a common core of goals; alternative approaches to specifying outcomes will be discussed; and sample lists of outcomes will be presented for three levels of second-language study.

Factors influencing goals and outcomes _____

The national need

During the past five years, the Helsinki Agreement, the President's Commission report, the Education for Exporting Act, and numerous individuals have emphasized the need for Americans to learn to communicate in other languages and called cultural understanding essential to international cooperation, the national security, and America's position in the business world. While the goals of communicative proficiency and cultural understanding are not new, they have never been achieved by the majority of foreign language students. The President's Commission observed: "The Commission views as a priority concern the failure of schools and colleges to teach languages so that students can communicate in them. The inability of most Americans to speak or understand any language except English and to comprehend other cultures handicaps the U.S. seriously in the international arena" (36, p. 11). The Commission also specified goals for the cultural component of instruction: " . . . foreign language instruction at any level should be a humanistic pursuit intended to sensitize students to other cultures, to the relativity of values, to appreciation of similarities among peoples and respect for the differences among them."

The goals of American education

A review of recent educational literature reveals several competing concerns in American education, including humanistic psychology, the interdisciplinary movement, career education, global education, and citizenship education. Learners of the future must develop effective strategies for learning, for communicating, and for meeting new challenges. They must clarify their values in the light of the values of other peoples, and they must understand social issues and the human condition around the world and throughout history. They must learn to manipulate abstractions and symbols, and they must prepare for their own careers. Clearly, education is expected to be both pragmatic and humanistic, general and specialized.

However two principal themes do recur; preparation for a changed future world, and the need to define "the basics." For those whose concern is the former, the key word is *world,* and the major change is toward interdependence among nations. Around the globe, Americans are viewing current events—revolutions, anti-American demonstrations, kidnappings, and invasions—with bewilderment. The role of second-language study in education for a global age merits an in-depth examination, which is provided in Chapters 4 and 6 of this volume.

The second major concern is the need to identify the basics. A group of educators representing several disciplines (7) concurs with the proponents of global education that "the essentials of education should be considered that set of experiences which enables learners to become aware of the world around them and to develop an understanding and appreciation of the interdependence of the many facets of the world" (pp. 379, 380). Among their recommendations, they state that students should acquire the ability "to use language to think and to communicate," and "to understand other languages and cultures." Schulz (32) recommends restructuring general courses so that students will realize the linguistic and cultural goals that have long been recognized but seldom achieved. Teachers must "present knowledge about other cultures and instill a critical awareness of our own; acquaint students with the literature, arts, and history of other peoples; give insights into the development, history, and common structural patterns of language; open views to career possibilities that require or are enriched by knowledge of or acquaintance with another language; increase tolerance toward customs and values different from our own; lessen provincialism; and, of course, start building a solid base in the communication skills of the target language" (p. 652).

Learners' needs and preferences

Several surveys of the views of students and other citizens reveal a common belief that cultural understanding and communication skills are two major values of foreign language study. McEwan and Minkle (19) report that after enjoyment and recreation, students rated "improved communication, global awareness, and culture" highest among their reasons for studying a language (p. 91). In third place were career-related reasons and self-improvement. Myers (24) presents the results of interviews with sixty-four Americans of all ages, who saw the main benefits of language study as increased cultural awareness, the ability to communicate in another language, preparation for careers, and a better knowledge of the English language (pp. 22–29). Rivers (30) reports that students basically want "to be able to communicate effectively" within another culture and "to know and be comfortable with the basics of a language so that they will have a firm foundation on which to build as future need requires" (p. 16).

Career education

Today's student is career oriented, seeking a place in the economy and hoping to find personal fulfillment as well as monetary rewards. Schools are attempting to lead pupils to career exploration and an awareness of their own talents, values, and interests. Elling (6) lists fourteen desired outcomes of career-oriented second-language study; in addition to being able to demonstrate knowledge about careers and their requirements and being prepared to seek employment in the target language, students should learn to function appropriately (i.e., with understanding of the culture-specific conventions of oral and written discourse) in social and work-related situations.

Career information can be expected to change during the next few years, as international business needs are evaluated in the light of international political and economic trends (Orr, 26; Thogmartin and Mann, 37).

The nature of language and language use

Since the birth of linguistics, second-language teaching has tended to follow the trends in linguistic theory. During the audiolingual movement, structural linguistics, together with behaviorist psychology, dictated both the content and the method of language teaching. A partial break in this pattern was effected by Chomsky's transformational-generative linguistics, with its approach to language analysis through introspection about the "ideal" speaker's intuitive grammatical knowledge rather than through observation. Although some applied linguists continued searching for implications for language teaching, Chomsky made it clear that there was no psychological basis for applying his theories to classroom instruction. Recent years, however, have witnessed a renewal of the relationship between linguistics and teaching as the source of linguistic description is no longer language in isolation from the real world but rather the meanings expressed through language as it is used for communication in social contexts. "Real" communication has, in turn, become a major concern of the foreign language teaching profession, which is seeking to define it in educational terms.

Several branches of theoretical linguistics provide insights about the nature of language and language use that may influence the specification of learning outcomes. Out of transformational grammar was born the field of semantics, which has contributed an awareness of the need to teach the meanings that are carried by words and signaled by grammatical forms and structures. Verb endings, for example, may be studied not only in terms of form and tense paradigms but for the ways in which they express relationships between events and time.

Further influences on language teaching are emerging from two related areas, discourse analysis and pragmatics, which investigate the uses of language in communicative exchanges. Native speakers control the social rules of discourse as well as the components of the linguistic system. The words, structures, tone, and gestures that are chosen for carrying out a communicative act depend upon the setting, the time, the topic, the participants in the exchange, and their roles and relationships, attitudes and moods.

At present, very little is known about what actually takes place in communicative encounters in particular cultures and societies. Furthermore, if this knowledge is to be applied to language learning and teaching, how much material should be included and how can it be organized and presented? Some approaches to solving these problems are being explored, particularly in Europe, in the form of functional/notional syllabus design and specifications for the "threshold level."

Language acquisition research

Research in language learning is reviewed by Stern and Cummins in this volume. The primary importance of research for goal-setting is that recent models of language acquisition point to the essentiality of language *use* for its acquisition; learners must practice communicating and develop strategies for learning and for communicating.

A consensus: Four principal goals

A closer examination and synthesis of the influences on goal-setting reveals four essentials, which may serve as a common core of goals for general-purpose courses:

1 Communicative functioning ability
2 Intercultural and international understanding
3 A knowledge of language and how it works, and the development of effective learning strategies
4 Career awareness

The next step in planning will be to translate these goals into priorities for basic courses. Even if language requirements are reinstated, a sequence of more than two years for the majority of students is a dream unlikely to be fulfilled immediately. In order to solve the problem of too much to do for too many students in too little time, it will be necessary to devise a system for making choices. Several approaches to determine outcomes are in existence or have been proposed, and they will be reviewed in order to gain additional perspective on the syllabus design and to seek guidance in specifying essential outcomes.

Approaches to specifying outcomes —————————————

The Structural approach

Most existing courses and materials have at their center linguistic forms and structures, selected and sequenced primarily on the basis of their frequency in the target language and the degree of complexity or difficulty that they might pose for second-language learners. Each feature is learned separately and for its own sake, reflecting an attempt to give a complete representation of the language (Valdman, 39, 40). Supplementary materials for study in other areas, such as "culture," art, or career education, may be added. Teachers and students everywhere have had ample opportunity to observe that this approach has not often led to communicative proficiency.

The Situational approach

Traditionally the alternative to the structural approach has been to situate the lessons in real-life settings such as the post office, a restaurant, or a library. The major difficulties with this approach are that very few of the settings for language use can be predicted, nor can one specify the communicative exchanges that take place within settings, beyond a limited set of typical expressions. As Westphal (45) has added, ". . . most things people say are appropriate in a variety of situations, and it would seem more efficient to teach items with a high potential for transfer first" (p. 121).

The Functional/notional approach

If what human beings choose to do and say as they communicate is not dictated by the settings in which they find themselves, it might be preferable to begin with the functions of language within a broad range of situations and to seek ways of teaching students to perform these functions. This approach has been receiving considerable attention, both in Europe and the United States. In England, Wilkins (47) has provided an exhaustive list of notions, or meanings and functions, that are expressed in English. He recommends that the linguistic items necessary to perform these functions be identified and applied and that the materials be sequenced according to a cyclical arrangement so that learners first acquire limited, relatively simple means of expressing each meaning or function, and at subsequent levels add more varied and complex possibilities to their repertoires.

For the Council of Europe's attempt at a unit/credit system for adult learning, collaborators from the participating countries have provided inventories of functions, notions, and the linguistic exponents necessary for carrying them out at the "threshold level," defined as the level at which one can "communicate non-professionally with foreign speakers in everyday situations on topics of general interest." This includes not only the ability "to survive, linguistically speaking, as tourists in a foreign country, or in contacts with foreign visitors" but "to establish and maintain social relations of however superficial a kind" (van Ek, 42, p. 2). Van Ek suggests that the threshold level "would provide a useful learning-aim for pupils unable to receive more than a minimum— say three years—of instruction" (p. 3). This statement exemplifies a major difference between European and American interpretations of "realistic" aims and reflects very different opportunities to learn.

While the functional/notional approach is seen as a possible solution to the problem of how to teach students to communicate, its application raises some difficult questions. First, based on what system of priorities does one select and order the functions to be learned? As Wilkins (47) points out, the future communicative needs of students in global courses are usually unknown. Second, what specific behaviors, linguistic and otherwise, are required for performing each function? Neither levels of linguistic proficiency nor the roles and behaviors that are appropriate for foreign learners within particular sociocultural contexts have been identified. What, exactly, is the threshold level in terms of linguistic proficiency, comprehensibility, and social appropriateness, and how much time is required to reach it? Is there such a thing as a "natural" threshold level at which learners are first able to express themselves and which can be reached relatively quickly through efficient learning and teaching strategies? There is a need to examine the functional/notional approach in the light of learning theory. Most important, how can linguistic features and functional categories be brought together? There is no direct relationship between communicative functions and specific utterances, forms, or structures. Any function can be performed through a variety of means that are available to the speaker. (These issues were discussed by the participants of the European/American Seminar on Communicative Approaches and Second Language Course Design (e.g., 5, 13, 39), the proceedings of which are forthcoming from the Indiana University Linguistics Club.)

An alternative approach, of course, is to maintain the structural core and apply the functions to it. Brumfit (5) proposes such a model, which would place stages of linguistic learning at the core of the course and add the functions in a spiraling arrangement, giving students practice with functions that can be expressed by the grammatical material at each level. Alexander (1) recommends a similar approach, which emphasizes the semantic and functional aspects of the grammatical core and adds to it related but ungraded patterns as necessary for communication. Guntermann (13) outlines a system for giving learners practice in using grammatical and lexical material for carrying out particular real-life purposes and provides examples of activities for various levels of study.

Interdisciplinary and humanistic approaches

Interdisciplinary education suggests a means to develop basic proficiency in a language while incorporating goals from other fields of study. Support for it may be found in the experience of bilingual programs in which language acquisition results from using the language to learn other subjects. Increasingly, interdisciplinary programs and courses are recommended as means to integrate the various parts of the curriculum and to meet the demands of global education (Elling, 6; Galt, 9). Second-language teachers at all levels can collaborate with their colleagues in other disciplines to bring languages together with area studies, career exploration, the examination of personal values, feelings and attitudes, and interpersonal relations (Galyean, 10). It remains for research to discover whether such practice results in increased effectiveness and efficiency of language acquisition.

Two state curriculum projects

Recognizing that essential learning outcomes can be specified for basic courses while at higher levels a greater diversification of options is desirable, the state departments of education in Minnesota and New York have published outlines of the material to be included for the initial stages of learning. For Minnesota a committee of eleven educators drew up a list of "foundation learnings" (34), representing "that point in foreign language learning when students can leave carefully graded and structured materials and begin working with nongraded and less structured materials" (p. 1). Divided into four sections—Language Use, Culture in the Language Classroom, Knowledge about Language, and Learning a Language—the document lists basic outcomes in descriptive terms designed to be organized into curricula and translated to specific objectives according to local situations. The foundation learnings for the speaking skill, reprinted below, demonstrate the level and types of outcomes presented in the document:

Speaking

1 Students control the sound system of the language well enough to be understood by a speaker of the language.
2 Students express experiences occurring in present, past, and future time.

3 Students retell, describe, and explain situations and ideas based on previously learned materials.

4 Students adapt learned grammatical patterns, vocabulary, and idiomatic expressions to express personal ideas, feelings, needs, and desires.

5 Students appropriately utilize one word or incomplete utterances as well as complete sentences.

6 Students choose a speaking approach to the situation—formal or informal, business or social, friendly or impersonal.

7 Students make effective use of English/target language dictionaries when their need for expression involved unknown vocabulary.

8 Students use context, structural cues, prefixes, suffixes and other associated vocabulary to supply intelligent guesses, or substitute forms when an unknown word is required (p. 3).

In addition to the skill specifications, affective counterparts are provided.

For the state of New York the publication *Modern Languages for Everyone* (21) outlines a foreign language program that begins with a basic course for all students and then divides into a variety of skill-development options for subsequent levels. Since the principal objective of the basic course is to expose learners to all four skills and help them to identify their strengths and interests, mastery of the stated objectives is not expected of all students. Some will continue to pursue "major sequences" toward state diploma credit in the four skills or choose between oral and written uses of language for in-depth study while others will turn to special-interest or skill-development courses for local school credit.

The Focus Approach

As Valdman has pointed out (39), a movement is afoot to reduce the unwieldy amounts of material presented in textbooks (Warriner, 43). Through the Focus Approach (Magnan, 18), a distinction is made between active and receptive learning outcomes, and the material to be taught for active use is selected and sequenced according to information that is available from research on pidginized forms of languages, which reflect natural language acquisition for communicative purposes. Grammatical structures are presented in their entirety at each level, but learners are encouraged to reduce these structures in the initial stages, gradually building them up as they are able. The principal advantage of this approach is that it allows students to progress in a natural way, communicating from the earliest stages without the frustration of attempting to demonstrate perfect control. It remains to be seen whether the ultimate result is superior performance and whether "fossilization" of deviant forms is a lesser problem with this approach than with others.

An Alternative approach

An alternative approach to specifying core outcomes for general courses begins with a search of related literature to identify the essential components of each of the four goals. These essential features are then translated into educational terms for classroom learning and sequenced on the basis of priorities determined by learning needs as well as learning difficulty. Through this process each of the goals will be divided, by levels, into outcomes ready to be broken down into performance objectives for specific situations and clienteles.

Definitions and outcomes

Communicative functioning ability

What does it mean to function in a foreign language and culture, and what are the most essential aspects of this ability for learners at basic levels? As previously stated, it is impossible to predict future communicative needs, and little information is available about the sociolinguistic behavior that is appropriate for specific communicative exchanges. The goal must be a general communicative proficiency that will allow learners to function for a variety of purposes within a broad range of social situations.

General communicative proficiency, like language use for specific purposes, raises the question of how to select, sequence, and integrate the grammatical, lexical, and functional aspects of communication. Does one begin with the linguistic features and add appropriate uses of language, or is it possible to first list the functions and then attach the grammar and vocabulary that are necessary for their execution? The answer to this question will depend upon the results of further research into functional/notional approaches and language learning/acquisition. While a system for placing functions at the center of the program may be developed in the future, at present it seems more reasonable to depend upon past experience with structural syllabuses. The grammatical material to be taught can be selected according to functional usefulness and learning difficulty and sequenced on the basis of difficulty, usefulness, and the relative essentiality for communication of the various semantic qualities of each feature.

The functional potential of a feature depends on its use for productive and/or receptive purposes and the frequency of its occurrence in the types of exchanges to be learned (e.g., conversation about topics of everyday interest). No feature should be included if it is seldom used, and it should not be required for productive use in the early stages if it is very complex or unnecessary for communication or if it is only one of several alternatives for expressing the same meaning, as in the case of the four ways to form questions in French (Valdman, 40). The most functional forms for both productive and receptive purposes are those that would be used for a variety of functions and those that carry the most referential or relational meaning, such as high-frequency nouns and the regular past-tense forms of common verbs. Less useful are features that are purely conventional, such as gender agreement in articles, which in themselves carry no referential meaning and are not controlled by most beginners. At an intermediate level, students should be expected to improve the accuracy of their use of such forms, since errors in gender agreement may affect listeners' emotional reactions (Guntermann, 11, p. 102). Likewise, syntactic arrangements should be simple at first and expanded gradually, as students become capable of controlling progressively longer and more complex structures (p. 121).

Sequencing of the grammatical material that has been selected as essential will depend again upon frequency or usefulness and difficulty as shown by learners' errors; it will also be determined by the relative essentiality of the various meanings that are signaled by each feature. For example, the regular present-tense forms, being relatively simple and useful, will be practiced early —first as indicators of habituality, since this is the most common meaning for the form, and later as signals of futurity (for English), present ongoing action (for Spanish), etc.

Once the linguistic features of the language have been selected and ordered, they can be practiced within the context of their functional uses. For example, the present-tense forms as indicators of habituality can be used as tools for carrying out a variety of purposes involving habitual actions: requesting and giving information ("When does the bank open?" "It opens at ten"); explaining how one approaches a task ("I make a list of things to do"); gossiping ("She always wears the same dress to every party"); complaining ("You always call on me!"), and many others.

Wilkins (47) has provided for the English language an exhaustive list of notions, or meanings, that may be used as a guide in selecting the semantic aspects of grammatical features. They are divided into three categories:

- *semantico-grammatical* categories, which are expressed through lexical and grammatical features, and include time, quantity, space, relational meaning, and deixis (which refers what is said to the context in which it is said, as in the case of the pronoun system's referring to the participants in a conversation).
- *modal meanings,* for which there are two scales: 1) a scale of certainty, which subsumes certainty, probability, possibility, nil certainty, conviction, conjecture, doubt, and disbelief, and 2) a scale of commitment, including intention and obligation.

- *communicative functions,* for which there is no direct relation to specific lexical or grammatical structures. These communicative functions represent what one *does* with language, not what one reports. The major subclassifications are Judgment and Evaluation, Suasion, Argument, Rational Inquiry and Explanation, Personal Emotions, and Emotional Relations.

Extensive inventories of functions and notions are also provided by Munby (23) and van Ek (42).

The learning outcomes that are related to communicative functioning ability will be stated in terms of semantic categories, the forms and structures used to express them, and the common communicative functions of language. At the beginning levels of study, both linguistic and sociological specifications will be limited and general, becoming more complex and specific to detailed communicative needs at higher levels. While the material will be language- and culture-specific, some examples can be provided here in English. To a sample list of linguistic features that are central to communication, semantic values are attached and ranked where appropriate, according to their essentiality for communication in a variety of situations. Common interactional functions are then applied to these linguistic-semantic features (see Table 1).

Once the linguistic, semantic, and functional materials have been matched, outcomes can be written in narrative form, stipulating performance levels (e.g., students at Level x can use singular and plural forms of nouns to express quantity in writing grocery lists; use the most common adverbs of time to announce everyday events; use common prepositions to express positional relations in hunting lost items). The final step in the application of the system will be to invent contexts and activities for practice. While this step is beyond the scope of this chapter, numerous ideas can be found in the foreign language education literature of recent years (e.g., Freeman, 8; Moscowitz, 22; Wattenmaker and Wilson, 44; Westphal and Joiner, 46).

All four skills can be developed within a communicative framework such as the one described above. The listening skill goes hand in hand with speaking in communicative exchanges, and students can be given opportunities to listen to each other and to native speakers carrying out these functions. Since native speakers cannot be expected to limit their speech to the productive repertoires of learners, and since there is evidence that extensive listening practice is a key to language acquisition, listening practice should include more lexical and grammatical variety and complexity. Purposeful listening in daily life is also often directed to discerning others' purpose or intentions in face-to-face interactions and to gaining information or entertainment from the media.

Similarly, "reading is communication, too!" (Phillips, 28) Students can learn to read signs, labels, instructions, advertisements, recipes, newspaper announcements, TV schedules, and letters, as well as the short stories, articles,

Table 1. Matching Linguistic, Semantic, and Functional Elements—Examples

Linguistic Features	Semantic Values	Functions
Singular and plural forms of nouns.	Quantity	Counting, inventorying items (I have three dollars; I need flour, sugar, and eggs).
		Describing, narrating events (The player[s] ran onto the field[s]).
		Making comparisons or debating topics (The boys are smarter than the girls).
Singular present tense forms of common regular action verbs	1 Habitual actions	Requesting and providing information, explaining how something works, gossiping.
	2 Timeless truths	Explaining natural laws.
	3 Conditional (present) actions	Explaining cause-effect relationships.
		Compromising; making deals.
		Placing conditions on promises, permissions.
	(This also requires complex sentence structure with a future construction in the second clause.)	
	4 Future action (not required for productive skills)	Understanding when others use these forms for planning, commanding, threatening, etc. (I go to the dentist tomorrow; tomorrow you do the work--or else!)
Adverbs of time		
(now, yesterday today)	Point of time	Clarifying, emphasizing times of events.
		Setting the scene for recounting an event.
(always, never)	Frequency	Giving advice (Always take your vitamins).
		Getting out of trouble, defending someone else (I always clean my room), (He never arrives late).
		Finding out or explaining rules of thumb (Always stand up when you meet another person).
(then, next, finally)	Sequence	Clarifying the order of events; asking for clarification.
		Explaining the steps for doing something.
		Explaining how something functions.
Prepositions		
(in, under, above, on, on top of, across, along, by, etc.)	Positional relations	Giving instructions, guidance.
		Describing locations.
		Helping someone to find a misplaced item.
into, out of, through, along, above, under, across, etc.	Motion in relation to static objects	Recounting events, telling stories.
		Giving instructions, directions.

and poems that textbooks traditionally present. They can use these materials to develop reading comprehension and interpretation strategies—contextual guessing, utilization of punctuation, rootwords, prefixes and suffixes, skimming, and relating the material to what they know of cultural values, conventions, and so forth. Finally, in developing the writing skill, learners should practice writing letters, notes, lists, outlines, step-by-step instructions, checks, applications and registration forms, addresses and telephone numbers, telephone messages, and other everyday written messages, as well as coherent paragraphs and compositions.

Intercultural understanding

During the 1970s a great deal of attention was devoted to the teaching of "culture." Jarvis (15), Nostrand (25), and Seelye (33) have provided what are undoubtedly the most comprehensive overviews to date on this very complex aspect of language teaching. The goals and objectives are myriad and varied; in addition to learning about "formal culture" (e.g., fine arts and literature), students are expected to achieve at least the following learnings about "deep culture."

Cognitive outcomes. The relation between language and culture, with emphasis on language use for communication, is obviously appropriate for study in second-language classes. For the sake of effective intercultural communication, a culture must be seen as a system of interrelated values, traits, patterns, attitudes, norms, and conventions, each of which belongs to the whole and serves in some way to meet the needs of the members of the society (Seelye, 33). Students should be able to observe, describe, explain, predict, and evaluate aspects of culture (Nostrand, 25) and their effects on people's communicative behavior. At the same time, they should understand that behavior varies with age, sex, time, social class, and place of residence (Seelye, 33) and observe that the participants' perceptions of these factors and of their own places in the cultural scheme will also affect the way they will interpret each others' words and actions and the way they act and react.

There is some evidence that stressing the similarities between cultures leads to decreased ethnocentrism while the study of cultural differences may have little effect (Tuttle et al., 38). Nevertheless, the differences should not be ignored, since it is difference in world views that often creates the culture shock and crosscultural conflicts that must be dealt with by citizens of a shrinking world. Americans must learn to understand culture shock and to relate the different cultural values and assumptions to conflicts between individuals, among groups, and even among nations.

In the past, much of the teaching about cultures in language classes has been limited to memorization of facts. To insure that all levels of cognitive functioning are activated when dealing with a cultural theme, one can apply a taxonomy such as Bloom's (3), which may serve as a guide for filling in the gaps between knowledge of facts and the ability to make informed judgments. The taxonomy provides for comprehension, application, analysis, synthesis, and evaluation of material to be learned (Guntermann, 14).

Skills. Skills for traveling, communicating, and researching other cultures should be developed. Communication requires the accurate interpretation and transmission of messages, which in turn requires attention to appropriate sociocultural behavior. Because of crosscultural differences, communication among members of different cultures requires that they speak in more explicit terms than in their native contexts, listen with more conscious attention in order to interpret accurately, and check constantly with each other through paraphrasing to insure mutual comprehension (Jarvis, 15). They must also learn what behaviors are acceptable and unacceptable in the target culture.

Research skills and learning strategies include hypothesis formation, data collection, and analysis by inductive reasoning. The Minnesota Committee of Eleven (34) presents seven steps for researching cultures:

1 Students perceive an aspect of the culture for researching cultures: materials, teaching presentations, or other sources.
2 Students make a statement about the culture as a result of this perception.
3 Students seek multiple sources for information related to the statement, such as newspapers, movies, slides, books, magazines, as well as other realia and native speakers.
4 Students question and compare their sources, examining them for potential limitations, such as publication date, intended audience, and purpose of the document; they describe and report their findings; they analyze their findings.
5 Students modify the statement, continue to seek additional information, and further refine the statement.
6 Students examine a related feature in their own culture using the process (steps 1-5).
7 Students compare their refined statements about their own and the other culture, describing similarities and differences (p. 7).

Affective goals. In addition to understanding the values and attitudes of both cultures, learners should develop greater curiosity, flexibility, and empathy (Jarvis, 15; Seelye, 33) to counteract ethnocentric attitudes. Curiosity is a two-sided goal. If directed, it may lead to fruitful research; if not, it may end in a view of the target culture as "quaint." The seven-step approach of the Minnesota group would seem to obviate such conclusions.

Flexibility includes a willingness to set aside one's own values, prejudices, and stereotypes, and postpone judgments indefinitely, knowing that many crosscultural observations cannot be easily explained. Flexibility implies the temporary acceptance of ambiguity and of one's own foreignness in others' eyes. It requires patience with oneself and others in the face of culture shock, and an effort to deal appropriately with one's own reactions to culture shock.

Empathy requires a willingness to examine the possible feelings and reactions of the "other" and to attempt to experience them. In order to empathize with others, one must first possess considerable information about them (Sarbaugh, 31); if empathy is to be of practical value, one must "see both sides" and seek a way to resolve conflicting interests to the participants' mutual satisfaction.

The specification of outcomes for the study of culture remains a problem; because there is no "theory of culture" appropriate to second language classes, it is difficult to determine which of these learnings are most essential. What are the variables of communication across cultures, and how do they interact? What are appropriate roles and behaviors for foreign learners within the context of the target culture? Such a theory may be forthcoming from the field of intercultural communication as it continues to explore "the relationship of culture to human interaction" (Asante et al., 2, p. 14).

Language and language learning

In order to develop an understanding of the nature of language, learners can be expected to acquire knowledge in the following areas:

- an overview of the linguistic features of the target and native languages—the sound systems, vocabulary, idiomatic expressions, cognates, morphology, and syntax
- semantic categories and relationships and the ways that they are signaled through the linguistic features
- the functions of language use in communication and the appropriate use of language within particular sociocultural contexts; how language varies with age, sex, social roles and relationships, place, time, and cultural values.

From these categories, outcomes and objectives can be derived for each level of study.

In addition to understanding the nature of language, students must be cognizant of the following aspects of their own language learning:

- the goals, outcomes, and objectives toward which they are working
- the various kinds of practice at their disposal for developing the language skills (e.g., drills, exercises, communication practice)
- the resources that are available and how to use them

- their individual preferences for particular learning strategies, and their needs for developing more effective or efficient strategies
- the value of confidence while practicing the use of the language for communication.

Career awareness

The two major outcomes of this goal are knowledge about available careers that involve a foreign language as a primary or ancillary skill and an awareness of one's own talents, interests, and preferences with regard to the requirements and working conditions of specific careers. In addition, certain skills related to jobs may be developed (e.g., writing letters of application, interviewing, writing reports). Many of the language functions can be performed with work-related topics. For example, seeking information can include interviewing foreign visitors about careers in their countries.

More information is needed on the careers for which a second language is desirable, the skills that should be developed, and the levels of proficiency that are desirable for particular careers and positions, Thogmartin and Mann (37) recommend that at the very least, "foreign language curricula should include courses with a more practical orientation" and "more emphasis, in fact, should be put on communications skills for foreign language majors."

Generating outcomes for designated levels of study _____

Under ideal conditions, the next step would be to specify minimal outcomes for real levels or stages of learning. While language acquisition research may succeed in identifying natural stages of acquisition in the future (Larsen-Freeman, 17), learning levels must be defined at present on the basis of communicative needs and teaching experience (especially with programs aimed at oral proficiency, e.g., Peace Corps training) and the realities of nine-month school terms. The common core of material to be studied will be selected from the four essential goals, the largest blocks of time being devoted to the two major areas, commmunication and culture. The task will be to provide for each level a block of studies complete in itself, so that students may either continue to the next level or leave the program having achieved at least a basic crosscultural understanding and the knowledge and skills necessary for survival and the enjoyment of travel. The following section consists of examples of outcomes for three conceivable but hypothetical levels; outcomes for specific languages, situations, and clienteles can be expected to vary with individual items or sections.

Waystage 1—Survival proficiency

This is the most basic level of proficiency, which allows learners to survive physically in the target culture and make friends, at least superficially. It should be reached by the end of the first year of study, at which time students will have achieved a solid foundation for further study, a level of proficiency and crosscultural understanding that should facilitate future travels and other encounters with native speakers, and an understanding of others that will make themselves wiser world citizens.

Speaking. At this level learners can express at least the following meanings, although they often resort to circumlocutions and gestures and must limit themselves to the simplest possible forms and structures:

- point of time: high-frequency adverbs
- duration: *for* a period of time, last week, this year
- time relations: simple present, past, and "going to" construction
- frequency: never, always, sometimes
- sequence: ordinal numbers, first, last
- quantity: plural and singular forms; articles; many; not many, much, not much, all of; numerals
- space dimensions: large, small
- location: in, on, near, under, behind, in front
- motion: to, from
- sentential relations: order of words, and other basic indicators of doer, object, and beneficiary
- description: common nouns and adjectives
- deixis: subject pronouns, possessive adjectives or *of* construction
- probability: probably, possibly, I don't know, I think (with indicative forms of verbs)
- negation
- obligation: have to, it's necessary to
- suasion: Please ____ ; do me the favor of ____ .

Students should also be able to carry out the following functions, which will be matched with the linguistic and semantic categories for communication practice:

- obtain food, shelter, and transportation for survival
- acquire through oral and written language information essential to their basic social and travel needs
- establish and maintain at least superficial friendships through greetings, farewells, and exchanges of personal information
- open or maintain conversations by inquiring or giving the most basic information about health, weather, the time, or the date

- carry out common classroom functions, such as requesting and giving information, asking permission, borrowing items, and solving simple problems
- express wishes (I want _____.)
- express ability and inability to do things
- recount past events and activities that are common to their daily lives, at least through the use of the simplest indicators of past time, such as the simple past tense forms and adverbial expressions
- describe places, people, and things well enough for them to be identified by a listener who is familiar with them
- make simple requests of others

Most students should be able to express these meanings in such a way that they could be understood most of the time, although listening to them will require some patience and effort from native speakers. For communication practice, the degree of required correctness of pronunciation, grammar, and vocabulary will depend upon 1) learners' ability to control particular forms and structures at this level and 2) the potential comprehensibility of utterances to native listeners. While learners will commit numerous errors of gender agreement, for example, these deviates seldom obstruct comprehension. Tense errors and mistakes in the choice of words may be more serious although native listeners are able to comprehend error-ridden sentences most of the time and even when no context is provided; for most survival-level purposes, precision of interpretation may not be required (Guntermann, 13). Students should see and hear correct models and receive feedback on their efforts to express themselves in order to avoid fossilization and so that their successes, together with an awareness of the possibilities for improved communication, will encourage them to continue their second-language studies.

Listening. Students are able to comprehend what is said and identify the purposes of native speakers within the bounds of the material they have studied. They can understand recombinations of this same material and are able to grasp meanings somewhat beyond the level of their speaking ability when listening to clear speech directed to them at normal speed, or when the speaker's gestures, the context, or other cues are available. They are unperturbed when exposed to the natural speech of native speakers in person or through the media; they are capable of discerning some words and phrases from the flow of speech.

Reading. Students command sound-symbol relationships and read recombinations of the material studied during the course; they are also able to gather some very basic information from newspapers and magazines, read with comprehension signs and other written material (including maps and schedules) encountered in the performance of the basic survival functions.

Writing. In addition to writing exercises for learning the grammar and vocabulary, students are able to spell the words and sentences that they can read and use orally, write short notes and messages, and fill out basic travel forms.

Culture. At this level much of the study of culture will be done in English. By the end of the course, students should:

- apply the seven steps for examining their own observations about the culture (see page 112)
- know that similarities and differences exist among cultures and that individual traits have their place in the cultural system
- explain the effects of age, sex, time, place, and social class on conventional behavior for carrying out such common functions as greetings and farewells
- imagine how members of the target culture might view certain behaviors that conflict with important cultural values and norms
- analyze their own reactions to cultural differences and observe that even among themselves, what they say and do depends upon their individual perceptions of the situation
- begin to identify the activities that they might enjoy among those that are available in the target culture
- attempt to express themselves as clearly, simply, and explicitly as possible in order to minimize miscomprehension.

The study of language. Learners at this level are cognizant of the phonemes and their principal distributions in contrast with English, and they know that intonation patterns also signal meanings. They know how verbs operate to signal present, past, and future time and that verbs should agree in person and number with their subjects; that pronouns can be subjects or objects; that nouns carry gender/number/case markers and that other forms should agree with them; that prepositions indicate various kinds of relationships; that languages vary in the details of the above features. They know that cognates are helpful although they may be pronunciation traps or "false friends." Finally, they know that the importance of accuracy in grammatical control for their level of study depends on the potential incomprehensibility of their errors.

Learning strategies. Students are aware of desired learning outcomes. They know that in order to control the grammar they must know the rules, engage in drill exercises, and monitor their speech; that to develop fluency, they need a great deal of practice in communicating. They have learned to seek simple means to express themselves and to resort to circumlocutions and gestures when necessary. They are able to apply contextual guessing to listening and reading and word-attack skills to vocabulary building. They know how to use textbooks, reference books, dictionaries, and human resources for learning. They are aware of important aspects of their own learning styles and strategies and actively seek to improve them.

Career information. Learners are aware of careers and jobs for which a foreign language may be useful or essential. They begin to note their own interests and whether or not these concur with the requirements of such jobs and careers.

In addition to the core outcomes, satellite areas—art, music, literature, history, economics, politics, geography, anthropology—may contribute material for enrichment. These areas provide opportunities for interdisciplinary cooperation and topics for functional skill development.

Figure 1 is a graphic representation of the interaction among the four goals for arrival at Waystage 1. Areas of the circle represent approximate percentages of time and emphasis. Broken lines indicate interaction between the elements; e.g., while there is no clear demarcation between communicative skill development and learning about language and language learning strategies, there is very little input to the central core from the satellite areas at this level.

Waystage 2—Expansion level

At this stage of learning, equivalent to the second year of study in most high school programs, learners will expand their alternatives for expressing the

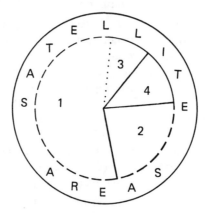

1. Communicative skill development: listening, speaking, reading, writing.
2. Culture study.
3. Language and language learning strategies.
4. Career awareness.

Fig. 1 Survival Level

meanings and functions of Waystage 1 and add new semantic, linguistic, and functional categories. Because they should be able to carry on simple, brief conversations without losing the attention of their listeners, they should establish and maintain closer relationships. Most of the time, their pronunciation does not distract listeners' attention or cause miscomprehension. With an opportunity to visit a country where the language is spoken, students who have reached this level should develop very rapidly greater fluency, comprehension, and vocabulary although their grammar remains incomplete. Their cultural understanding will have grown considerably, both in depth and in breadth. Errors are still numerous as learners attempt to incorporate new forms and structures into their speech and writing. In communication practice the teacher selects for correction those errors that would cause miscomprehension or elicit extreme emotional reactions; emphasis is still on basic communicative potentialities more than "rightness" or "wrongness."

Speaking. At this level learners can express the following:

- additional time relations: additional adverbs and prepositions; present perfect, past perfect, progressive forms of verbs, and contrasts between various past forms
- quantity: a lot of, a little, some, any, none
- space: measurements in inches, feet and miles and/or in metrics; height; still more adverbs and prepositions of location and motion in space
- distance: close, far away
- sentential relations: object pronouns, the most useful conjunctions, some common reflexives
- certainty, belief, probability, possibility, nil certainty, intention (with verbs in the indicative mood and impersonalized expressions).

They should be able to perform the following functions, many of which are additional alternatives for carrying out the functions listed for Waystage 1:

- maintain relationships at a deeper level: introduce and meet people; share experiences, opinions, common problems; express personal feelings; issue invitations and accept or decline; make social plans
- influence others' actions: request help, get others to do things, give and respond to instructions (expressed through indicative or other simple forms), give advice
- agree, disagree
- make excuses
- request and report information on matters of common interest related to their daily lives
- identify and describe people, places, objects; compare and contrast

- paraphrase and summarize, within the limitations of the topics and materials studies
- request information by telephone

Listening. During the second year of study, listening practice should be expanded to include many more exercises at the *macro* level (i.e., language as it is spoken naturally). Learners should be able to comprehend more than they can say. When listening to native speakers, radio and TV broadcasts, movies, or tapes, they can identify the topic and attitudes of the speakers when the material is familiar, concrete, nontechnical and when the speech is clear. Even when much of wht they hear is new to them, they are able to decipher parts of the message as they recognize words and phrases.

Reading. At this level, students read short, carefully edited stories and articles and peruse newspapers and magazines for specific information. They comprehend nontechnical instructions; simple invitations, notes, and letters written by native speakers; advertisements; and jokes and cartoons containing material within their proficiency limitations.

Writing. Students write simple telephone messages, friendly letters, paragraphs, and very short compositions; and they can fill out forms related to travel, school, and so forth.

Culture. Some of the culture study is now conducted in the target language with visual props and realia. Students continue to research the target culture and learn about culture-based conventions surrounding communicative exchanges. They study cases of crosscultural conflicts, and in addition to learning facts, they apply, analyze, and synthesize their cultural learnings to form hypotheses and solutions regarding crosscultural conflicts. They are willing to suspend judgment as they analyze how speakers of the language might think and feel.

Language and language learning. Learners know that forms signal meaning and that time relations are expressed in many different ways; they understand the uses of the tense forms they have studied. They are aware that messages can be expressed in a variety of ways and that there is usually a simpler means of saying or writing what they want to express. They have set their own learning goals and know what they have to do to achieve them.

Career exploration. Learners are apprised of careers requiring languages, the proficiency levels necessary in careers that interest them, and their own interests and preferences. Those who have identified a possible career are helped and encouraged to seek out appropriate vocabulary and apply it in their language-development exercises.

Figure 2 represents Waystage 2. There is now more interaction between language development and culture study; the latter contributes some topics for functional practice while the former provides a channel other than English

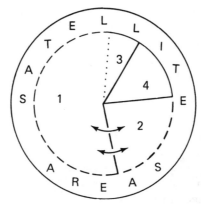

1. Communicative skill development: listening,
   speaking, reading, writing.
2. Culture study.
3. Language and language learning strategies.
4. Career awareness.

Fig. 2 Expansion Level

for learning about culture. At this level there is more emphasis on orientation
to possible careers than at Waystage 1.

Threshold level—Basic communicative proficiency

By the end of the third year, learners will have filled in most of the gaps in
their knowledge of important aspects of the linguistic, semantic, and functional
systems so that they can find a way to express most of their everyday needs,
ideas, and feelings. Their fluency has improved greatly; and although they
typically continue to commit many errors, they are able to correct themselves
much of the time. During the last portion of this year of study the teacher may
correct many more errors, and students are encouraged to monitor their
speech more carefully. Emphasis is now given to the higher expectations that
native speakers may have of advanced students.

Speaking. Learners add the following meanings to their repertoires:

- expression of more specific time: at exactly 6:00; on Thursday the 12th of
  May, 1980; since . . . ago; whenever
- additional descriptive terms for space dimensions: round, square, three-
  dimensional; _____ miles/kilometers away
- additional adverbs and prepositions of location and motion: underneath,
  above, towards, throughout, wherever
- passive voice

- further work with reflexive and related constructions
- probability, possibility, negation, belief (with contrast between indicative and subjunctive)
- conjecture (I wonder . . .)
- contrary-to-fact (If I were you . . .)
- commands.

They should be able to perform many new functions, including the following:

- express approval, disapproval, and blame
- report on current school events and major world events
- explain facts and relationships such as cause-effect
- make suggestions and recommendations
- give directions and instructions
- influence others: command, request, beg, insist, permit, prohibit, threaten, etc.
- express (and hide) emotions and respond to others' feelings
- joke; share leisure activities; apologize; argue
- make guesses and predictions.

Listening. Learners can now comprehend enough of any clear, standard message dealing with an everyday topic to surmise the message most of the time. They are able to identify others' purposes and intentions within the bounds of their own experience with the target language and culture. They can converse at some length on topics of everyday interest, although native speakers must often restate their messages in more than one way for comprehension to be complete.

Reading. While students continue to read carefully edited messages, they also read simple stories and articles and illustrated material on their own for enjoyment as well as for specific information. With the aid of a dictionary, they can read with general comprehension unedited words in standard, nontechnical language.

Writing. Students are now capable of writing outlines, instructions, short plays, longer letters, narratives, and essays.

Culture. Learners are able to relate cultural conventions to the purposes for which they are practiced. They know the major traits, patterns, and values of the culture and are able to identify them in case studies. They can solve many crosscultural problems; and when they are unable to solve them, they know to develop hypotheses and attempt to understand the other's point of view rather than invent generalizations. When they do not understand each others' meanings or intentions, they are able to check with each other through paraphrasing ("I think you're saying. . . . Is that right?") They also attempt to understand their own views and reactions in the face of cultural differences.

Language and language learning. They have an overview of the linguistic system and the semantic categories of the language and have developed the most efficient, effective approaches to language learning that these have to offer. They know how language and culture interact in communication; and they know that intercultural communication requires sensitivity, understanding, and patience. They are aware of the goals yet to be met.

Career awareness. Learners continue to seek information on careers, and those who identify a possible career seek further information about it and its linguistic requirements. They practice some skills related to their own areas of professional interest.

At this level the areas of study interact considerably as students are able to use the target language to gain information about careers, the culture, and related topics from the satellite areas. The curriculum is much more integrated.

At subsequent levels the core will become fused with the satellite areas, as local and individual needs and interests dictate the material to be studies.

Research questions

The major questions for research and reflection that have been raised in this chapter are, by topic:

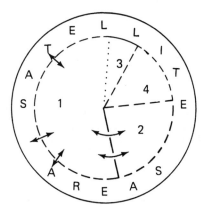

1. Communicative skill development: listening, speaking, reading, writing.
2. Culture study.
3. Language and language learning strategies.
4. Career orientation and preparation.

Fig. 3 Threshold Level

Communicative functioning ability:
- What are the most important functions at each level of proficiency within particular cultures? How can they be identified?
- What linguistic and extralinguistic behavior is appropriate for foreign language learners as they attempt to carry out these functions? Which of these behaviors are most and least difficult to learn?
- Are there "natural" levels of second-language learning/acquisition that can be identified and described?
- What are the effects on learning of reducing the grammatical material and increasing the functional practice for all four skills?
- Can functions/notions comprise the core material; i.e., can a system be found for selecting and sequencing functions and drawing from them the linguistic elements to be taught?

Intercultural understanding:
- What are the essential variables of intercultural communication and how do they interact?
- What cultural knowledge, skills, and attitudes are most important for learners to acquire at various levels of study? How can they best be learned?
- Which aspects of cultural learning are most appropriately combined with foreign language study?

Language and language learning:
- What would be the effects of acquiring an overview *about* the language before attempting to develop skills in using it?
- What are the most efficient and effective learning strategies and how can they be developed?

Career awareness:
- For what careers is knowledge of a second language required or useful either as a primary or an ancillary skill?
- What types and levels of proficiency are necessary for particular careers and jobs?

Conclusion

In this chapter a procedure has been demonstrated for specifying desirable learning outcomes for second-language study. The process consists of 1) synthesizing information from areas related to foreign language education to identify a common core of goals; 2) defining the goals more specifically in order to identify the essential components; 3) translating the resulting material into terms compatible with educational reality and existing information about learners' potential and limitations; and 4) sequencing the material according to essentiality and difficulty, by levels of study. Figure 4 provides a graphic representation of the process.

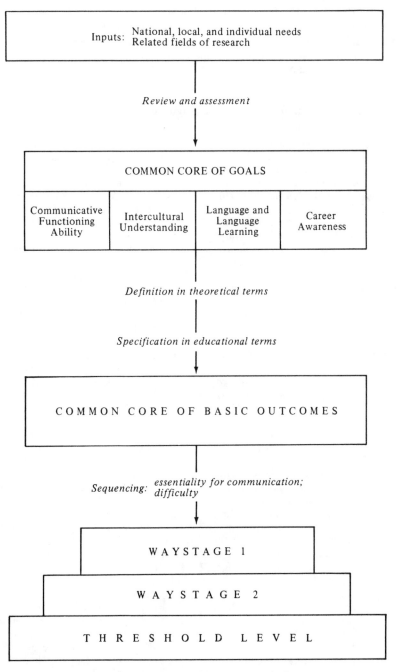

Fig. 4 The Specification of Outcomes: The Process

The levels that are identified and the examples of outcomes that are presented here are both general (in that they do not represent any given language) and tentative (in that research can be expected to bring further insights for the identification of the essential components of the goals as well as information on language learning processes).

References, Learning outcomes in the language classroom

1 Alexander, L. G. "Where Do We Go From Here? A Reconsideration of Some Basic Assumptions Affecting Course Design." *English Language Teaching Journal* 30 (1976): 89–103.

2 Asante, Molefi Kete, Eileen Newmark, and Cecil A. Blake. *Handbook of Intercultural Communication.* Beverly Hills, CA: SAGE Publications, 1979.

3 Bloom, Benjamin S., Max D. Englehart, Edward J. Furst, Walker H. Hill, and David R. Krathwohl. *Taxonomy of Educational Objectives. Handbook I: The Cognitive Domain.* New York: David McKay, 1956.

4 Born, Warren, ed. *Goals Clarification: Curriculum, Teaching, Evaluation.* Reports of the Working Committees of the Northeast Conference on the Teaching of Foreign Languages. Middlebury, VT: Northeast Conference, 1975.

5 Brumfit, Christopher. *From Defining to Designing: Communicative Specifications versus Communicative Methodology in Foreign Language Teaching.* [Paper presented at the European/American Seminar on Communicative Approaches and Second Language Course Design, New York, October 1979.]

6 Elling, Barbara. "Special Curricula for Special Needs," 83–115 in June K. Phillips, ed., *The New Imperative: Expanding the Horizons of Foreign Language Education.* ACTFL Foreign Language Education Series. Skokie, IL: National Textbook Company, 1980.

7 "The Essentials of Education." *Foreign Language Annals* 12 (1979): 379–80.

8 Freeman, G. Ronald. *101 (Plus) Ways to Stimulate Conversation in a Foreign Language.* [ACTFL Materials Center, 2 Park Ave., New York, 10016.]

9 Galt, Alan. "Realizing the Potential, Broadening the Base," 117–32 in June K. Phillips, ed., *The New Imperative: Expanding the Horizons of Foreign Language Education.* ACTFL Foreign Language Education Series. Skokie, IL: National Textbook Company, 1980.

10 Galyean, Beverly. "A Confluent Approach to Curriculum Design." *Foreign Language Annals* 12 (1979): 121–27.

11 Guntermann, Gail. *An Investigation of the Frequency, Comprehensibility, and Evaluational Effects of Errors in Spanish Made by English-Speaking Learners in El Salvador.* Columbus, OH: The Ohio State University, 1977. [Doctoral Dissertation: DAI 38: 11 (1978)]

12 _____ "Purposeful Communication Practice: Developing Functional Proficiency in a Foreign Language." *Foreign Language Annals* 12 (1979): 219–25.

13 _____ "Some Factors to Be Considered in Specifying Target Levels of Communicative Proficiency." [Paper presented at the European/American Seminar on Communicative Approaches and Second Language Course Design, New York, October 1979.]

14 _____ "A Suggested Approach to

Determining Cultural Objectives." *Hispania* 59 (1976): 87–92.

15 Jarvis, Donald D. "Making Cross-cultural Connections," 151–77 in June K. Phillips, ed., *The Language Connection: From the Classroom to the World.* ACTFL Foreign Language Education Series, Volume 9. Skokie, IL: National Textbook Company, 1977.

16 Lafayette, Robert C. "Coping with 'Innovative Overchoice': A Curricular Model." *Foreign Language Annals* 11 (1978): 247–56.

17 Larsen-Freeman, Diane. "An ESL Index of Development." *TESOL Quarterly* 12 (1978): 439–48.

18 Magnan, Sally Sieloff. "Reduction and Error Correction for Communicative Language Use: The Focus Approach." *The Modern Language Journal* 63 (1979): 343–49.

19 McEwan, Angela, and Roger Minkle. "Why Am I Studying Spanish? An Evaluation of Student Response." *Hispania* 62 (1979): 89–97.

20 Medley, Frank W., Jr. "Identifying Needs and Setting Goals," 41–65 in June K. Phillips, ed., *Building on Experience—Building for Success.* ACTFL Foreign Language Education Series, Volume 10. Skokie, IL: National Textbook Company, 1979.

21 *Modern Languages for Everyone.* Albany: NY: State Department of Education, 1978.

22 Moscowitz, Gertrude. *Caring and Sharing in the Foreign Language Classroom.* Rowley, MA: Newbury House, 1978.

23 Munby, John. *Communicative Syllabus Design.* New York: Cambridge University Press, 1978.

24 Myers, Pamela J. "Profiles and Perspectives," 17–49 in June K. Phillips, ed., *The New Imperative: Expanding the Horizons for Foreign Language Education.* ACTFL Foreign Language Education Series. Skokie, IL: National Texbook Company, 1980.

25 Nostrand, Howard L. "Empathy for a Second Culture: Motivations and Techniques," 263–327 in Gilbert A. Jarvis, ed., *Responding to New Realities.* ACTFL Foreign Language Education Series, Volume 5. Skokie, IL: National Textbook Company, 1974.

26 Orr, Ethan. "Up the Multinational Ladder." *Sky* (Delta Airlines, June 1979): 141–44.

27 Panetta, Leon E. "The Importance of Foreign Language Study." *Bulletin of the Association of Departments of Foreign Languages* 11 (1979): 3–4.

28 Phillips, June K. "Reading is Communication, Too!" *Foreign Language Annals* 11 (1978): 281–87.

29 "Report on the MLA Task Force on the Commonly Taught Languages." *Foreign Language Annals* 11 (1978): 635–641.

30 Rivers, Wilga M. "The View on the Way Up: A Wider Perspective," 11–18 in Warren C. Born, ed., *The Foreign Language Learner in Today's Classroom Environment.* Northeast Conference Reports. Middlebury, VT: Northeast Conference, 1979.

31 Sarbaugh, L.E. *Intercultural Communication.* Rochelle Park, NJ: Hayden Book Company, 1979.

32 Schulz, Renate A. "Back to the Basics in the Foreign Language Classroom?" *Foreign Language Annals* 11 (1978): 647–55.

33 Seelye, H. Ned. *Teaching Culture.* Skokie, IL: National Textbook Company, 1975.

34 *Some Essential Learner Outcomes (Foundation Learnings) in Modern Foreign Languages.* Minnesota Department of Education. Curriculum Bulletin/57. Fall 1977. Code VIII-A-E-C-30.

35 Steiner, Florence. *Performing with Objectives.* Rowley, MA: Newbury House, 1975.

36 *Strength through Wisdom: A Critique of U.S. Capability.* A Report

to the President from the President's Commission on Foreign Language and International Studies. [New York: ACTFL Materials Center, 1979.]

37 Thogmartin, Clyde and Jo An Mann. "Business Needs for Foreign Languages: A Survey of 219 Employers." *Bulletin of the Association of Departments of Foreign Languages* 10 (1979): 32–33.

38 Tuttle, Harry Grover, Jorge Guitart, Anthony Papalia, and Joseph Zampogna. "Effects of Cultural Presentations on Attitudes of Foreign Language Students." *Modern Language Journal* 63 (1979): 177–82.

39 Valdman, Albert. *Communicative Ability and Global Foreign Language Course Syllabus Design.* [Paper presented at the European/American Seminar on Communicative Approaches and Second Language Course Design, New York, October 1979.]

40 _____ "Communicative Use of guage and Syllabus Design." *Foreign Language Annals* 11 (1978): 567–78.

41 Valette, Rebecca M., and Renée S. Disick. *Modern Language Performance Objectives and Individualiza-*

tion: *A Handbook.* New York: Harcourt Brace Jovanovich, Inc., 1972.

42 van Ek, J. A. *The Threshold Level for Modern Language Learning in Schools.* London: Longman, 1977.

43 Warriner, Helen P. "High School Foreign Language Texts: Too Much Between the Covers to Cover." *Foreign Language Annals* 11 (1978): 551–57.

44 Wattenmaker, Beverly S., and Virginia Wilson. *A Guidebook for Teaching Foreign Languages: Spanish, French, and German.* Rockleigh, NJ: Longwood Division, Allyn and Bacon, Inc., 1980.

45 Westphal, Patricia B. "Teaching and Learning: A Key to Success," 119–56 in June K. Phillips, ed., *Building on Experience—Building for Success.* ACTFL Foreign Language Education Series, Volume 10. Skokie, IL: National Textbook Company, 1979.

46 _____ and Elizabeth G. Joiner, eds. *Developing Communication Skills.* Rowley, MA: Newbury House, 1978.

47 Wilkins, D. A. *Notional Syllabuses.* London: Oxford University Press, 1976.

6

Broadening the middle school curriculum through content: Globalizing foreign languages

Lorraine A. Strasheim
Indiana University

Introduction

Not since the advent of audiolingualism, which arose from within the ranks of foreign language educators, has there been the kind of professional excitement global education is generating among second-language teachers. The challenges of global education, however, differ radically from those of audiolingualism. First of all, global education encompasses all disciplines in K–12 curricula; it is a multidisciplinary phenomenon providing foreign languages with an opportunity to become integrated into the total school curriculum in ways not possible in the past. Second, global education is focused on what to teach—the content—rather than on how to teach—the method.

As the profession is defining the role of foreign languages in global education, there is another curricular challenge demanding the profession's attention, a problem Adcock (1) has defined clearly and succinctly:

> Foreign language programs at the middle and junior high levels must take into account the unique developmental characteristics of the emerging adolescent, especially keeping in mind that the rate of cognitive growth differs greatly from student to student. A simple extension of a senior high program down into the middle and junior high school has been done frequently in the past, with little or no regard for the special

Lorraine A. Strasheim (M.A.T., Indiana University) is Coordinator for School Foreign Languages at Indiana University, where she teaches undergraduate and graduate methods. A former president of ACTFL, she has published in *Foreign Language Annals, The Modern Language Journal,* and a variety of professional publications. She is presently serving as a member of *The Modern Language Journal* editorial board.

characteristics of the learners. The uniqueness of the middle school's clients demands a unique curriculum, and that includes the foreign language curriculum. (pp. 302–3)

The emergence of global education is providing foreign language teachers with an opportunity to construct curriculum from the ground up rather than from the roof down, an opportunity to avoid the failures of foreign language in the elementary school by fitting the curricula to the needs of the learner and the functions of the school level. To proceed to add random global education components to various parts of the sequence will result neither in globalized offerings nor in addressing the real problems of attrition, especially between levels one and two. What is called for is a reasoned approach to restructuring the foreign language sequence, beginning with level one in the middle or junior high school, and then moving to level two and beyond in progression, with minima defined for each level in so far as the foreign language skills are concerned, a graded approach to the teaching of culture, and a careful "matching" of objectives, learning activities, and evaluation instruments.

There is time to do the necessary learning and the necessary planning. We need to take our watchword from the Roman emperor Augustus, "Make haste slowly," for the emergence of global education has led many foreign language specialists to three interrelated misperceptions: 1) that foreign languages are *de facto* global education and need few changes to become globalized; 2) that global education is essentially another of the "Monday morning" ideas typical of the seventies and the decade of innovative overchoice; and 3) that workshop leaders and materials developers can, with minimal "homework" of their own, speed teachers into classroom implementation.

While most of our middle school and junior high school colleages can provide us with the knowledge we need about the emerging adolescent and the kinds of learning experiences he or she needs, we must begin planning with them rather than imposing on them. At the same time, all of us need to do a sizable amount of learning, unlearning, and relearning to prepare ourselves for global education. We need time to assimilate and internalize the philosophy and concepts of global education, for our "world" has been western Europe and this hemisphere, our "world" languages have been branches of the Indo-European family only, and our maps have centered this hemisphere between two ragged halves of the rest of the nations on this planet.

What are the "bare bones" facts about global education?

If the 47 million young Americans in our schools are to be prepared for life and citizenship in an interdependent world, Lee Anderson (3) argues, the content, the methods, and the social context of education must be changed.

In collaboration with Charlotte Anderson (4), he sets as the goals of this changed or *global* education: developing "the students' understanding of themselves as individuals, members of the human species, inhabitants and dependents of planet Earth, and participants in a global society" and helping them to acquire the competencies required to function "intelligently and responsibly" in these roles (p. 8). The Wisconsin State Social Studies Curriculum Study Committee (23) calls this phenomenon of global education an effort at a "more holistic and multidimensional" preparation for students, while King and Condon (10) characterize it as "learning . . . centered around four basic themes, or concepts: change, communication, conflict, and interconnectedness" (p. 4).

But global educators do not stop with a definition of goals. Leestma (12) elaborates on the sensitivities and competencies needed for the rest of this century and beyond, defining them as:

- some basic cross-cultural understanding, empathy, and ability to communicate with people from different cultures
- a sense of why and how mankind shares a common future—global issues and dynamics and the calculus of interdependence
- a sense of stewardship in the use of the earth and acceptance of the ethic of intergenerational responsibility for the well-being and fair chance of those who will come after us (p. 6).

Global educators then proceed to define the learning outcomes desired in terms of cognitive, perceptual, emotional, and social *capacities,* which are further broken down into *abilities.* What follows is an extremely short example from the massive work that has been done. Anderson (3) is defining one of several capacities contributing to perceiving one's interconnectedness or interdependence:

Competence in Perceiving One's Involvement in Global Society

requires the CAPACITY to	perceive that peoples at all levels of social organization —from the individual to the whole society—are both "cultural borrowers" and "cultural depositers"; they both draw from and contribute to a "global bank of human culture" that has been and continues to be fed by contributions from all peoples, in all geographical regions, and in all periods of time
which involves the ABILITY to	a) conceptualize culture as a human creation varying among particular groups and societies, but serving universal objectives; b) trace the historical and geographical origins of — the technologies — the institutions — the languages — the beliefs

c) identify contributions (technologies, beliefs, institutions, languages) made by one's own community, region, religion, or ethnic group to the "global bank of human cultures" (p. 345).

Despite these highly refined competencies and learning outcomes, global education is not conceived as a new program to be imposed on a crowded curriculum in a time of decreasing enrollments; it is rather planned to be implemented through the addition of global components to many of the disciplines within that curriculum.

Isn't global education in conflict with Back to Basics?

Just as global education is not an effort at world federation, it is not in conflict with Back to Basics. Sadly enough, this misperception compelled Becker's (5) assertion: "We consider basic skills of reading, writing, and arithmetic to be essential to citizenship development for participation in a global society" (p. 45).

It is important to remember in this context that while drills are necessary to the development of skills, foreign language is, as Phillips (21) has argued, "a contentless discipline." And, as King and Condon (10) advise, ". . . skills development is much more likely to be improved when students are dealing with subject matter that is real to them and inherently interesting" (p. 4). It should be unnecessary to point out that although grammar may be "basic" to learning a language, the idea content is "basic" to motivating the student to persist in his or her studies until some real skills have been acquired.

Isn't global education too idealistic and too utopian to succeed?

However idealistic and utopian global education may seem, it can succeed *if:*

- its proponents begin to respond more realistically to the political and psychological barriers that hamper the development of global perspectives. There must be further study, in both foreign language and in the social studies, of the obstacles Torney (27) has identified, those arising within the individual student and those originating from without—in schools, in families, through government policies, and through the media
- entire faculties and the community are involved in planning for global education from the outset
- there are some clear-cut definitions of how the United States will be better served by citizens with global perspectives

- there are efforts by all the educational and communication channels to address that part of the population not enrolled in schools and colleges. As Gardner (8) has indicated, "Social change is a learning process for all concerned. It always requires re-education of large numbers of people to accept new objectives, new values, new procedures . . ." (pp. 27–28)
- the leadership fits its proposals to the realities of the schools today, focusing particularly upon declining student populations
- teachers are given opportunities—and time—to examine, test, and accept the philosophy and are not rushed into implementation
- it retains a focus on issues and values and does not devolve into an educational "world tourism"
- what Longstreet (15) calls "an ongoing tentativeness" can be maintained. Global materials, to be authentic and effective, will probably have a three- to five-year life.

Global education only seems too utopian and too idealistic to those teachers who habitually cite goals without "matching" them to instruction and evaluation.

Should foreign language teachers become involved with global education?

Teachers of all languages and at all levels should seriously consider becoming involved with global education. First of all, it is not easy to dismiss the K–12 recommendation of the President's Commission (26), which asserts that students "must grow up with more knowledge about our interdependent world, keener awareness of other people, and greater sensitivity to those peoples' attitudes and customs" (p. 48). This recommendation was reinforced by the public, for in the last Gallup Poll of the Public's Attitudes Toward the Public Schools (7) 60 percent of those surveyed indicated that they felt that the "interdependence of nations—foreign relations" were "essential subjects" (p. 40).

Foreign language specialists should also be interested in global education because of its potential impact upon the educational construct. Overly (20) sees it as an "all encompassing organizer for general education, inclusive of all other subjects" (p. 2). Leestma (12), too, speaks of the centralizing force of global education, although in a different context:

Global education is a challenge that has the potential to rival Sputnik in re-invigorating American education with a sense of mission. Taken as a whole, it offers the closest thing in education to a moral equivalent of war. The concerns involved convey the full complexity and fascination of world reality as well as the imperative element of survival (p. 5).

Not to consider becoming involved with global education is to deny the *raison d'être* of foreign language education.

But why aren't foreign languages already global education?

The global education goals relating to cultural awareness and crosscultural understanding frequently mislead foreign language teachers into assuming that their courses are already globalized offerings because they also have cultural goals. As Robinson (22) has argued, however, the claims for the teaching of culture have "rarely been reflected in specific instructional and evaluative practices of the foreign language classroom" (p. 135) because "ideas have housed the language rather than the reverse" (p. 138).

Teachers may be overestimating the amount of culture teaching they actually do, for Moskowitz (17), whose data includes observations in eighty-eight classrooms, found that even outstanding teachers tend to all but overlook culture. Nerenz (18), reinforcing the Moskowitz report, learned that Wisconsin teachers she studied spent only 7 percent of their instructional time teaching culture. When these data are contrasted with the stipulations that a globalized course is one in which one-third of the instructional time is spent on transnational issues and/or crosscultural contrastive studies (Ochoa and Strasheim, 19), it becomes clear that foreign language specialists have much to do in restructuring their content focuses and their instructional priorities if they wish to take any substantive role in global education.

Pleading the communication goals for foreign language offerings does not alleviate the problem, for as Edmund Glenn (9), Chief of Interpreting Services for the U.S. Department of State, emphasized:

If you want to be understood, truly understood, by people of a different culture, of a different language, it is not enough to use their vocabulary, their grammar, and even their pronunciation. You also have to use their logic. Otherwise they will not understand you (p. 16).

What can a teacher who is interested in global education do?

The foreign language teacher who is interested in global education should begin by doing his or her "homework." This can include the following "learning activities":

* Write to your state department of education or public instruction to see what publications are available from that source.
* Write to Global Perspectives in Education to ask a) for a list or catalog of their publications and b) to be put on their mailing list. Address: Global Perspectives in Education, Inc., 218 East 18th Street, New York, NY 10003.

- Study one or both of these basic resources:

  1 Lee Anderson. *Schooling and Citizenship in a Global Age: An Exploration of the Meaning and Significance of Global Education.* Bloomington, Indiana: Mid-American Program for Global Perspectives in Education, 1979. Orders should be prepaid with a check for $6.00 made out to Indiana University and sent to The Social Studies Development Center, Indiana University; 513 North Park Street; Bloomington, IN 47401.

  2 James M. Becker, editor, *Schooling for a Global Age.* New York: McGraw-Hill Book Company, 1979.

- Study any textbooks the school's social studies department can provide on global education or world cultures. Get a teacher's edition if possible in order to be able to study objectives and learning activities in some depth.

As they do this "homework" on global education, foreign language teachers should also review resources on the teaching of culture and begin to sort out some of their teaching priorities. This process might include: 1) re-evaluating the textbook's "optional" cultural readings currently being ignored; 2) taking special care to teach vocabulary both with visual cultural referents and with some attention to cultural meanings; 3) discussing what the use of such phenomena as polite and familiar pronouns tell us about the value system of the people, thus teaching the *whys* as well as the *hows* of cultural behavior; and 4) approaching readings from the standpoint of the idea content rather than from the grammar. With the resulting shifts in emphases, that one-third instructional time criterion for globalized offerings becomes far less threatening. Also it might well be that our middle and junior high school students would be more motivated in their studies; for, as it stands now, the content of our first-year books—numbers, colors, parts of the body, members of the family, and so on—roughly parallels the K–3 curricula.

Where does the interdisciplinary or multidisciplinary aspect come in?

It is highly unlikely in times of contrained school budgets and declining student populations that many schools will be able to offer team-taught experiences, although the middle school is more flexible in this regard. But there are other modes of cooperation. In an earlier article (24) I suggested that social studies and foreign language teachers meet to determine 1) where there is "overlap" in the two disciplines where both are teaching the same things and 2) a sharing of responsibilities and objectives. It is my belief that such meetings could lead to the identification and preparation of materials to be used in both disciplines as well as some class and teacher exchanges.

One does not have to leave the foreign language department, however, in order to begin interdisciplinary cooperation. Such materials as the Elkins, Kalivoda, and Morain (6) audio-motor unit on the picnic provide a marvelous opportunity for more meaningful interaction and cross-fertilization within or among languages.

Teachers can also utilize what I call "curricular complements" (25) to achieve a measure of multidisciplinary cooperation. A curricular complement is one discipline's approach to a topic considered in another discipline. While curricular complements need not be taught simultaneously, teachers can use their knowledge of the other disciplines' activities as a review of prerequisite knowledge and to expand and reinforce student learnings. Some sample curricular complements are

- *Foreign Languages:* food, meals at home and in restaurants, table etiquette, table settings, and the like
- *Home Economics:* the preparation of foods from the cultures represented in the foreign languages offered
- *Social Studies:* the food chain, calorie consumption around the world, global food quality and related matters.

Surveying the faculty on three to five such topics will result in more faculty cohesion as well as a set of curricular complements.

Here are sample curricular complements gleaned from materials in the social studies and foreign languages:

Tracing a Family Tree: A Social Studies Approach

Grade Level: 4 and above.

Source: James M. Becker *et al. Indiana in the World.* Indianapolis: Division of Curriculum, Indiana State Department of Public Instruction, 1978, p. 10.

Objectives: 1 Students will trace their ethnic heritage by developing a family tree.

2 Students will discuss how families can be affected by their cultural/ethnic heritage.

Procedure: Have students construct a family tree tracing their family's history as far back as possible. They will present these family trees to the class. Students might also compare family trees. (Since certain students might be sensitive about this, it would be best if they volunteer this information.) Students should be encouraged to discuss specific family customs and to compare these with the customs of other students' families. Students might also be asked to speculate on:

- how living in the United States has affected the customs of their family
- how their cultural/ethnic heritage has affected their family life

- why specific family customs developed
- how their ethnic group has influenced life in their community
- the impact of members of their family on the community.

Ethnic Smorgasbord

On a particular day, have students bring in a food or artifacts representative of their ethnic background. They should describe each "ethnic dish" or artifact. You may want students to speculate on the origin of particular recipes or artifacts. To conlude the activity, have students discuss the similarities and differences among the various foods and artifacts.

Der Stammbaum (A Family Tree): A Foreign Language Approach

Grade Level: Level one, middle, junior high, or high school

Source: Susan Hunt-Smith, William Blaisdell, and Esther Stockdreher. *Der Apfel Fällt Nich Weit vom Baum.* Indiana University: Summer Foreign Language Workshops, 1975. [Mimeograph.]

Objectives: 1 To personalize some German information learned—names, family members, family relationships, and dates.

2 To demonstrate that other cultures approach things differently.

Instructions: Make a three- or four-generation family tree. It might be wise to use posterboard (half size) or a large piece of construction paper. You will have to ask relatives for information, for you should include the birthdays and years of birth in German form and the maiden names of your female relatives as well as the relationship of each person to you. You may, if you prefer, make up an imaginary family.

Hint: Work out your family tree on scratch paper before you begin the final copy.

Remember:
- German dates put the day first, then the month, then the year. If you were born August 24, 1966, you write it:

  24.   8.   66

  day month year
- If your mother's maiden name was Schulz and her married name is Sauerkopf, you would write "Maria Sauerkopf geb. Schulz." *Geb.* stands for "born."

You may want to use circles to represent female relatives, squares to represent males. You might want to use an actual tree shape. You could, if you wished, "illustrate" your family tree with magazine pictures, cartoon faces, or photos (if your family doesn't mind).

Teachers who delve into curricular complements may well be pleased by the creative and constructive ideas they learn.

What might this middle school curriculum "look like"?   _____

If teachers begin defining the middle or junior high foreign language curriculum in terms of minima, using a design like that proposed by Lafayette (11), which consists of a definition of "core" materials to be mastered by all plus reinforcement and enrichment activities, they will have both a basis for articulating with the next level and a construct into which some global education components can be built.

A footnote is appropriate here. Teachers tend to add what they call "supplements" to the basic teaching materials. While most argue that their texts have deficiencies, the real motivation is more likely a desire to interact with the course and the materials, to put one's personal stamp on the offering, as it were. But adding materials year after year of a textbook adoption period can distort the objectives and the instruction; teachers must learn to *subtract* and to *replace* as well as to add.

Given the definition of the language and skills "core" and minima, the teacher is ready to define the culture "core" or minima, for culture is to be an integral part of the foreign language experience. The beginning year of the language experience should aim at devoting 20 to 25 percent of the instructional time to cultural learnings, including vocabulary, grammar, and reading activities with cultural dimensions. Beyond those activities, the focus should probably be upon cultural awareness in the form of cultural behavior (greetings, etiquette—the kinds of content already included) and the global education concept of interconnectedness (interdependence). As teachers proceed in their planning, they should include objectives, learning activities, and evaluation. Students will learn only what is tested and graded.

As they plan, foreign language specialists should learn from a variety of social studies people. While we are quick to seize upon such statements as Torney's (27) "that the years before age fourteen may be thought of as a kind of critical or optimal period in the acquisition of knowledge and attitudes about international organizations and processes" (p. 86), we do not respond as readily to advice of the kind offered by Morris (16):

> . . . I have become increasingly convinced that to be effective any realistic program of global education for children must have much of its roots in their own daily lives and the relationships of their own communities to the rest of the world. Everyone lives in some local community on this globe, and as valuable as it most certainly is to see the world from space to gain new perspectives, we must not overlook the individual child and his/her experience base in a given part of that global whole (p. 141).

From Adcock's (1) fine discussion it becomes clear that middle or junior high "schoolers" require learning activities which they do rather than those the teacher does for them. These students, for example, will benefit far more from devising a map of those nations that are Spanish- or French-speaking than from seeing a map or bulletin board devised by the teacher.

If we strive to help students perceive their interconnectedness, relating the learnings to the students' environment with an emphasis on student doing, we might come up with a series of lessons as in this outline:

I   *Our State's Historic Connections to the World's Peoples*
   A The origins of objects and articles used in everyday life (bed, book, shoe, tableware, etc.)
   B Towns and cities in the state with names of French, German, Latin, Russian, or Spanish origin
   C Parallel (short) descriptions of the city in the target culture and the one in the home state
   D Patterns of foreign settlements in the state
II *Our State's Linguistic Connections to the World's Peoples*
   A The families of languages in the world (*N.B.* The world's languages extend far beyond the Indo-European family of languages. The teacher should present the Indo-European family and let students research the other families for a mural, a frieze, or a bulletin board.)
   B English word borrowings coming through time
   C Derivations from the target language in familiar English usage
   D Foods from the target culture(s) familiar to Americans

This approach represents the author's "creative borrowing" of the concepts in *Indiana in the World,* the source of the curricular complement cited earlier. This work, and comparable ones in many states, are patterned after *Columbus and the World* which was produced by Chadwick Alger and the Staff of the Mershon Center (2); under the nurturing hand of the Chief State School Officers, most state departments of public instruction/education have these resources available. They are excellent guides in working toward the last part of the outline.

III *Our State's Business and Industry Connections to the World's Peoples*
   A Multinational businesses
   B Foreign-owned businesses
   C The state's involvement in import and export

Students who have explored these kinds of "connections" should be better prepared to see the value of acquiring language skills.

These types of learnings could constitute a good segment of an exploratory program or, in schools where no such courses are offered, they can be made a part of the "core" for the beginning year. These lessons, in conjunction with a focus on cultural behavior—greetings, table etiquette, getting around in another country, shopping and currency, and the like—need one other component in the middle or junior high school sequence:

IV *Career Awareness*
   A Learnings centered around jobs and careers in the target culture(s) and the way in which work is regarded
   B The wide range of careers in this country and abroad requiring or recommending second-language proficiency as a primary or secondary skill

The key lies in the teacher's permitting the students to learn for themselves and to teach one another. Teacher-prepared materials might be more comprehensive—and even more attractive—but in the long run the students' own efforts will provide less stultifying and more meaningful learnings.

What projections can be made for the second year and beyond?

Beginning foreign language curriculum planning from the ground up instead of the top down (thus almost guaranteeing few if any changes in the advanced levels) would permit teachers to spiral or "grade" the cultural as well as the linguistic learnings. In the second year, students could be introduced to contrastive cultural studies in which they study some of the linguistic differences and some of the differences in social behavior, beliefs and values, and contributions of at least three of the societies using the target language. It is gratifying to see that textbooks are beginning to show the "seeds" of some of these approaches even if the learnings involved cannot yet be considered globalized.

Third-year classes might well study beliefs and values in some depth. Loew (14) proposes an excellent activity for contrasting values in American society and the target culture, an activity that uses newspapers and magazines—contemporary print media. Advanced students, too, could use the print media to contrast different world views and to gain some perspective on how the United States is viewed through the world.

As foreign language teachers are seemingly about to embark upon integrating culture teaching into their course offerings, simultaneously increasing the amount of instructional emphasis and time given to it, there is a need for more research like that of Tuttle *et al.* (28) to determine the effects of teaching similarities and differences in an effort to find ways of teaching cultural differences without creating distance and alienation.

What can the professional organizations contribute in this process?

Leestma (13) establishes a three-phase agenda for global educators. The first phase, to be completed by 1980, is basically a period of creating a professional awareness of global education. While foreign languages have tentatively entered this arena, there is still much to be done, particularly in moving toward responsible planning for future implementation. Leestma's second phase, due to end in the mid-eighties, involves the establishment of inservice opportunities, development of preservice options, involvement in student and teacher exchange programs, and formation of a research agenda. Associations like ACTFL should establish some standing committees both to set this kind of agenda and to deliberate it with colleagues in other disciplines; for Leestma's phase three, to be accomplished in 1990, calls for district programs, teacher certification, and school accreditation as well as local, state, and national assessments of the program made.

Since the global components of the foreign language class should be an integral part of the program and not left to chance, they should be incorporated in any minimal goals that might be established nationally. It is imperative that the various professional organizations act responsibly to guide teachers over the next ten years rather than to develop workshop sessions and professional articles leading to another curriculum that "just growed like Topsy."

Conclusion

While foreign language specialists have rather piously cited the characteristics of learners at different age levels, there has been no concerted effort to develop curricula for these learners. The process has been one of "transplantation" despite the learner differences, the variety of period lengths and contact times, and the development of adversary relationships between the teachers at the various school levels. Replicating the "sins" of the FLES era in the middle or junior high school can only lead to the same outcome—the disappearance of second languages in this environment.

The confluence of a variety of powerful forces—the President's Commission, the emergence of global education as a force in the schools, the increased cooperation among the various professional organizations within and outside foreign languages, and the call for national minima can all be brought to bear upon the proficiency, motivation, and attrition problems the profession would not discuss until very recently.

While high school foreign language specialists have, to a great extent, asserted their independence from their colleagues in colleges and universities by claiming rightly that their task was more than mere college preparation, they have not been willing to concede that their middle and junior high school colleagues also have some special needs. More often than not middle school and junior high school teachers have been cast in the roles of "second-class professionals"; they are expected to accept content, materials, and pacing imposed by the sequencers in the level above them. Teachers at these middle school levels, too, have had few pages in the professional literature or few podia at professional meetings to plead their special curricular needs. And the same publishers who would never consider issuing the same texts for seventh- and tenth-grade use in English, math, or social studies have also contributed to the problems.

While much is being made of the need for public awareness today, one of the things of which the public is very much aware is that great numbers of children enter middle or junior high school offerings each year only to find that their French, German, or Spanish is coming at them in amounts they cannot handle, at paces they cannot maintain, and through teaching approaches that do not facilitate the learning.

And while it is currently popular to advocate foreign language programs in the elementary school, it is impossible to see how we can accommodate learners at that level when we cannot at the middle or bridging level. We have to learn to keep posing one question to ourselves at each stage of the foreign language sequence: "If the learner were to stop at the end of this year, what skills and what learnings will he or she have that can survive twenty years hence—until the time that he or she assumes citizenship, family, and career roles?" And as professional language teachers, we also should be far more concerned with questions like these:

- Where do we have the greatest mass of our students?
- What kinds of learnings should we be providing for the mass that are now saved for only those who reach the advanced levels?
- What attitudes toward second language learning are we creating in the school patrons of today and those of the future through our enormous attrition rates?
- Do all of our students have opportunities for skill-using or are these activities deferred until only the "majors" are left?
- What ideas have my students considered in the course of their foreign language study?

One of the prime areas requiring research in foreign language education is the role that idea content plays in motivating students to continue in their language studies.

In some schools, some well-organized and caring schools, each of the disciplines will be asked to define those global education objectives that its department can achieve, and students will be given options in the ways in which they fulfill the minima established. In the great majority of schools, each department—even each teacher—will be left to define those objectives that are appropriate to the discipline. What this means, sadly, is that until textbooks incorporate global learnings into the basic materials, many American students will be receiving an education more fit for their grandparents' time than their own.

If we refuse to recognize the unique characteristics of the emerging adolescent and devise curricula for that level, if we permit culture teaching to devolve to the other disciplines in the curriculum (either because we have "declined" involvement in global education or because we have persisted in devoting under 10 percent of our instructional time to the teaching of culture) we shall lose all that interdisciplinary cooperation we have begun to build, the school roles we have professed to want; and we shall be making foreign language an end in itself for the foreseeable future. If, on the other hand, we confront the challenge, setting a professional agenda extending to 1990, we shall be demonstrating to the educational world and our students that we do not regard these challenges as some of Pogo's "insurmountable opportunities," that we want to be a full partner in the development of more holistic educations for America's young people, and that we do want to aid all our students in preparing to live more successful and productive lives in the future. Most important, we shall be demonstrating that language is the medium, and culture is the message.

References, Broadening the middle school curriculum through content: Globalizing foreign languages

1 Adcock, Dwayne. "Foreign Languages in Elementary and Emerging Adolescent Education," 289–326 in Gilbert A. Jarvis, ed., *An Integrative Approach to Foreign Language Teaching: Choosing Among the Options.* ACTFL Foreign Language Education Series, Volume 8. Skokie, IL: National Textbook Company, 1976.

2 Alger, Chadwick, and the Staff of the Mershon Center. *Columbus and the World.* Columbus: Mershon Center, Ohio State University, 1975.

3 Anderson, Lee. *Schooling and Citizenship in a Global Age: An Exploration of the Meaning and Significance of Global Education.* Bloomington: Mid-America Program for Global Perspectives in Education, Indiana University, 1979.

4 _____ and Charlotte Anderson. "A Visit to Middleston's World Centered Schools: A Scenario," 1–51 in James M. Becker, ed., *Schooling for a Global Age.* New York: McGraw-Hill Book Company, 1979.

5 Becker, James M. "The World and the Schools: A Case for World-Centered Education," 33–57 in James M. Becker, ed., *Schooling for a Global Age.* New York: McGraw-Hill Book Company, 1979.

6 Elkins, Robert J., Theodore B. Kalivoda, and Genelle Morain. "Teaching Culture through the Audio-Motor Unit." *Foreign Language Annals* 6 (1972):61–67

7 Gallup, George H. "The Eleventh Annual Gallup Poll of the Public's Attitudes Toward the Public Schools." *Phi Delta Kappan* 61 (1979):33–45

8 Gardner, John W. *No Easy Victories.* New York: Harper and Row, 1968.

9 Glenn, Edmund. Quoted by Tora Tuve Ladu, "Teaching for Cross-Cultural Understanding," 14–17 in Lorraine A. Strasheim, ed., *Foreign Language in a New Apprenticeship for Living.* Bloomington: Indiana Language Programs, Indiana Uni-

versity, 1971.

10 King, David C., and Larry E. Condon. "Introduction to the Humanities Series," 2–6 in Judith M. Barnett, *Culture's Storehouse: Building Skills through Folklore.* Intercom Series #90/91. New York: Center for Global Perspectives, 1978.

11 Lafayette, Robert C. "Coping with Innovative Overchoice: A Curriculum Model," *Foreign Language Annals* 11(1978):247–56.

12 Leestma, Robert. "Education for a Global Age: What Is Involved?" *Vital Issues* 28: 7(1979). [*Vital Issues* is a newsletter published by the Center for Information on America, Washington, CT 06798.]

13 _____ "Looking Ahead: An Agenda for Action," 232–43 in James M. Becker, ed., *Schooling for a Global Age.* New York: McGraw-Hill Book Company, 1979.

14 Loew, Helene Z. "Tuning In: Popular Culture in the Second Language Classroom." *Foreign Language Annals* 12(1979):271–74.

15 Longstreet, Wilma S. "Open Education—A Coming to Terms with Uncertainty," 124–40 in Norman V. Overly, ed., *Lifelong Learning: A Human Agenda.* Washington, DC: Association for Supervision and Curriculum Development, 1979.

16 Morris, Donald N. "Elementary School Programs," 111–51 in James M. Becker, ed., *Schooling for a Global Age.* New York: McGraw-Hill Book Company, 1979.

17 Moskowitz, Gertrude. "The Classroom Interaction of Outstanding Foreign Language Teachers." *Foreign Language Annals* 9(1976):135–43, 146–57.

18 Nerenz, Anne. "Utilizing Class Time in Foreign Language Instruction," 78–89 in David P. Benseler, ed., *Teaching the Basics in the Foreign Language Classroom: Options and Strategies.* Skokie, IL: National Textbook Company, 1979.

19 Ochoa, Anne S., and Lorraine A. Strasheim. "Toward Continued Cooperation Between the Social Studies and Foreign Languages." *Global Perspectives* 1 (April 1980). [Newsletter published by the Center for Global Perspectives, 218 East 18th Street, New York, NY 1003.]

20 Overly, Norman V. "A Perspective on Global Studies," 1–8 in Norman V. Overly and Richard D. Kingston, eds., *Global Studies: Problems and Promises for Elementary Teachers.* Washington, DC: Association for Supervision and Curriculum Development, 1976.

21 Phillips, June K. "Introduction: Language Is the Link," 1–6 in June K. Phillips, ed., *The Language Connection: From the Classroom to the World.* ACTFL Foreign Language Education Series, Volume 9. Skokie, IL: National Textbook Company, 1977.

22 Robinson, Gail L. "The Magic-Carpet-Ride-to-Another-Culture Syndrome: An International Perspective." *Foreign Language Annals* 11(1978):135–46.

23 State Social Studies Curriculum Study Committee. *Global Studies for Wisconsin Schools: Definitions and Directions.* Madison: Wisconsin Department of Public Instruction, 1979. [Mimeo.]

24 Strasheim, Lorraine A. "An Issue on the Horizon: The Role of Foreign Languages in Global Education." *Foreign Language Annals* 12 (1979):29–34.

25 _____ "Professional Concerns—Interdisciplinary Cooperation: Will Teachers in 'Average' Schools Be Left Out?" *Foreign Language Annals* 13(1980):59–61.

26 *Strength through Wisdom:* A Report to the President from the President's Commission on Foreign Language and International Studies. Washington, D.C.: Superintendent of Documents, U.S. Printing Office, 1979.

27 Torney, Judith V. "Psychological and Institutional Obstacles to the Global Perspective in Education," 59–93 in James M. Becker, ed., *Schooling for a Global Age.* New York: McGraw-Hill Book Company, 1979.

28 Tuttle, Harry Grover, Jorge Guitart, and Joseph Zampogna. "Effects of Cultural Presentations on Attitudes of Foreign Language Students." *Modern Language Journal* 63 (1979):177–82.

7

The international high school:
A challenge for scholars

Dorothy B. Goodman
Glynis Scott
Washington International School

"Monolingualism, always strong, is spreading," wrote S. Frederick Starr (28) in the *Chronicle of Higher Education* in 1976. The world is beginning to laugh at the United States: *"Sprachlose Weltmacht,"* chuckled a recent headline in the *Frankfurter Allgemeine Zeitung* (25). Each time the distressing statistics are mentioned, the confidence of the modern language profession, hardly strong in recent decades, sinks further: "What are we doing that is wrong? Why are we failing?"

It is not your fault. The malaise goes deeper than the decline in languages. Yours is only one of the professions affected. Historians, as well as geographers, mathematicians, biologists, chemists, physicists, and your close colleagues, the teachers of English language and literature, suffer from the same malaise. Our disciplines are not being systematically studied in the schools. We have retreated in disarray and left the field to psychologists, sociologists, and,

Dorothy Bruchholz Goodman (Ph.D., University of London, England) has been director of the Washington International School since she co-founded it in 1966. A graduate of Bryn Mawr College, she won a Fulbright grant to study at the School of Slavonic and East European Studies in London. She later taught history at American University and Howard University in Washington D.C. She serves on the Geneva Council of Foundation of the International Baccalaureate (I.B.) and on the boards of the International Schools Association, the U.S. Commission for the United World College Schools, the Fulbright Alumni Association, the I.B. North America, and the Council on International and Public Affairs.

Glynis Scott (B.A., University of London, England) is Assistant (Publications) to the Director. She has worked for the British Council in South America, been a Moral Tutor at the University of Durham, England and taught English Language and Literature at the Washington International School, at the community college level in England, and at the university level in Santo Domingo, Dominican Republic and Bogotá Colombia. She has also written a travel book on Colombia and various pieces of journalism.

yes, philosophers (many of whom are pale followers of John Dewey) whose disciplines are not school subjects. We have been told that we do not understand children, that we do not believe in the education of the masses, that we do not understand the relation between schools and politics, and, most cutting of all, that we do not believe in democracy. Our critics seem to have forgotten that among those great "democrats" who, like them, have conceived of the school as an instrument of social and political conditioning rather than intellectual training are Frederick the Great, who believed that peasants would make better soldiers for the conquering of all Europe if they could read and write, and Lenin, who preached that education and politics were inextricably intertwined. It does seem odd that the North Atlantic basin, and particularly the United States, should let itself be led by authoritarians rather than by John Stuart Mill (16) who warned 120 years ago about too close an association between government and schools because government schools, being efficient, would cultivate conformity, and conformity would lead to tyranny. (Mill did not foresee that government schools might be *in*efficient.) It is not languages alone that are suffering. It is the general decline in academic instruction in schools that chiefly accounts for the present plight of languages and "international studies."

Skeptical of "global education," the Council for Basic Education (18) has pointed out that most Americans pass into middle and old age ignorant of many of the simplest facts of the world beyond:

Who can name the countries of Africa, much less say where they came from or where they are going? Those who can may nevertheless be dismayed by such facts as those Fred Hechinger cited in the *New York Times* last March 13: 27 percent of high school seniors think Golda Meir was president of Egypt, for example, and 40 percent think Israel is an Arab nation. Can anyone sensibly hold that education has no responsibility for overcoming this form of isolationism? It has the greatest responsibility. The question is, how will education meet the responsibility . . . We do not believe that global education will eliminate [isolationism]. And although proponents will probably argue that it would enhance basic education, we suspect it would enfeeble the disciplines of basic education. Might not virtue be better safeguarded and education farther advanced if the energy, time, and money a global thrust would gobble up were devoted to the preserve and inservice preparation of teachers in language, history and geography, the arts, sciences and mathematics? It will be, in our view, a poorly prepared teacher who is unaware of the global implications of those subjects as the United States moves into a third century.

This is a sound prescription, not a glamorous one.

The background

The Helsinki Accords of 1975 had made it incumbent upon the signatories "to encourage the study of foreign language and civilization as an important means of expanding communication among peoples." This led to the appointment, in 1978, of the President's Commission on Foreign Language and International Studies. Meanwhile, in October 1977 at Georgetown's Conference called "Language in American Life," Starr (29) suggested that the way to revive the teaching of languages in the United States was to organize "international high schools," one in each major urban center of the country, initially twenty, growing to sixty. A Yale classicist turned Slavic scholar and historian, Starr was aware of the Russian use of special language schools in which, from the middle elementary through to university level, children pursue all their subjects, except the Russian language itself, through English, French, or German with extraordinary effectiveness. He was of course also aware of the many European examples of schools—be they *lycées* or *gymnasia*—where several languages are taught simultaneously to adolescents who emerge able to work well in at least two or three of them. The immediate model for United States reform in this country might be, he suggested, the Washington International School (26, 27).

The Washington International School

The Washington International School (WIS) opened in 1966 with three children in the basement of a private house. Now fourteen-years old, the school serves 540 Washington children of over eighty nationalities, ages three to eighteen. Pupils, 50 percent of whom are Americans, come from every segment of the community, international and local. The school is multinational in staff and curriculum. Texts and teaching materials come from five continents, the school's ninety teachers from over thirty countries.

At the primary level pupils are required to follow their regular school subjects through two working languages, at present English and French (about two-thirds) or English and Spanish (about one-third). Mother-tongue classes in Arabic and Dutch are under way, with help in prospect for the latter from the Dutch and Belgian governments. Classes in Japanese and Chinese are being considered for the future. The secondary classes are complete, and pupils prepare for the International Baccalaureate, which gives access to major universities of the world and sophomore standing at Harvard, Bryn Mawr, and most North American colleges.

In the belief that the monolingual child is an underprivileged child, the school gives all its young children two working languages. Another central aim of the founders was to use the pool of international teaching talent in the community to enrich the cultural and educational lives of Washington children and thereby to raise the academic standards of local education. Science is stressed at the secondary level. This is the only school in the metropolitan area, and probably in the country, that requires each pupil from age eleven through age sixteen to study systematicallly each year biology, chemistry, and physics. The same is true for history and geography, art, and music, as well as the pupil's two working languages. At least two years of Latin are also required. At age sixteen, the program narrows to allow for some specialization within the International Baccalaureate (IB) prior to college. The intellectual aims of the school have broadened since its founding in the sense that, beyond using syllabuses and teachers from the rest of the world to reinvigorate U.S. education, the school now sees itself as a pioneer in establishing worldwide standards of scholarship for schools.

Origins

Many threads are woven into the origins of the School. The needs of the international civil servant were one thread. Their children must be able to enter a school on arrival in Washington without losing a year or more and on departure to transfer to the home country, or to a third country, without losing time. Above all, it is important to international civil servants and to diplomats that their children be eligible for the universities of their choice. There is a precedent. At the founding of the League of Nations, the pioneers of the international civil service banded together to establish the International School of Geneva, known as Ecolint. The idea was based on good, healthy self-interest. They could serve themselves while serving the world. They would draw together the best elements in the world's educational systems, both in structure and in content, which they in their persons represented. Their school would be a true *école pilote,* better than any one national group of parents and teachers, or any one government could possibly create. They shared Ralph Waldo Emerson's vision of education: its purpose was to blow the cobwebs of parochialism from our minds. For a start, well-educated people were by definition multilingual, or at least bilingual. To them the world's *linguae francae* were French and English. Of course children must be taught systematically the history of the world, not just the history of one narrow national segment thereof. They went farther: it was not just the right of international civil servants to found such a school; it was their duty and their responsbility. On their fiftieth anniversary in 1974, having initiated the International Baccalaureate, they published a book (6). The frontispiece read:

> Voici la mémoire vivante
> des 50 années initiales
> d'une école dont les élèves
> viennent de tous les horizons de la Terre.
> Première école internationale de l'histoire,
> née a l'ombre de la Société des Nations,
> elle tente,
> toutes frontières mentales abolies,
> de dialoguer avec le petit de l'homme,
> quel qu'il soit
> et d'où qu'il vienne (p. 6).

Similar concerns prompted the founders of the United Nations International School in New York (15) and the United World Colleges (see below).

Another thread is what might be called domestic reform. There were those among the founders of WIS who had taught in U.S. colleges and universities and who were only too aware of the low standards of the U.S. high school graduate. Other Americans had chafed, during their own high school days, under a system in which the pupil is always picking up and putting down subjects, and there is too little language too late. If they had studied abroad, as several had, they were aware that no system except the North American followed this *à la carte* pattern; that many countries asked children to start a second language in the elementary school, and that all of the rest of the world's education systems had a menu of subjects followed to a terminal point, after which one specialized.

Then there was what one may call the world peace thread. One of the Washington International School's founders had worked with the International Refugee Organization in occupied Austria and Germany after World War II. She visited camp after camp of displaced persons. Ukranians, Poles, White Russians, Serbs, Croats, Czechs, Slovaks had established, in the miserable hovels in which they lived, separate schools for their children. Cheek by jowl, Serbs and Croats, Poles and Ukranians were teaching their children quite different versions of the same history. From the standpoint of scholarship it was nonsense; and from the point of view of the survival of the planet, it was intolerable.

Then there was the local thread, the "equal educational opportunity" thread. It was clear twenty years ago that the standards of the public schools in the District of Columbia were declining precipitously. Having been one of the top systems in the United States—Thomas Jefferson had been the president of Washington's first Board of Trustees of Public Schools, and the city had the magnificent "M Street" (later Dunbar) high school in the early decades of the twentieth century—Washington schools were being mired in local politics. It was becoming increasingly difficult for bright, or just plain hard-working, black or white children to get a first-rate education in the public sector. When one added to this the social problem of being a black child confronting the children of the white establishment running the most powerful country in the world, even independent schools had a hard time creating a favorable environment for young blacks. For them, it would be a very special experience to study along with the children of international civil servants, children who were being deliberately encouraged to retain their cultural roots rather than lose them in a North American melting pot.

In the early 1960s a group of staff families of the World Bank, the International Monetary Fund, and the Inter-American Development Bank began to explore the possibilities of establishing a first-rate school in Washington, D.C. to serve both the international and local communities. They collected information on the principal educational systems of the world, especially on requirements for university entrance, and on the experience of existing international schools in other important centers. One of the purposes was to determine whether it would be feasible to devise curricula and teaching methods that would permit children of different nationalities to enter the school at various stages of their education or, having spent a period at the school, to resume their education at home. If the school were to be truly international in character and meet these objectives, it should be a unified school rather than a collection of national schools set up under one roof; that is, it should offer a curriculum that would enable the children of many nationalities to pursue broadly the same course of study, preferably in more than one language. The experiences of the International School of Geneva, the United States International Schools (founded in the late forties), and the six schools of the European Community were studied carefully as they seemed most relevant to the purpose. The chairman of the European Community Schools, which offered the special advantage of teaching each child in two European languages, was invited to Washington for discussions; later, he was one of three consultants who assisted in preparing a feasibility study of the proposed Washington International School under grants from the three financial institutions (22).

The sponsoring agencies decided not to adopt the proposed school officially, for the major national governments represented on their boards could not agree on an international plan. So the school started independently in 1966, modeling itself closely on the feasibility study and the advice of the consultants.

The Ford Foundation, which had early expressed an interest in the project, in 1969 gave $500,000 for the purchase from the District of Columbia of a former public school building with one acre of land in Georgetown. An Act of Congress was required to permit the District of Columbia to sell the premises to the school without offering it at a public auction. Considerable interest in the school was expressed by members of both Houses during the hearings on the bill.

One of the conditions that the Ford Foundation attached to its grant was that within five years the school's enrollment should be one-sixth scholarship children from the inner city of Washington, expressing a concern that the school should not cater solely to the relatively high income families of the international and local communities but should also help to serve the evident need of Washington to provide for the education of its less privileged children. The Foundation was also interested, as was the school, in observing the result of providing a common education for a group of children of mixed social, economic, and cultural backgrounds.

From the very beginning it was planned that the school would take children all the way from nursery school (age three) through to college entrance. The school added a class a year until the first students took the International Baccalaureate examinations in 1977, one obtaining the full diploma. There were twenty students in the 1980 "leaving" class, of whom eighteen have earned the full International Baccalaureate diploma. The school is a "common school" in the Horace Mann sense. Children not only come from some eighty-five countries but also from a variety of social and economic backgrounds. There are children of diplomats and international civil servants; there are inner city children on scholarship who may be black, white, Hispanic, or Asian in origin, and there are middle class Americans seeking a more scholarly education than national schools offer. Of the 50 percent American pupils, one-third come from the inner city on financial aid. (For the structure of the school, see Table 1.)

U.S. Public Schools			Washington International School	
Elementary		Age 3	half day nursery	*Junior House*
		Age 4	half or full day nursery	
	Kindergarten	Age 5	Junior A	
	First Grade	Age 6	Junior 1	
	Second Grade	Age 7	Junior 2	
	Third Grade	Age 8	Junior 3	
	Fourth Grade	Age 9	Junior 4	
	Fifth Grade	Age 10	Junior 5	
	Sixth Grade	Age 11	Middle 1	*Middle House*
Junior High	Seventh Grade	Age 12	Middle 2	
	Eighth Grade	Age 13	Middle 3	
High School	Ninth Grade	Age 14	Tutorial 1	*Tutorial House*
	Tenth Grade	Age 15	Tutorial 2	
	Eleventh Grade	Age 16	Tutorial 3	
	Twelfth Grade	Age 17	Tutorial 4	

Table 1. A Comparison of the Structure of U.S. Public Schools and the Washington International School

Curriculum: Language

At the time the School was being planned, in the early and mid-sixties, there was extensive discussion of the language pattern for the future school (11).

The Working Committee started its deliberations in 1964 with the aim of imitating the European Community School pattern. At that time, the Common Market Schools used German, French, Italian, and Dutch. Each child went to a polyglot kindergarten in which languages were mixed indiscriminately and no attempt was made to teach children to read and write. In the primary school, ages six to eleven, the children spent about 80 percent of their time in their "mother tongue" with one period a day in a second language, in Europe's case, either French or German. In the secondary school, from eleven to eighteen, most academic subjects were pursued in the child's "mother tongue." This was true whether the pupil opted for the science/mathematics stream, for classical languages, or for "modern studies." However, pupils were obliged to study geography, history, and biology—descriptive subjects in which vocabulary is extensive—in their second language. Based on the European Community pattern, our original Washington plan was to use French, Spanish, and English as working languages and to require each child to do his geography, history, and biology in whichever of the others had been chosen as the pupil's second language.

It became increasingly evident that this European Community pattern would not be adequate for monolingual Washington. Even in Europe, standards of history, biology, and geography suffered because the children's knowledge of the second language was not good enough; the emphasis on language in the elementary school would have to be heavier in order to give the children a viable second language at the secondary level. We wrestled at length with the question of how to do this. To what extent should the second language be taught as a subject—the way it is in national schools across the world—and to what extent should it be used as the medium of instruction?

Importance of the early start

Other considerations come into play. We became acquainted with the work of Penfield, the great Canadian neurologist, who believed that the human brain can develop alternate speech centers up to the age of ten or eleven and therefore learn a second and indeed third languages as easily and accurately as the first. At a later age language learning by any method is, almost without exception, more difficult and it is nearly impossible to learn to speak with the accent, intonation and inflection of a native speaker. The younger child, on the other hand, absorbs and reproduces language without being aware of what he or she is doing, without "half-trying" (19, 20).

We are aware of arguments that a second language introduced early only confuses a child and that he or she does not learn to read or write well in either. We do not find this to be the case. Mankind has after all known for millenia that the time to learn languages is as early as possible, and affluent families have seen to it throughout history that their children learned at least two or three languages. Of course environmental factors are enormously important. If children come to believe through the attitude of their parents, their teachers, their church, or what they see on television, that it might be damaging to them to learn another language, performance suffers. We find that if the families are immigrants and keen to shed the old and adapt the new, this may, and indeed usually will, affect the children. We have to our sorrow lost a number of very bright children whose parents wanted above all to Americanize them. This, needless to say, is society's loss, and thousands of dollars may be spent years later on these very same children who as young adults want to become area specialists.

There is one distinction that should be made. In countries like Switzerland or the Cameroons where everyone must, for survival, know two or three languages, there appears to be little relation between IQ and ability to learn language. Everyone succeeds. In an environment where the pressures are all monolingual, it is admittedly much easier to teach bright children two or three languages than less bright ones. And even with the bright ones, the school must be fanatical about academic standards. As in every other human intellectual activity, it is very easy to learn a great deal superficially. Our own experience at the Washington International School has been that, with rare exceptions, the child's first language is actually enhanced by early exposure to a second. For instance, it is easier for the Washington International School to teach inner-city American children Castilian Spanish or Parisian French than to teach them standard English. After they have learned some Spanish or French and become conscious of the importance of enunciation and of grammar, the school has tools with which it can tackle the English. We have also noted the greater ease with which a "bilingual" child approaches a third language at a later stage of schooling as compared with a monolingual child beginning after puberty a second language (that is, a first foreign one). Moreover, our experience confirms Penfield's conviction that acquiring new languages enhances the general intellectual ability of children. We have also found that instruction in the second working language should not necessarily be restricted to descriptive subjects; that analytical subjects such as mathematics and physics may be imparted through the second working language. The Washington International School believes that both should be part of a child's program in the course of his or her career. We have discussed this point of whether the second vehicular language should be used for descriptive or analytical subjects with our independent colleagues—those not restricted by governmental policies—at the Toronto French School, the French-American Bilingual School of Boston, and the Ecole Active Bilingue of Paris. Everyone believes every carrot of enticement should be used.

Partly, therefore, for intellectual reasons and partly for administrative and cultural ones, the straight bilingual pattern for the primary school in which each child pursues all subjects through two working languages was selected. At age three, children attend a morning nursery class in either French or Spanish. Since English is the dominant language, if not in the child's own home, then certainly in the immediate environment, it is French or Spanish that needs the earliest introduction or reinforcement. At age four, the program consists of half a day in French or Spanish, and, if a family opts for the full-day program, the other half in English. Numbers and letters are introduced in both languages. From age five to age eight the children follow a pattern of "alternate days"—one day in English and then one in French or Spanish. At nine and ten a half day pattern prevails, making homework schedules easier to supervise. The regular primary school curriculum is thus followed fully in two languages and by the end of Junior House the child can speak, read, and write both languages fairly fluently and accurately and follow nonlinguistic subjects in either language. It is very important to use native-speakers experienced as primary school teachers at the elementary level, for one is essentially using the "mother's knee" method for injecting the language. The Washington international community provides a rich talent of teachers from which to draw. While not every international high school will have the advantage of drawing on a group of children so well prepared linguistically in their elementary school, some such pattern is the ideal. A system of "feeder" elementary schools where children have had the advantage of learning other languages easily at an early age would raise the potential academic level of the international high school considerably. There is some indication that language teaching at the elementary level is about to have a renaissance. (See below, under Practical Steps.)

Language at the secondary level

The original plan for the secondary school—when academic disciplines, as distinct from the basic skills of "the three Rs," become so very important—had been to alternate, annually, the pupils' two working languages in each subject. For instance if Mary did history and geography in Spanish in 1978-1979, she would do them in English in 1979-1980 and again in Spanish in 1980-1981. This may still be the ideal plan, but until comparable materials—in all three of our working languages—are available, this alternation is proving difficult to achieve.

From the staffing standpoint, there are problems as well, for our using this plan means that pupils already departmentalized by subject at a fairly tender age must change language, materials, and teacher each year. Curricular problems of coordination increase geometrically. Furthermore, this requires equal strengths of the pupil in both working languages. This may be possible for children who have come through the whole of our primary school and also for the few who arrive in Washington at twelve, fourteen, or sixteen with a good command of English and French or English and Spanish. However, older children coming with two of the school's working languages are the exception rather than the rule.

After weighing these factors, the Washington International School has decided that it should adopt, at the secondary level, a pattern for language closer to that of the International Baccalaureate rather than continue the strict bilingual plan of the elementary school. This requires a knowledge of two languages and of the "relevant culture and civilizations" but provides for a pupil's sitting examinations in other academic subjects in his or her best language, "Language A." This means not that a pupil follows all his nonlinguistic subjects in the same language, but that for some pupils increasing weight is given to Language A, through which most but never all academic subjects will be studied. As M. René-François Lejeune, former Director-General of the Geneva International School, put it when he visited Washington a few years ago, ". . . . the ideal is that the school, in consultation with parents and pupil, should decide which subjects are followed in which language."

Currently the Washington International School is not able to offer all secondary subjects in all three languages: mathematics, physics, chemistry, and biology are usually offered only through English. Geography and history are carried consistently throughout in all languages. Children who have come successfully through the primary school (Nursery to Junior 5) can continue their history and geography in French or Spanish. Their French or Spanish is usually of a sufficiently high standard so that they can write an IB history examination in French or Spanish while doing math and chemistry in English *or* they can do *two* Languages A. Either route gives them bilingual IB diplomas—without academic standards having suffered. Linguistically our aim remains what it has been since 1964: that students emerge from their secondary education with a solid command of two working languages. And if they have a third, so much the better!

Other subjects

Latin is required for at least two years in the Middle House because the school believes that one cannot learn language, any more than one can learn medicine, unless one studies both the living and the dead. We are somewhat shamefaced after fourteen years to have only Latin as our classical language. (We have had some Greek and Chinese but only very extracurricularly.) Our aim is to offer choices among Latin, Greek, Sanskrit, Arabic, and Mandarin Chinese. We rely heavily on British materials, notably what is called "Cambridge Latin," which was developed by the Nuffield Foundation. It is bolstered—for it is chiefly Latin by the "direct" method—with grammatical exercises. In the third and optional year, original Latin texts are used. Pupils not continuing in Latin begin a third modern language. We are working on a single grammar syllabus that will encompass Latin and the three working languages of the School, English, French, and Spanish. Children being children, knowledge is compartmentalized all too easily. In line with traditional practices, our children meet a grammatical idea first in French, then (other children, of course) in Spanish, and last in English. It is usually possible, though for only a small minority of the pupils, to study one's Latin through French or Spanish.

Since this is essentially a chapter about the humanities, we shall not dwell on mathematics and the sciences. The traditional U.S. mathematics syllabus is just that: traditional rather than scholarly. The pattern of algebra in the ninth grade, Euclidian geometry in the tenth, and algebra again in the eleventh was established when the U.S. system went "mass" or "universal" at the turn of the century. One Ohio superintendent of schools, himself a mathematician, remarked at a recent International Baccalaureate conference that this is a very good scheme for engineers but hardly one that suits the generalist or the would-be professional mathematician. Intellectually, it is better to weave the topics of mathematics together, as we do in Washington, so that from Middle 1 (grade 6) onwards, mathematics is a spiral with all the topics studied continuously at increasingly higher levels of difficulty until IB Mathematics is reached. But the U.S. pattern of mathematics teaching seems, despite "new math," to be engraved in granite, for publishers are all tied now to producing mathematics texts in the algebra/geometry/algebra pattern and school boards, superintendents, and teachers to buying those texts. What everyone should be doing is discovering why Japanese children learn mathematics so much faster and so much better than children anywhere else in the world, both at thirteen and eighteen, as shown in the Swedish study of the mid-sixties. Admittedly, at the time the study was done it was not possible to study mainland Chinese children. There is some evidence, particularly from Singaporean schools, that children whose literary language requires them to memorize pictographs or ideographs are better in mathematics than children who deal only with alphabets. The school is not aware of any serious research on this question; Stryker's thesis does not mention it (30).

Students at the Washington International School also pursue a broad range of subjects continuously through the secondary school—eight to ten subjects, compared with the four or five in a U.S. high school—until the onset of the International Baccalaureate program in Tutorial 3 (11th grade) at sixteen years of age.

"International studies": History and geography

One of the problems with the terms *international studies, international education,* and *international school* is that they mean so many different things to different people and on different occasions. Does *international* mean "among nations" or "worldwide"? Any trip longer or more serious than mere tourism can be "international education"—like the nineteenth century European Grand Tour. Sending individuals abroad for technical training to be applied at home for national development is also "international education"—Japan did this with remarkable success at the turn of the century. And what is an "international school"? Many national schools overseas are called "international" simply because they are outside their home country. Even if they enroll children of several nationalities, they serve a particular expatriate community, whether U.S. or German or French, and follow the national curriculum of the home country.

What is a genuinely international school? We would cite several criteria:

- that the teaching staff be of several nationalities
- that the children be of many nationalities, including both privileged and underprivileged of the host community
- that each child use at least two working languages
- that the syllabuses accommodate at least two national traditions
- that textbooks and teaching materials be drawn from several countries
- that the school prepare its students for colleges and universities in more than one country.

Lambert (14) makes some useful comments about the various meanings of "international studies" leading to an "international perspective" at the undergraduate level. They can of course be simply "foreign" language study. They can also be area studies, learning facts about a particular part of the world, usually an area outside the North Atlantic basin. They can be disciplinary, such as an economic analysis of the developing world's problems. Or they can be the teaching of attitudes or perspectives leading to "transcultural empathy" (p. 15); this is often called "global education." The reader will have gathered from our extended quote from the Bulletin of the Council for Basic Education that the Washington International School is not enthusiastic about "global education" but believes staunchly in history and geography as essential school subjects.

At eleven, twelve, and thirteen the school teaches regional geography— Asia, the Americas, Europe and Africa—in successive years. It is extremely difficult at the moment to find texts in regional geography in any European language, for regional geography is out of fashion in Francophone and Hispanic countries as well as in the English-speaking world. Some written in English were eventually located in Fiji. Tutorial 1 (age fourteen) does physical geography, and Tutorial 2 (age fifteen) does human geography, both on a worldwide basis. This year the International Baccalaureate syllabus in geography is being initiated; heretofore only the IB history syllabuses under Category 3 "Study of Man" were done.

World History Project ———————————————

In the discipline of history, the need for telling a common story to the planet's young is particularly compelling. The world is technologically one, and it is hardly sensible to be continuing to give the children of any one country a myopic or distorted view of the world as a whole.

In 1964–1965, in preparation for the founding of the school, a start was made in the collection of school syllabuses from as many countries as possible. A cursory review of these early materials confirmed the conviction of the school's founders that the world educational systems were moving in a direction contrary to that of all other areas of human life. In technology, in music, in agriculture, and of course in science, human beings are busy studying and emulating one another. Not so in primary and secondary education where the premium is put on being as different as possible.

It was not until the early seventies, when the school had gathered sufficient institutional strength to look for research funds and write proposals, that it approached the (U.S.) National Endowment for the Humanities and asked for help in making a beginning, with history. In December 1974 the school was awarded an NEH grant to enable it to devise syllabuses and bibliographies in the "history of mankind" for school children everywhere. As WIS reported to the International Schools Association (31), school syllabuses of a majority of UN member nations have been collected in large measure through the co-operation of UNESCO regional offices, under the leadership of Mr. Ryon Kim of the Paris headquarters. Caroline Ware, one of the authors of UNESCO's own *History of Mankind,* has been an adviser to the Project. It was decided to plan to teach the history of the world in a spiral pattern: *Cycle 1*—stories for 5–9 year olds; *Cycle 2*—a chronological narrative for 10–14 year olds, pre-history to the present; *Cycle 3*—comparative themes, such as the history of religious institutions, which return through the theme to ancient China, India, etc., at ages 15–16.

The International Baccalaureate syllabuses in contemporary history, are of course used at ages 16–18. This fits Alfred North Whitehead's scheme of romance (Cycle 1), precision (Cycle 2) and generalization (Cycle 3).

The first year and a half of the NEH grant were spent in expanding and bringing up to date the collection of national syllabuses; in writing long chronological charts that were completed except for the continent of Africa; and in compiling bibliographies of myths, legends, and stories of as many countries and cultures as possible—"mankind's self-images" as the UNESCO *History of Mankind* puts it—to be used chiefly with the younger children. In the autumn of 1976, the charts and bibliographies were given experimentally to a number of our own teachers at different levels, ranging from age five to age thirteen. We quickly hit a serious snag deriving from our own inadequate schooling: we teachers found we were, in Norman Cousins's phrase, "half-educated" (5). Even those of us born and bred in Asia—one particularly good

Burmese teacher springs to mind—knew too little about ancient China to teach young children from charts and bibliographies. And so we plunged into "curriculum development," an infinitely more time-consuming process.

A complete secondary-level teaching program for "ancient" history up to 500 B.C. is now ready and was used in its entirety for the first time in 1979-1980. Its nine topics include the introduction; Sumer; the Babylonians, Assyrians and Persians; the Egyptians; the Hebrews; the Minoans and Mycenaeans; ancient China; ancient India; and the early Americas. Also ready for use outside as well as inside the school are East and South Asian materials on the "classical" period, 500 B.C. to 500 A.D. Meanwhile the collection of stories for the younger children as well as syllabuses and bibliographies for the whole of the "classical", "medieval" (500 A.D. to 1500 A.D.), and most recent (1500 A.D. to the presnt) periods, organized on a worldwide basis, are in use in the school. Part of the completed "ancient" materials are in use at the Oyster School, an English-Spanish bilingual public school in the District of Columbia and at the Nishimachi International School, Tokyo. Inquiries have been received from all over the world about the history materials, particularly as the result of an article published by the *International Herald Tribune* (17). We are now negotiating with a publisher who is interested in putting out a common core for all English-speaking countries, with different supplementary materials for different pedagogical traditions. These chronological materials are usable at any secondary level, including that of the International Baccalaureate; although of course IB students supplement them with extensive use of the bibliographies prepared for teachers. During 1980 and 1981 the school proposes to seek new funding to intensify the research and writing on the classical, medieval, and modern periods, to allow for appraisal by university scholars, and to devise a permanent system for keeping abreast of bibliography. It is extremely difficult to get materials for children, particularly on Asia and Africa, in English. It is almost impossible to find them in other languages. When found they tend to disappear from print. We hope to be able to use the worldwide representatives of the Library of Congress to help.

Misery loves company, and it may be some comfort to the "ailing U.S. language establishment" (Lambert 14, p.17) to learn that the historical establishment is also ailing, that many young Americans are entering adult life without ever having learned any history—even American history—despite state requirements. They do not know in which century George Washington was born (31). True, we have the skeleton of American history at, usually, the fifth, eighth, eleventh and twelfth grades, and this "exposure" to U.S. history, however ineffective and biased, has proved a remarkably hardy plant since the middle 1890s.

Since the 1920s, "groups," "movements," and "societies" were studied; and individual human accomplishments, so often the meat of this historian, were ignored. Nor was there any attempt to develop in children a sense of historical development in the rise and fall of human institutions. Geography also got lost in the shuffle as those of us know who have taught "college" history to students not quite sure whether Buenos Aires is in Asia or Africa.

The Mountbatten World Textbook Library ———————

In a world technologically one, it is a curious anomaly that educational systems deliberately build walls around themselves. E.B. White's *Charlotte's Web* and Virginia Haviland's delightful collections of stories do indeed cross national frontiers and are translated into many languages, but textbooks hardly budge. In Washington, D.C., it is not possible to purchase or even to examine texts published in Toronto, let alone in London, Melbourne, Moscow, or Peking. How can one be scholarly about school curricula without being able to compare materials, to weigh and sift the evidence? The essence of scholarship, the first vital steps, are surely to assemble and assess.

Some countries do have centers that act as national clearinghouses. EDMARC, the acronym for the Educational Materials Review Center of the U.S. Department of Education, receives texts and materials from over 100 commercial publishers in the U.S. and very occasionally seeks out adventurous materials from the United Kingdom: readers printed in Pitman's Initial Teaching Alphabet have, for instance, been displayed there. National textbook collections also exist in England—the University of London's Institute of Education has the National Textbook Reference Collection—and in France where the Ministry of Education has organized the *Institut Pédagogique National* in Paris. As in the case of EDMARC, these British and French collections are national ones, coming from British and French publishers.

There are also certain collections specialized by discipline. In Brunswick, Germany, there has been a textbook center, the Georg Eckert Institut für internationale Schulbuchforschung, for more than thirty years with a collection of history and geography texts. There has also been a UNESCO center and collection in Hamburg. As of this writing the condition of these collections is uncertain. It is not known whether they are being kept up to date. There is also a magnificent collection of scientific and mathematics materials at the University of Maryland, where Professor David Lockard of the Botany Department and the School of Education has had for more than a decade an international clearinghouse that publishes bibliographies.

However, to the best of our knowledge, there is no general collection anywhere in the world founded with the deliberate aim of reflecting the best current educational practices in all corners of the globe and, ultimately, of bringing the textbooks of one country to the children of another. What better way, for instance, for U.S. children to gain a perspective on their world of the twenty-first centry than by cutting their reading teeth on the Maoris of New Zealand through a New Zealand primer?

The objectives of the Mountbatten World Textbook Library are:

1 to assemble a specimen collection of primary and secondary school text-books and teaching materials, in all disciplines, from the 152 members of the United Nations; and to keep the collection up to date
2 to display these texts and teaching materials for visiting scholars, teachers, and educational administrators
3 to make available to interested individuals and organizations critical bibliographies of the collection.

Clearly the collection cannot be comprehensive. A former Assistant Director-General of UNESCO once tried to discourage us altogether from embarking on the textbook collection: "It would be like re-inventing the Library of Congress!" Such gargantuan proportions may be avoided by adhering to a theme and choosing only books of a highly demanding intellectual level to match a particular chronological one. This immediately rules out many titles in North America where a process of "didactic dilution" has been underway for the better part of a century. For countries such as France where standards tend to be uniform, there is to be no attempt to collect *all* grammar books for, say, the *sixième,* but rather perhaps two—one a "traditional" grammar and another a "functional" one. Nor shall there be an attempt to duplicate Brunswick or Maryland. We shall, however, proceed to develop a selective union catalogue of other international collections.

Such a textbook collection is of course not a new departure for the Washington International School. We have been informally assembling texts and teaching materials for the fourteen years of our institutional existence. At present the volumes number approximately 15,000 including those in the lower school library on Olive Street, Georgetown. Teaching materials and texts are examined and ordered from French-, Spanish-, and English-speaking countries and are catalogued upon arrival in the School's library. Since the School is American in its setting, a particular effort has been made to use non-American books and materials in the classes conducted in English: *e.g.,* grammar books and poetry collections from Great Britain and geography texts from New Zealand.

The collection was formally christened as the Mountbatten World Textbook Library on December 13, 1979, by the British Ambassador, Sir Nicholas Henderson. The Library is dedicated to one of the great men of the twentieth century, Earl Mountbatten of Burma, who devoted the last years of his life to "international education" in the true scholarly sense and in particular to the International Baccalaureate. He was fond of saying, "not every child can have an international education but the potentially élite *must* have" (3). And by élite he always meant bright, hard-working, idealistic young people of every social and economic walk of life, and from every nation on the face of the earth. He wanted those young people who had studied together the syllabuses of the

International Baccalaureate to meet one day in the Parliament of Man. He was the International President of the United World Colleges of Wales, Canada, and Singapore. These are international sixth form boarding-schools where 700 sixteen-to-eighteen year olds, chosen by some sixty national committees and the majority on full financial aid, study together toward the International Baccalaureate.

What is the International Baccalaureate?   ———————————

The IB is a set of syllabuses and examinations in the major academic disciplines (10). It has been developed with the financial assistance of foundations and governments (including France, Germany, Great Britain and the United States) and the scholarly assistance of professors, teachers, government officials, and examining bodies in Europe, North America, and the developing world. The American critic, Clifton Fadiman, has said:

> The underlying importance of the International Baccalaureate is that it institutionalizes for the world's youth a truth which, since the Renaissance, we have forgotten. During the High Middle Ages all students were members of a great Western Community. They had a common education; they understood each other; they understood their world. Now, as the globe shrinks, as mobility increases, it becomes necessary to reinstitute, in a modern setting, this great idea of a universal education. The IB is a giant step in the direction of a truly international and humane, rather than a provincial, education for the best young minds of our country—and indeed all countries. It embodies an idea whose time has come. (7, p.1)

Philosophically the IB planners are devoted to ". . . the balanced . . . development of those mental powers and capacities which can make of all of us more sensitive and human persons and of some of us scholars and intellectual innovators" (21). The scheme is uncannily similar to the "core curriculum" recently promulgated by Dean Rosovsky of Harvard.

The syllabuses and examinations, available in English and French are divided into six parts and are usually studied for a two or three-year period between the ages of sixteen and nineteen. Each academic discipline, within which there is a wide range of subjects, must be represented in order to obtain the full diploma. The young humanist cannot escape mathematics, nor can the young scientist ignore language and literature. Students choose major minor areas of study and are examined accordingly at Higher and Subsidiary Levels. Fields include:

1 A first language and its literature, Language A. World literature is also studied through the student's Language A

2 a second language and its literature, Language B. (Languages A and B need not be English and French—they could be Tamil and Portuguese or Russian and Chinese.)

3 "Study of Man": history, geography, economics, psychology, philosophy, or anthropology

4 an experimental science: physics, chemistry, or biology

5 mathematics

6 an optional subject, from within the five fields above, or in music or the plastic arts.

Also required, but not examined, is a course in the theory of knowledge and some time spent in the arts, in physical education, and in community service.

The IB diploma qualifies the student for entrance to major universities of the world such as the Sorbonne and Oxford, and for sophomore standing at most North American colleges. Soon it will be practicable for an able student of any nationality in any sixth form in Britain, or *lycée, gymnasium,* or senior high school on the continents of Europe, America, Asia, or Africa to enter universities in any country. Why should students from Kansas not go to Oxford, the Sorbonne, or even Peking? (10)

After a decade of carefully controlled work in twenty-two schools in fourteen countries, the IB has emerged from its experimental period and now boasts some 5,000 diploma holders of 125 nationalities who, with some 5,500 others who have individual IB certificates, have gone to over 200 universities in some 45 countries. In the past five years the number of participating schools has quintupled.

In sum, the International Baccalaureate Office of Geneva, Switzerland (IBO) is a nongovernmental international institution that is both a research center and an examining board. Its work is important for international schools and peripatetic families; for developing countries that do not wish to imitate a colonial pattern of education; and for national systems of education, which, however feebly, are beginning to think about "internationalizing" themselves (13).

Nationwide "International High School": How to begin   ——

Channel 9 in Washington D.C. put out a program called "Prisma" about bilingual education in the summer of 1980. It was mostly about the poverty end of the spectrum. But at one stage, Representative Paul Simon of Illinois, who did so much along with his colleagues Representatives Panetta, Fascell, and Fenwick to launch in 1978 the President's Commission on Foreign and International Studies, was interviewed on the lawn of the Capitol. "Today we are the only country in the world," said Congressman Simon, "which allows a young person to go through elementary school, high school, college and *on to the Ph.D.* without ever having to study a language other than English. Let us make this a day in the past . . . ."

The Washington International School is clearly a special case. Assuming that the School is on the right, the ideal, road—even if it has not yet arrived at its destination—is its experience relevant to the some 23,000 high schools scattered across the continental United States? It has no political constraints (only economic ones) so its usefulness as a model to the public sector may be limited. But there are steps that can be taken. Let us turn to some practical suggestions for making the "international high school" a significant landmark, or series of landmarks, on the national scene. What can a public school do? What can an independent school do? How about local school boards, state authorities, the federal government? And what can colleges and universities do? And let us think in the short-, the medium-, and the long-term.

Practical steps

Secondary Schools

The first and most obvious recipe for becoming an international high school is to join the International Baccalaureate. (Twenty-eight schools, twenty public and eight independent or parochial, have already done so.) Write to Mr. H. Gilbert Nicol, Director; International Baccalaureate North America, Inc.; 680 Fifth Avenue; New York; NY 10019. There is a formal application process, and the school has to satisfy the headquarters of the International Baccalaureate Office in Geneva, Switzerland, that it is strong enough academically to carry the IB program. This is not, as Mr. Nicol likes to say, a "quick fix for promoting international understanding . . . schools adopt the program as a practical means for attaining standards in education recognized throughout the world." The Language B Higher Level syllabus guarantees a high standard in the second language; the syllabus is based on studying that language at least two, usually three, and sometimes four years before the student begins the IB syllabus itself. The syllabus for Language A, the student's best language, which would for almost all schools in the United States be of course English, includes "world literature in translation" with, at the Higher Level, five selections from at least three continents other than the one on which one is situated and at the Subsidiary Level three selections from at least two continents.

As for "international studies," I.B. has an excellent syllabus in recent world history. One examination paper deals with broad worldwide themes such as the causes and effects of wars in the twentieth century, the North-South dialogue, religion and politics in the twentieth century, economic developments between World Wars I and II and so forth. All history students, at both Higher and Subsidiary Levels, study these topics. The other paper, for the Higher Level only, gives a choice among major regions of the world from 1750 to the present or from 1890 to the present. The regions are East Asia, South and West Asia, Europe including the U.S.S.R., Africa, and the Americas (note, not "the United States"). Moreover, the IB syllabuses in mathematics, physics, chemistry, biology, and history of art have all been "internationally" developed; that is, collegial groups of university scholars and teachers from a score of counties have participated in formulating them. This is probably the most important single fact about the IB: one immediately becomes, as a teacher or a principal, part of a worldwide scholarly community concerned with what is taught at the secondary level. Even were it not for the strong emphasis on language and world history, the International Baccalaureate enforces the "internationalizing" of the teaching staff. One can no longer remain only a member of a small localized school community. Suddenly one has colleagues all over the world with whom to share one's concerns. **N.B.** Be sure to leave room in the budget for getting your staff to international meetings; airfares are high, and the IB has not succeeded in obtaining serious reductions from any of the large companies.

In the meantime:

- Tighten graduation requirements. The District of Columbia has just decided (spring 1980) to make one year of a language mandatory for the high school diploma. This is, of course, minimal but it will at least make Representative Simon's statement untrue for the nation's capital. More sophisticated school systems can immediately demand two years, and the really strong ones can demand three.
- Join, for $100, Professor John Means's self-instructional program (Temple University, Philadelphia). This advisory service, formerly presided over by Professor Eleanor Jorden of Cornell, who remains a member of its board, helps colleges and when needed senior high schools to choose materials for teaching oneself, particularly in the "critical" languages. A native speaker must be available to meet with the student once or twice a week. Professor Twarog's Ohio State program is also available for help with individualized materials that enable a given high school class to include pupils of different levels. This could help with the more common languages, such as German, or with advanced levels of French and Spanish.
- Plan to buld on whatever linguistic strengths the junior highs and the community possess. In the latter regard, circumstances will vary; there may be a language significantly represented in the community but not

served in an academic classroom at all. Provided there is a means of cir-
cumventing local regulations on teacher certification—that teachers must
be American citizens, that they must have diplomas from certain teachers'
colleges, and so forth—some first-rate language classes can probably be
organized overnight. Here we are thinking chiefly of the "critical" languages. For the common ones, there are probably not any certification
problems at the secondary level.

- Send for the WIS history syllabuses; they are available for the cost of
  reproduction to no more than twenty-five schools. (Copyrights have not
  yet been cleared.)

Medium-term:

- Introduce a course in philology like the one devised by Lois Sandison of
  the Brearley School, New York, in the 1930s and 1940s. Drawing on the
  children's knowledge of English, Latin, and French, she trained them,
  through carefully selected sight passages from Spanish, Italian, German,
  Dutch, and the Scandinavian languages, to come to grips with Teutonic
  and Latin roots and to do a good deal of educated guessing about most
  Indo-European languages, provided they are written in the Latin alphabet.
- Carry on systematically, at the secondary level, whatever languages the
  elementary and junior high schools may have begun.
- Require at least two years of a classical language, beginning with Latin
  and perhaps adding Greek.
- Require a full three years of a modern language or two years each of two
  modern ones.
- Start requiring readings through other languges in advanced history
  courses.
- Require geography throughout the high school (it does not
  have to be five periods per week).
- Teach at least one complete course through another language. Some
  school systems, like Arlington, Virginia, have done this very successfully
  in history. Of course, allow only the "target" language to be used in the
  classroom of an advanced literature course.

Long-term (five to ten years):

- Arrange to offer at least one classical language in addition to Latin/
  Greek: Sanskrit, Mandarin Chinese, or Arabic.
- Offer two to three "critical" languges: Russian, Japanese, Swahili, for at
  least three years each.

Independent schools

These can model after Washington International School, for most do not have
to worry (much) about teacher certification, "buying American" for textbooks,
following state requirements for courses, and so forth. We stand ready to help

with selecting French and Spanish materials and science texts as well as providing history syllabuses and bibliographies. Open a branch of the Mountbatten World Textbook Library.

If the independent school has waiting lists, admissions can be geared to:

- previous knowledge of one or more common languages
- previous knowledge of a critical language and determination to continue it
- willingness to undertake the study of a classical or a critical language.

For the independent school with a boarding department, arrange to have summer language schools in critical languages to train a) students who will have a running start when they return in the autumn to their ordinary high schools and b) teachers at the beginning, intermediate, and advanced levels. The old NDEA Institutes are the model. A two-day language retreat in cooperation with a local public school can be organized as Phillips Academy, Andover has done.

It hardly needs to be mentioned that public, independent, and parochial schools should put parents to work promoting overseas exchanges through groups such as the Experiment in International Living and the American Field Service for summers, Christmas and spring vacations, and whole years abroad during high school or between high school and college. The Lycée du St. Germain-en-laye near Paris has had a number of programs combining a vacation with two or three weeks in regular French classrooms and vice-versa for French students coming here to school. PTAs can also work to get teachers abroad, regularly, in the summer. Funds are available but one must dig diligently and write proposals eloquently to find them. You can get exchange students from the "common language" countries, even Russia and China. Again, Phillips Academy, Andover, has pointed the way.

Elementary schools

Short-term:

- Develop a "buddy" system with a local school, public or independent, that *is* strong in other languages. Many urban centers have independent schools with strong traditional language programs beginning in the kindergarten.
- Reintroduce Foreign Languages in the Elementary School (FLES) before/after school financed by PTAs or during school if funds are available. This is the program pioneered by Theodore Andersson of the University of Texas at Austin (2).
- Create an atmosphere of glamor and prestige surrounding the new language. As the U.N. International School's director put it:

[The second language] as I would like it to be taught at this age is music, magic, power. It is the language of incantation, and charade, and pantomime. It is the tongue of a select people which enlarges us when we learn their secrets. And when by repetition and reaction, it's come into our heads by ear as naturally as our first learnt tongues, then we read and and write (in that order) and discover new spells and spellings. . . .

If you teach a second language first to enlarge the imagination and awareness of young children, they can start in this way at any age from 4–11. All of this stage is a preparation for the rational under-standing of another people and their ways of thought and expression, which is the secondary stage of language learning. [The second language] mustn't be just a subject or a drill like any other. It should be the most lively, the most active, the most prestigious thing in the school for newcomers (4).

- It does not really matter what methods are used. Find the most effective ways for the situation. Finocchiaro regrets the passion generated over methods. It is as if God had called Moses back to add an eleventh commandment: "Thou shalt teach language in only one way!" (8) There is only one golden rule: use native speakers at the elementary level.
- Work with local junior high schools to be sure they have the capacity to carry on the language(s) begun at the elementary level.
- Send for the Washington International School's history syllabuses, Cycles 1 and 2.

Medium-term: Introduce a "total immersion" class on the Canadian pattern or a "bilingual" one on the Cuban pattern developed at the Coral Way School in Miami in the early 1960s. The immersion pattern is appropriate if none of the children in your community speaks the "target" language. The bilingual pattern is usually more appropriate if you have a strong mixture of Anglo-phones and, say, Francophones. For more information about the immersion and bilingual patterns write to:

The Association to Cure Monolingualism
c/o Washington International School
3100 Macomb Street, N.W.
Washington, D.C. 20008
Attention: Mrs. Elizabeth Williams

or

Professor Joshua Fishman
Yeshiva University
New York, N.Y.

The Association to Cure Monolingualism was organized in March 1980 in conjunction with the Georgetown University Roundtable on Languages and Linguistics. Its charter members are a half dozen schools, public and independent, that have bilingual/immersion programs at the elementary level or who teach "critical" languages. As we searched across the country for strong programs, we often found that districts that had strong elementary school language also had an IB school—Milwaukee, Chicago, and Cincinnati are examples. At both elementary and high school levels languages are being used to attract middle class families back into the cities and into the public schools. This indication that languages are becoming "fashionable" is one of the healthiest signs on the horizon.

Before beginning the immersion class, try to make sure it can be carried straight through the sixth grade. If you cannot, start the immersion class anyway and hope for the best.

Long-term: Convert the whole school to the immersion or bilingual pattern. Make provisions for late entrants. Organize special intensive classes to bring newcomers up to par or, if it is decided to "immerse" new arrivals in the regular classes, arrange tutorial help through teachers' aides.

Remember always Penfield's point, that the elementary level is *the* time to learn languages effortlessly and to pave the way for still other languages in later life (19, 20); and Reischauer's, that learning another language is one of the best ways for a young child to gain an "emotional awareness" of another culture, and to escape from the "our gang" approach of a national school (23).

Colleges and universities

Here of course resides the most leverage over school programs, for colleges are the consumers of the products of the schools.

Undergraduate

Short-term:

- Raise, however slightly, any entrance or exit requirement. A senior Harvard professor once remarked that if Harvard raised its exit requirement from 550 to 600 on the language Achievement Test and made a noise about it, this would probably help a great deal nationwide, out of proportion to the actual raising of the language standard on the Charles River.
- Announce you will raise the requirements a great deal more by 1985, still more by 1990.
- Through your alumni/ae clubs, give language "book prizes" at local school commencements in the name of the college.
- Start requiring readings in other languages within literature, history, economics courses. (An introductory economics course might read some of Say in the original—or Karl Marx.)

- Make certain all your language and literature courses are taught through the "target" language.
- Start paying attention to language departments and school principals in your area—give lectures at the schools; offer seminar space; if your own French department is putting on a Molière play in French, invite high school students to come.
- Encourage history departments of the schools nearest to you. Help them to start at least a two-year sequence in the history of the world/non-North Atlantic basin.
- Start eliminating any institutional prejudices you may have about schools. Remember that in all other countries of the world the pecking order divides not between tertiary and secondary, but between secondary and primary. The great philosopher Henri Bergson taught for many years in a lycée.

Medium-term (2–5 years):

- Require more language, and some world history, from candidates for admission from schools that can provide it, that is, differentiate among the schools. Continue of course to admit bright youngsters from schools that do not have good language and world history. (Over time the weaker schools will copy the stronger.)
- By 1985, admit no one who has not had at least two years of Latin *or* a strong modern language.
- Institute course requirements in at least one modern language—from which one could be excused by examination.
- Start a modest exit requirement if, like Yale, you do not have one at all.

Long-term (5–10 years):

- Require for admission two years of a classical language and three of a modern: competence to be confirmed at least by College Board Achievement Tests and preferably by Advanced Placement. Take out and dust over the pre-1942 college boards, which were essay, not multiple-choice.
- Strengthen the exit requirement until you arrive at the ideal: two modern languages, one common and one critical, to be judged by both written and oral examinations taken not earlier than the junior year (to make certain that the student retains whatever school proficiency he/she may have had).

We are quite aware, of course, that many undergraduate colleges are hurting for bodies since the baby boom is no longer with us. So it is difficult to make entrance or exit requirements more demanding. But the Ivy League, Stanford, and many others are not short of candidates and the responsibility lies chiefly with them to undertake the measures suggested. There will also be a few brave souls (perhaps some of the women's colleges?) who will venture to follow the prescriptions even though they are not overwhelmed with admission candidates. And they will be rewarded, ultimately, for their courage.

Graduate

Short-term:

- Insert into all Ph.D. requirements a reading knowledge of at least one language other than English (some institutions, of course, already do this—and more) to be met by written examination, never by the mere taking of a course. Let students translate passages about their specialties with a dictionary at hand. (A physicist might do one passage on black holes and another on relativity.) Since many words are cognates, at least in alphabetical languages, the student ought to be able to master enough in an intensive six weeks course to pass the test.
- Require for the M.A. a one-year course in a language, which one could exempt.

Medium-term (2–5 years):

- For the Ph.D. extend the requirement for one language to two, as above under "Short-term."
- For the M.A., transform the course requirement into an examination requirement, as under the "Short-term" requirement for the Ph.D.

Long-term (5–10 years):

- For the Ph.D. extend the requirement for written examination in two languages to include a sight passage in one, a dictionary passage in a subject other than the student's specialty in one, and an oral test in one of the two languages. By the time most undergraduate colleges have implemented their long-term prescription, graduate students—we are now in the 1990s—can be expected to be fluent in at least two modern languages—one common, one critical; both oral and written.

And what of governments?

Local school boards should push and prod their schools to do something serious about languages. Communities behind these boards may want to examine governance of their schools. In too many districts, getting elected to a school board is the obvious first step on the political ladder—with disastrous effects on scholarship in the schools.

A practical measure, both at local and state levels, is to do something about the certification of teachers to see to it that the best educated people, American or "foreign," get into the schools as teachers. One large mid-western school system to whom we talked when we were founding the Association to Cure Monolingualism said that in order to get around the teacher certification problem they had invented something called the "bilingual competence policy." If you were a native speaker of high academic quality of a language other than English, were well-educated yourself, and had teaching experience, they could get you into their schools without any certification whatsoever. Unfortunately, we have been following narrowly defined certification procedures for nearly two generations in this country.

What can the federal government do to implement Helsinki promises?

It can designate the twenty public schools that are authorized to offer the International Baccalaureate as International High Schools. The IB forces the immediate strengthening of "foreign language and international studies." Presumably this should be done by the new Secretary of Education, Judge Shirley Hufstedler. A Presidential/Congressional proclamation would be helpful. These schools are fairly well spread across the country and so fit the Starr mandate:

Barrington High School, Barrington, IL
Bellaire High School, Bellaire, TX
Francis Lewis High School, Flushing, NY
Great Neck North High School, Great Neck, NY
Hamden High School, Hamden, CT
Harlingen High School, Harlingen, TX
Jamaica High School, Jamaica, NY
James Madison High School, Brooklyn, NY
Jerome I. Case High School, Racine, WI
Lincoln Park High School, Chicago, IL
Morris Hills School District, Rockaway, NJ
Rufus King School for the College Bound, Milwaukee, WI
Southfield Senior High School, Southfield, MI
Southfield-Lathrup High School, Southfield, MI
South Shore High School, Brooklyn, NY
Valley High School, Las Vegas, NV
Wausau East High School, Wausau, WI
Wellesley High School, Wellesley Hills, MA
Westfield High School, Westfield, MA
Withrow High School, Cincinnati, OH

There are too many in New York; the Pacific Coast is not represented; and only Harlingen, Jamaica, Rufus King, and Withrow could count as "inner city." But it is a beginning, and new ones can be strategically placed.

It can discard the myth of the sanctity of the public school. What is sacred about wending one's way through the political process? Schools, contrary to what Lenin believed, have nothing to do with politics. The intervention of the state may well have been useful during a stage of historical transition in order to make certain that equality of opportunity was recognized. But no one could deny the principle of equality of opportunity in 1980. That battle is won; we are flogging a dead horse. The question has become how to channel taxpayers' funds into institutions of independent, nongovernmental control—a kind of reverse TVA—and an independent yardstick for the public sector. Perhaps we might take a leaf out of the British book; they had for decades "grammar" and "direct grant" schools, run by private boards of trustees, receiving both public funds and parents' fees.

It was a great disappointment to find that the President's Commission report left out the non-public sector altogether. And yet that is where the great language strengths reside. Barely one half of 1 percent of all U.S. children go to independent schools, about 7½ percent to religious or sectarian ones; over 90 percent are in the public schools. Yet out of the top 56 schools in the country, ranked in terms of numbers of Advanced Placement examinations taken in Latin in 1978, 26 or nearly 50 percent were independent schools and another 11, or 20 percent, Roman Catholic—*nearly 70 percent non-public*. The figures were comparable in 1979. The figures in French language (50%) and literature (40%), in Spanish language (23%) and literature (28%), and in German (32%) were less dramatic but still significant.

Given the strong performance in languages of the non-public sector, why was it excluded from the report of the President's Commission? There can be no answer other than a political one. If we are interested in educating individual young human beings and providing experienced linguists for government and business in the future, perhaps we had better have another think; in any human endeavor it is only sensible to build on existing strengths. For a start, extend the "international high school" designation to the independent and Catholic schools authorized to do the International Baccalaureate. They are

The Anglo-American School of New York (formerly the Franklin School), NY

The Daycroft School, Greenwich, CT

Detroit Country Day School, Birmingham, MI

The French-American Bilingual School, San Francisco, CA

Immaculate Conception Cathedral High School, Memphis, TN

Kent School, Kent, CT

United Nations International School, NY

Washington International School, District of Columbia

The government could work out a system of incentive grants for independent schools with a strong track record in languages, world history, and/or geography. For example, $25,000 might go to Andover for scholarships of $1,000 each for youngsters who will agree to study Russian; another $25,000 to Concord for student who will study Chinese; we here in Washington would be glad to do the Japanese if this kind of help were available. Other incentives could be devised for history and geography.

Or the government could supply some, though never all, of the funding for a new Carnegie Committee of Ten—which last met in 1892. The Committee of Ten were the last group of scholars to look at the curriculum of the U.S.

primary and secondary school *as a whole*. After nearly a century, it is time someone had another look.

A final word: The role of the scholar

This chapter began with an exhortation to scholars, and so it will end. The schools, all of them, should be put back into the hands of scholars. The control of any educational system must be lodged with the most learned men and women in the country. The real reason for the decline of languages, the disappearance of geography after the sixth grade, and the increasing parochialism of the American history course is the country's espousal, since the turn of the century, of social goals for education rather than intellectual ones. Social and political concerns should have nothing to do with educational concerns directed at the greatest possible development of the individual child's abilities. In a 1979 report on the National Science Foundation's curriculum work, a panel of the American Association for the Advancement of Science recommended that

> . . . a commission of the highest quality with nationally recognized and respected leadership should be established to reexamine in depth the goals and purposes of American elementary and secondary education and to issue a ̇ major new statement to establish a framework for education and to provide a rationale and justification for new directions. . . . The Committee of Ten was able to redirect education through its efforts over 85 years ago. . . . The proposed commission should be free of bureaucratic and institutional constraints and provided with support staff and time to conduct their study. It would be desirable for the commission to be created by presidential appointment and preferably to be funded from nongovernmental agencies. . . (1)

The model would be the 1892 Committee of Ten, which organized carefully selected groups of scholars of the various disciplines who met, by discipline, in different centers: Latin and Greek at the Univesity of Michigan; English at Vassar; "other modern languages" at the Bureau of Education, Washington, D.C.; mathematics at Harvard; physics, astronomy, chemistry and natural history at the University of Chicago; history, political economy and civil government at the University of Wisconsin; and so on. They stayed in private houses to conserve funds, and the National Education Association, which did some of the organizing work, negotiated some reduced railroad fares ". . . but the reductions obtainable were less numerous and considerable than the National Council of Education had hoped." The English conference commented, incidentally, ". . . that the best results in the teaching of English in high schools cannot be secured without the aid given by the study of some other language; and that Latin and German, by reason of their fuller inflectional system, are especially suited to this end." Their chairman was President Eliot of Harvard; they were funded by Carnegie. They spent the grand total of $2500—and they laid out the curriculum (Carnegie units) for the schools for a century. One half of the members came from universities and about one half from schools, public and non-public (24).

It would be wrong to ignore the fact that it will be difficult to persuade university scholars to take the kind of responsibility for the schools that they were willing to assume at the end of the nineteenth century. They have had many discouraging experiences in the twentieth—not least the post-Sputnik reforms, of which virtually nothing is left. But if quality is to be restored and if we are to have once again college freshmen who are literate; those of us who believe with Fitzgerald (9) that the task of the school is to transmit, just as efficiently and thoroughly as possible, this generation's store of knowledge to the next, must roll up our sleeves and get to work.

References, The international high school: A challenge for scholars

1 American Association for the Advancement of Science. *A Report on the Implications for the Science Community of Three National Science Foundation-Supported Studies of the State of Pre-College Science Education,* June 1979.

2 Andersson, Theodore, and Mildred Boyer. *Bilingual Schooling in the United States,* Volume 1. Austin, TX:Southwest Educational Development Laboratory, 1970.

3 Berthoud, Roger. "Lord Mountbatten at 75, aiming now at creating an international sixth-form elite." *The Times* (20 June 1975):18.

4 Cole, Desmond. Personal Communication. 27 April 1966. [Letter.]

5 Cousins, Norman. *Confessions of a Half-Educated Man.* [Paper presented at the Mountbatten meeting of the United World Colleges, Princeton University, October 1975.]

6 *Ecole Internationale de Genève, 50e Anniversaire, 1924-1974.* Geneva: Ecole Internationale de Genève (1974):6

7 Fadiman, Clifton, quoted in *Paidei* 3 (Fall 1974):1. La Salle, IL:The Hegler Institute.

8 Finocchiaro, M. "Myth and Reality in Bilingual Education Programs," 123-137 in Renzo Titone,ed., *Bilingual Education and Foreign Language Teaching Today.* Milan:Oxford Institutes Italiana, 1979.

9 Fitzgerald, Frances. *America Revised.* Boston:Little Brown, 1979.

10 Goodman, Dorothy B. "An Idea Whose Time Has Come." *Exchange* 12 (Fall 1976):35-40. Washington, DC:U.S. Department of State.

11 __"The Language Pattern: Past Present and Future." *Newsletter of the Washington International School* 3: 2(April 1973):1-2.

12 Husén, Torsten, ed. *International Study of Achievement in Mathematics.* New York:Wiley, 1967.

13 "International School to Offer International Baccalaureate." *Bank Notes* (June 1975):3. Washington, DC: World Bank Group.

14 Lambert, Richard. "The Curricular Challenge," 13-17 in Robert Black, ed., *The Role of the Scholarly Disciplines.* New York:Change Magazine Press, 1980.

15 Malinowski, Halina W., and Vera Zorn. *UNIS: Its History and Devel-*

opment, New York:The United Nations International School, 1973.

16 Mill, John Stuart. "On Liberty." *On Liberty and Other Essays*. New York: Macmillan, Modern Readers' Series (1926):126 [First printing 1859].

17 Mintz, Anita. "History Courses Taught Without National Bias." *International Herald Tribune*(8-9 September 1979):International Education Supplement, p. 1.

18 "The Parade: Global Education." *Basic Education*. Washington, DC: Council for Basic Education (November 1979):3-5.

19 _____ and Lamar Roberts. *Speech and Brain-Mechanisms*. Princeton, NJ:Princeton University Press, 1959.

20 Penfield, Wilder G. "The Uncommitted Cortex: The Child's Changing Brain." *Atlantic Monthly* 214:1 (July 1964):77-81.

21 Peterson, A.D.C. *International Baccalaureate*. London:Harrap (1972) 36.

22 *Proposal to Establish an International School in Washington: Feasibility Study*. 1818 H Street,N.W., Washinton, DC:Working Committee for an International School, 1965.

23 Reischauer, Edwin O. *Toward the Twenty-first Century: Education for a Changing World*. New York:Vintage Books, 1974.

24 "Report of the Committee on Secdary School Studies." *National Education Association*. New York:Arno Press, 1969. [Reprinted from the 1893 edition issued by the U.S. Government Printing Office.]

25 "Sprachlose Weltmacht," *Frankfurter Allgemeine Zeitung* (22 January 1980):Feuilleton section.

26 Starr, S. Frederick. "Foreign Languages in the American School," 9-14 in *President's Commission on Foreign Languages and International Studies: Background Papers and Studies*. Washington, DC:U.S. Government Printing Office, 1979.

27 __ "International High Schools: Their Time Has Come." *Phi Delta Kappan* 60(June 1979):743-44.

28 __ "Needed: A Cure for Provincialism." *Chronicle of Higher Education*. 12(8 March 1976):32.

29 __ "Why Not International High Schools?" 127-131 in E. Michael Gerli, James E. Alatis, and Richard I. Brod,eds., *Language in American Life*. Proceeding of the Georgetown University-Modern Language Association Conference, October 1977, Washington, DC:Georgetown University Press, 1978.

30 Stryker, Shirley Letts. *Bilingual Peer Interaction in the Washington International School*. Washington, DC: Catholic University of America, 1975 [Doctoral Dissertation.]

31 "Washington International School's World History Project." *International Schools Association Bulletin* 88 (September/October 1979):11-14.

8

Modest proposals for second and foreign language teacher education in the 1980s

Charles R. Hancock
University of Maryland

Introduction

Teacher education in the United States is at a critical juncture. Teacher surplus, sparse financial resources, pervasive low morale, and declining enrollments in schools and colleges are realities reflecting the seriousness of that juncture. Teacher "burn-out" has also become a pervasive reality.

Since second language teachers, in both foreign language education and in bilingual programs, live with the same constraints as other educators, the following paragraphs describe the general status of teacher education models, rather than those specific to second language education.

Joyce et al. (21), for example, have argued that performance-based teaching models must be examined so as to reveal more sharply defined teaching roles; field-based, systematic training in specific competencies; and more empirical research on teaching effectiveness. Nash and Ducharme (25) have argued that educators must broaden their perspectives "beyond mere classroom teaching competence" to help individuals in a variety of extra-classroom settings find "power and meaning in their personal and professional lives."

These perspectives define the focus of this chapter—*conventional,*

Charles R. Hancock (Ph.D., Ohio State University) is Associate Professor of Foreign Language Education at the University of Maryland (College Park). He has taught French and Spanish at the high school level and has worked in the field of teacher education since 1971. He has served on the ACTFL Executive Council and the Board of Directors of the New York State Association of Foreign Language Teachers. His publications have appeared in *Foreign Language Annals, French Review, Language Association Bulletin, Modern Language Journal,* and the *TESOL Quarterly.* His professional affiliations include ACTFL, AATF, TESOL, the Maryland State Foreign Language Teachers Association, the Greater Washington Association of Foreign Language Teachers, and the Washington Area Teachers of English as a Second Language.

competency-based (or performance-based, for those who prefer the latter terminology) and *humanistic* models of teacher education. It is, of course, not intended that these be construed as mutually exclusive categories.

The primary goal of the chapter is to describe the current status of second language teacher education models and to propose directions for the 1980s.

Conventional models of teacher education programs

Previous volumes of this series have clearly substantiated the notion that foreign and second language teacher education is dynamic. Thus, the title of this section must not be construed to be negative. It is intended that "conventional" be understood to mean "widely practiced." Wing (33) made a similar thrust in her 1975 ACTFL Series Chapter, particularly the section on procedures and practices to achieve commitment and competence. She also urged that the profession view preservice and inservice education as a continuum. A few years later, Bailey (2) reviewed practices within teacher education, particularly techniques that are used within a teacher education program for foreign language teachers. Loew (23) cautioned that our profession must accept change in society as a constant and develop coping strategies for harnessing our collective efforts to benefit our students.

In a recent publication, Jorstad (18) and Knop (22) have described some contemporary approaches to professional development of foreign and second language educators. Their chapters present analyses of current practices in the profession and identify needed research and development activities.

It is obvious from studying these publications that most foreign and second language teacher education programs have been carefully conceived and represent some of our best thinking within the constraints of particular institutions with which they are associated. Such analyses also reveal many basic similarities in our training programs. One synthesized model of such programs is presented in Figure 1. While particular situational factors might result in modifications in this model, it is probable that most of what can be called "conventional" in foreign and second language teacher education falls within this schematization. To be sure, much diversity occurs within individual programs, especially with respect to the content and mode of presentation for the various courses. This type of model for second language teacher education is not likely to change fundamentally within the near future.

One constraint inhibiting change is the *economic* factor. Foreign and second language teacher education programs in most institutions of higher education are not likely to be expanded. The money for such activities is simply not available in most cases. In fact, many existing programs are being told to establish priorities and/or cut-back. In other cases, we are being urged to apply research paradigms to our programs to increase efficiency and contribute to

Figure 1.
A Synthesized Model of a Second Language Teacher Education Program

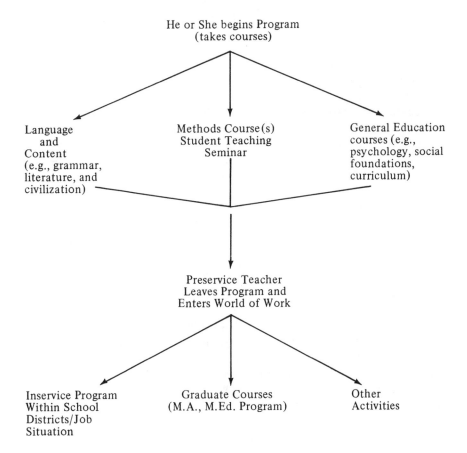
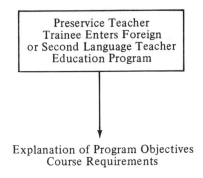

the theoretical research base that is not as adequate as many second language educators intuitively know it should be.

It seems logical to conclude that those who work in teacher education must respect local constraints in formulating updated guidelines for the training of professionals in foreign language, English as a second language, and bilingual education. It is beyond question that existing guidelines for the preparation of specialists in these three fields should build upon existing statements. The Guidelines for Teacher Education Programs in Modern Foreign Languages (12), the National TESOL Guidelines for Programs in English as a Second Language (13), and those of the Center for Applied Linguistics for bilingual/- bicultural education (14) are ideal points of departure in any updating of "guidelines." However, continuous updating is essential because the realities facing the foreign and second language educator have drastically changed since the 1960s, when many of these statements were drafted. A proposal for a national conference dealing with this topic and related issues will be described later in this chapter.

Movements towards a fundamental skills emphasis in most schools and colleges, mainstreaming of learners with handicaps (Public Law 94-142), increasing numbers of foreign students and immigrants in the schools, increased interest in ethnic studies (*Roots*) and multicultural education, and most importantly the need for political astuteness/awareness on the part of teachers are just a few realities facing all teachers, but particularly those involved in second language education.

While these realities may be considered *content*-related, rather than *format*-related (or model-related), they cannot be denied in today's world. It is quite possible that the relationship between content and format of foreign and second language teacher education might reveal some fundamental, desirable changes in both, with appropriate attention as always, to the constraints within which any modifications must be considered.

Competency-based models

Background

The accountability movements of the 1970s stimulated revisions in foreign and second language teacher education programs, bilingual education, and most academic training programs. Previous publications have amply documented the breadth of the PBTE (performance-based) or CBTE (competency-based) movement in foreign and second languages education. Interested readers may refer to chapters by Andrews (1), Bailey (2), DeLorenzo (6) and Fanselow and Light (8).

Key ideas

While it is not feasible to review the contents of all of the areas just mentioned, it is useful to recapitulate some key points:

- CBTE/PBTE is a systems approach training model.
- It includes the establishment of measurable learning outcomes for the trainee.
- The above outcomes fall into three categories—knowledge, attitudes, and behaviors.
- The training components include a delivery system composed of both cognitive and affective elements in a variety of learning environments.
- Mastery of the competencies by each trainee must be demonstrated prior to the exit from the training program.

These five aspects are shown schematically in Figure 2:

Figure 2. A Schema of Competency-Based Teacher Education Components

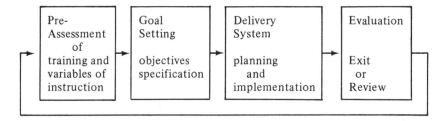

| Pre-Assessment of training and variables of instruction | Goal Setting objectives specification | Delivery System planning and implementation | Evaluation Exit or Review |

Guidelines

The model in Figure 2 has been widely used, particularly in states like New York where there was a strong movement during the mid-1970s towards revising all certification-based training programs. Each of the campuses of the State University of New York where foreign and second language teachers were trained were obliged to revise programs along competency-based lines. In an effort to provide leadership in this matter, the New York State Association of Foreign Language Teachers' Professional Development Committee devised the *Minimal List of Competencies for Foreign Language Teachers: Suggested Guidelines for Foreign Language Teacher Preparation* (Hancock et al. 17). As the title implies, these guidelines were published to assist institutions in revising foreign and second language teacher training programs to a competency-based model. Basic (minimal) competencies in a broad range of areas are identified: practical command of language, language analysis, culture, teaching-learning process, and professional awareness. A sample page from the document is reprinted here. The excerpt reveals a format that follows the schema.

Similar "guidelines" produced by the International Association of English as a Second Language Teachers, TESOL (13), and the Center for Applied

Figure 3. Culture

COMPETENCY	INDICATOR (Assessment Procedures)	ASSESSMENT CRITERIA	ASSESSOR
The candidate can:			
1. Demonstrate the research skills needed to locate and organize information about the foreign culture to acquire a knowledge base which will include but not be limited to aspects of the geography, history (including political), education, and plastic and visual arts of the countries where the FL is spoken.	Candidate will indicate knowledge of the location and be able to organize information concerning the target culture.	Selecting an aspect of the foreign culture (as identified under Competency), the candidate will prepare a written report on that aspect and indicate at least ten sources to validate the conclusions reached.	The faculty member teaching the course in culture and civilization would assess this effort (in collaboration with a member of the FLED staff).
2. Describe how people behave in the most common, mundane, and crisis situations in the foreign culture.	Candidate will indicate a knowledge of specific contemporary daily patterns of life concerning such topics as recreation, work, modes of transportation, school, and human relationships in countries where the FL is spoken.	In an interview situation (test) in which 5 areas of contemporary life are specified previously thereto, the candidate will identify contemporary patterns of behavior exhibited by persons who speak the FL natively.	A panel consisting of a number of the appropriate FL department, a member of the FL education department, and a secondary school FL teacher will assess the candidate's competency.
3. Evaluate statements describing aspects of behaviors concerning the foreign culture.	Candidate will be able to discriminate the accuracy of statements relating to the culture and civilization in which the FL is spoken.	Given a set of statements concerning aspects of behaviors in the foreign culture, the candidate will correctly comment of the accuracy of each statement.	The FL specialist in the culture of the specific language appointed by the department chairperson will assess this effort.
4. Describe the principal ways in which people within a foreign culture behave as contrasted with that of the U.S. and how these patterns relate to the context of the total target culture.	Candidate will be able to describe the foreign cultural pattern related to the content of the total culture and compare it to that of the U.S.	Given a cultural concept (e.g., time-space, leisure time activities), the candidate will list real life activities in which the target and source cultures exhibit differences and similarities.	College instructor of civilization/culture course.

(Language Association Bulletin March, 1978)

Linguistics for the Preparation and Certification of Teachers of Bilingual/ Bicultural Education (14) were also disseminated during the 1970s. The three documents reveal many similarities in content (language proficiency, linguistics, culture). However, the delivery system and the criteria for mastery are not specified in the TESOL and Bilingual/Bicultural guidelines.

Interim assessment

While the national attempts at CBTE have not yet run their course, it is useful to take stock of some recent trends. One of these trends is an apparent drop in the thrust for full competency-based training programs. There are many clues that suggest the theoretical base for competency-based education may not yet exist. A great deal has been learned about specifying knowledge, attitudes, and behaviors expected of teachers, particularly when these expectations are substantiated by role analyses. We have also learned much about the need for improved communication between the trainees and all of those whose job it is to help them develop into functioning professionals.

However, many aspects of a CBTE-PBTE model remain troublesome. The current knowledge base has not allowed for determination of a comprehensive list of essential competencies for foreign/second language teachers. In fact, where extensive lists exist, they are frequently unmanageable. We cannot begin to get a handle on those intangible competencies like "classroom presence" and "flexibility," and the complex knowledge-skill-attitude that a teacher must *be* in order to demonstrate "presence" and "flexibility." Even if we knew how to identify such competencies, which many agree are at the heart of successful teaching, we are not even close to being able to measure them objectively.

It is not surprising then to note that many gallant efforts at competency-based second language teacher education have been abandoned. This does not at all imply that those efforts have not left their mark on the profession. Perhaps we were, as a profession, simply unprepared to cope with many unanswered questions about what training programs were capable of achieving. One positive outcome of CBTE efforts is a clearer notion of the many facets of the role of a second language teacher. This information allows for continuous reexamination of how our training programs reflect (or do not reflect) such role diversity.

We in second language education must attend to matters related to designing, evaluating, and developing dynamic teacher education programs. Too little cross-fertilization within our profession has occurred. Is it not appropriate that it be enhanced in the 1980s?

Humanistic teaching models _____

Unlike competency-based models of teacher education, humanistic models per se are not widely encountered. Instead, many teacher education programs are designed to train "sensitive" professionals at both the preservice and in-service levels. This sensitivity is presumed to be practiced as a teacher interacts with students.

Patterson (27) has identified the primary qualities of the humanistic teacher, which include three basic characteristics: *genuineness* or *authenticity, respect* or *warmth,* and *empathic understanding.* Most of these characteristics are self-explanatory, with the exception of empathic understanding. By this term, Patterson refers to a particular kind of understanding that requires a teacher to put him- or herself in the learner's place and to try to perceive the latter's perceptions or feelings.

Davis (5, p.100) identified similar characteristics, stating that the humanistic teacher is "an authentic human being interfacing with other human beings...."

The parallel movements in the fields of psychology and pedagogy towards emphasis on the *person* began in the mid-1950s, when a field called humanistic psychology emerged. Some facts and dates are worth reviewing:

1954 The first general sketch of humanistic psychology appears as the heading of a mailing list compiled by Abraham H. Maslow: "People who are interested in the scientific study of creativity, love, higher values, autonomy, growth, self-actualization, human need gratification, etc."

1955 The term "humanistic psychology" in its current usage is first used by Hadley Cantril in "Toward a Humanistic Psychology."

1956 Abraham H. Maslow publishes an article also called "Toward a Humanistic Psychology."

1958 *Humanistic Psychology,* a volume by John Cohen, stresses that the subject matter of psychology is distinctively human and that its starting point must be the phenomena of experience. Maslow designates humanistic psychology as "the Third Force."

1961 *Journal of Humanistic Psychology* is founded in the United States by Anthony Sutich.

1962 American Association for Humanistic Psychology (AAHP) is established.

The name Maslow is well known to those in the field of psychology. The concept of "basic needs" of every individual, which is now widely accepted, was published in 1968 in Maslow's *Toward a Psychology of Being* (24). In that book, he presented the diagram in Figure 4.

Rivers (28, p.64) has stated that:

Since any genuine communication requires that one feel at ease in the situation, these Maslow-type needs among students and between teach-

Figure 4. The Maslow Hierarchy of Needs

4
Self-
Actual-
ization*
- - - - - -

3
Respect,
Esteem,
Approval,
Dignity, Self-
Respect
- - - - - - - - -

2
Belongingness as in a
family, community, clan;
friendship, affection, love
- - - - - - - - - - - - - - - - -

1
Protection, Safety, Security
(Basic Needs)

*Self-actualization is considered the highest need; it includes freedom for the fullest
development of a person's talents and capacities.

ers and students affect the success of the communicative interaction,
even apart from differing levels of language control.

If one is to follow the recommendations of Maslow and Rivers, the psycho-
emotional needs of foreign and second language learners must be dealt with.
But how are we training teachers to deal with such needs?

A search of some of the profession's most carefully conceived recent books
failed to show models of humanistic education being implemented in teacher
education programs in any systematic manner. Strevens (32), for example,
presented a solid description of basic principles of teacher training in both
Britain and the United States, but he did not deal with training teachers to
respond to those issues raised by Rivers.

Joyce et al. (20) conducted a survey of teacher education programs and
described the results in a series of position papers on major dimensions in preservice education. These include: 1) the structure and content of preparation
programs, 2) the characteristics of faculty and students in teacher preparation
programs, 3) governance and decision-making processes in institutions that
prepare teachers, and 4) cost factors and sources of revenue for teacher education programs. The descriptions of value and attitudinal aspects of the
programs provide many insights for us in foreign and second language

education. One thing we might do in the 1980s is to study such reports and seek appropriate applications in our discipline.

Fanselow's FOCUS model

Fanselow's work concerning the "teaching act" shows excellent potential for helping us to investigate the rules that govern communication. The model is implemented in at least one TESOL master's program and in many programs whose teachers Fanselow has helped to train. FOCUS (Foci for Observing Communications Used in Settings) is a conceptual framework and one way of classifying, creating, and evaluating communications in a wide range of settings. Fanselow (7, p.3) has concluded that the term "teaching act," which is at the heart of all teacher-learner interactions, must be broader when discussing language teaching than when discussing other types of teaching. He stated that "studying the teaching act of a language teacher must include study of how we communicate in non-teaching settings as well as teaching settings since part of our job is to teach our students how to communicate outside of the classroom."

The following chart illustrates the primary elements of the Fanselow model (Figure 5). It is suggested that the reader first examine the five questions at the top of the chart and then study each vertical column.

Essentially, what Fanselow proposes is a system wherein teachers are trained to investigate the teaching act. It is a promising means towards raising teachers' awareness to the point where they are able to specify many heretofore intangible or unexplained aspects of both successful and not-so-successful lessons. It is a model that we should definitely examine more closely in the 1980s.

The Silent Way and Community-Language Learning

Teachers who are trained in and teach using the "Silent Way" and "Community-Language Learning" are often on different wavelengths from those who are not informed about the philosophies of either Gattegno (9) or Curran (4). Elsewhere I have synthesized current efforts of "humanizing" second language teaching (16). Yet, despite their uniqueness, such programs must not be ignored by our profession. Instead, as professional teacher educators, we ought to seek deeper understanding of them so as to determine the ways in which their precepts agree with those of the teacher education program with which we are associated.

While many, many second language teachers have attended workshops,

Figure 5. Five Characteristics of Communications in Settings*

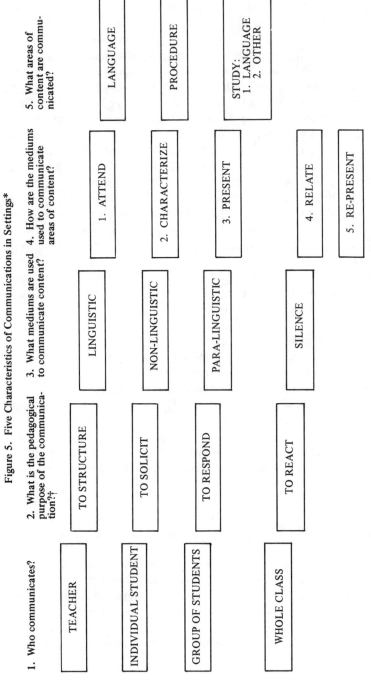

1. Who communicates?	2. What is the pedagogical purpose of the communication?†	3. What mediums are used to communicate content?	4. How are the mediums used to communicate areas of content?	5. What areas of content are communicated?
TEACHER	TO STRUCTURE	LINGUISTIC	1. ATTEND	LANGUAGE
INDIVIDUAL STUDENT	TO SOLICIT	NON-LINGUISTIC	2. CHARACTERIZE	PROCEDURE
GROUP OF STUDENTS	TO RESPOND	PARA-LINGUISTIC	3. PRESENT	STUDY: 1. LANGUAGE 2. OTHER
WHOLE CLASS	TO REACT	SILENCE	4. RELATE	
			5. RE-PRESENT	

*Table 5 is an excerpt from John F. Fanselow, *Breaking Rules: Alternatives for Language Teachers.* Longmans, to be published in 1981.
†These four pedagogical purposes are from Bellack.

conference sessions, and mini-courses on topics such as the Silent Way and Community-Language Learning, such approaches are only now finding their way into the conventional models of teacher education. A study of current programs also reveals that where these approaches are included they tend to be English as a second language rather than foreign language teacher education programs. Perhaps one plausible explanation for such differences is that English as a second language programs have traditionally included adult learners. Both the Silent Way and Community-Language Learning are likely to be most successful with adults, or at least more mature language learners. To be sure, at the knowledge or information level such approaches are included in programs, but are they internalized by the teacher? While a clear negative response must be registered for the typical second or foreign language teacher, there are many of us who are inspired by the "whole person" approach espoused by Curran and by the need for teacher "silence" exposed by Gattegno. This is not the place for a full description of either view of teaching. One of the best recent publications for this purpose is Stevick's *A Way and Ways* (30). Gattegno's *The Common Sense of Teaching Foreign Languages* (9) is also useful.

The aim of good teaching is, according to Gattegno, "to make students independent, autonomous, and responsible" (9, p.45), and learning a language "is one more step towards being a freer person" (p.55).

Is it appropriate to paraphrase the ideas for the teacher in training? Are the references not also applicable to teachers? If so, why has the field of second language education remained steadfast in its emphasis on the language, rather than the people who are learning and teaching it. Can we hope for any changes in this matter in the 1980s? Are our teacher training programs systematically training teachers to internalize these types of humanistic models for teaching? Many questions.... few answers!

Douglas Brown, President of TESOL (3), predicted that the 1980s will bring a set of continua (rather than one right answer). This is nowhere more clearly evident than in the area of teacher education models. Thus, a modest proposal is offered in the final section.

A modest proposal

There are many signs for optimism within foreign and second language education circles, despite some serious constraints. One definite sign is the report of the President's Commission on Foreign Language and International Studies. While it is still too early to make a final judgment on the results of that commission's activities, it is already evident that foreign and second language education has been bolstered by the "good press" that it has recently received.

Legislation in support of foreign and second language education has been initiated, especially by Representatives Paul Simon (Illinois) and Leon Panetta (California). ACTFL, in conjunction with the Joint National Committee (JNCL) has established a Washington Office to lobby for foreign language. (See Mendelson's study in Chapter 3.)

How are teachers in training internalizing information such as the above? How do teacher education programs integrate such high priority areas as political action strategies into preservice teacher education programs? Must such insights and involvement await inservice efforts? These are some of the questions one can raise concerning at least one area of a foreign or second language teacher's education.

However, many more areas are equally deserving of consideration. In fact, the wide variety of programs identified by Strasheim (31) in "Foreign Language Programs: Reaching Toward the Twenty-First Century" reveal wide variety of program options for which we simply have not, as a profession, prepared teachers in the past. Two areas to which we need to devote immediate attention are exploratory and immersion programs. Will we have foreign and second language teachers ready to work in such areas when they are needed?" The answer is probably no. Are we ready to guide non-language decision-makers who need our advice in establishing training programs that reflect these other "innovative" approaches to foreign and second language education?

Hammond and Sims conducted a survey of model programs published in 1980 under the title *Prescriptions for Success* (see 15 for progress report). We need to study the teacher education programs in which participating teachers were trained; we must study as well their subsequent inservice training. Such a study is potentially quite revealing.

The Proposal

The least we can do in the training of teachers of foreign and second languages is to seek to implement the following types of approaches that might be labeled "energizers" for the 1980s:

- Think about past successes and use them in the future.
- Treat teachers as thinking beings—thinking *human* beings.
- Emphasize teaching as a problem-solving skill.
- Emphasize decision-making skill development.
- Encourage an emphasis on *linguistic* and *communicative* competency.
- Work closely with other disciplines to take advantage of opportunities for interaction.

One aspect of this modest proposal, and even more importantly the issues that most affect our profession, is a high-powered national conference on second language teacher education. National associations are the most likely sponsors of such a conference. It is the type of conference that might easily cross academic boundaries and lead to the type of serious look at our teacher training programs that is needed.

Summary

In summary, this chapter represents a call for action in the 1980s. As we continue to face the challenges of training second and foreign language teachers to respond to the *whole-person* student at all instructional levels, let those of us who design the training programs implement those that free our own students to achieve their fullest capabilities as they enter the realities of the teaching profession. We must establish a theoretical base for what we do, but we must also establish flexible models of teacher education, models that will allow various designs—conventional, competency-based, humanistic.

References, Modest proposals for second and foreign language teacher education in the 1980s

1 Andrews, L. O. "Developments in Preservice and Inservice Teacher Education," 353-96 in Gilbert A. Jarvis, ed., *The Challenge of Communication.* ACTFL Foreign Language Education Series, Volume 6. Skokie, IL:National Textbook Company, 1974.

2 Bailey, Leona G. "Teacher Education for a Changing World," 179-210 in June K. Phillips, ed., *The Language Connection: From the Classroom to the World.* ACTFL Foreign Language Education Series, Volume 9. Skokie, iL:National Textbook Company, 1977.

3 Brown, H. Douglas. "TESOL— 1980's: Some Predictions." [Paper presented at the Spring Meeting of the Washington Area TESOL Association, May 1980.]

4 Curran, Charles A. *Counseling-Learning: A Whole-Person Model for Education.* New York:Grune and Stratton, 1972.

5 Davis, David C. *Model for Humanistic Education: The Danish Folk High School.* Columbus, OH:Merrill Publishers, 1971.

6 DeLorenzo, William E. "New Teachers: Developing Flexible Foreign Language Teachers," 64-115 in Warren C. Born, ed., *New Contents, New Teachers, New Publics.* Reports of the Working Committees of the Northeast Conference on the Teaching of Foreign Languages. Middlebury, VT:Northeast Conference, 1978.

7 Fanselow, John F. *Breaking Rules: Alternatives for Language Teachers.* Longmans, forthcoming.

8 ___ and Richard Light, eds., *Bilingual, ESOL, and Foreign Language Teacher Preparation: Models, Practices, Issues.* Washington, DC:TESOL Publications, 1977.

9 Gattegno, Caleb. *The Common Sense of Teaching Foreign Language.* New York:Educational Solu-

tions, Inc., 1976.

10 Goddu, Roland. "Pursuing Continuing Education as a Foreign Language Teacher: An Overview," 327-50 in Gilbert A. Jarvis and Alice Omaggio, eds., *Choosing Among the Options*. ACTFL Foreign Language Education Series, Volume 8. Skokie, IL: National Textbook Company, 1976.

11 Grittner, Frank, ed. *Learning a Second Language, Seventy-ninth Yearbook of the National Society for the Study of Education, Part II*. Chicago:University of Chicago Press, 1980.

12 "Guidelines for Teacher Education Programs in Modern Foreign Languages." *Modern Language Journal* 50(1966):342-44.

13 "Guidelines for Preparing Teachers of English as a Foreign Second Language." TESOL Association, Washinton, DC, 1973.

14 "Guidelines for the Preparation and Certification of Teachers of Bilingual/Bicultural Education." Arlington, VA:Center for Applied Linguistics, 1974.

15 Hammond, Sandra B. and William D. Sims. "The ACTFL Survey of Successful Programs." *Foreign Language Annals* 13(1980):91-92.

16 Hancock, Charles R. *Humanizing the Second Language Curriculum*. Concord, MA:Heinle and Heinle Publishers, forthcoming.

17 ___ et al. *Minimal List of Competencies for Foreign Language Teachers: Suggested Guidelines for Teacher Education Programs* (Revised Edition). Schenectady, NY:The Language Association Bulletin, 1978.

18 Jorstad, Helen L. "The Education and Reeducation of Teachers," 168-85 in Frank M. Grittner, ed., *Learning a Second Language, Seventy-ninth Yearbook of the National Society for the Study of Education, Part II*. Chicago, IL:The University of Chicago Press, 1980.

19 Joyce, Bruce, and Marsha Weil. *Models of Teaching*. Englewood Cliffs, NJ:Prentice-Hall, Inc., 1972.

20 Joyce, Bruce *et al.* "Preservice Teacher Education." Washington, DC: U.S.O.E., 1971. [EDRS:ED 055 485]

21 ___, Jonas F. Soltis, and Marsha Weil. *Performance-Based Teacher Education Design Alternatives: The Concepts of Unity*. Washington, DC:American Association of College Teachers of Education, 1974.

22 Knop, Constance K. "The Supervision of Foreign Language Teachers," 186-207 in Frank M. Grittner, ed., *Learning a Second Language, Seventy-ninth Yearbook of the National Society for the Study of Education, Part II*. Chicago, IL: The University of Chicago Press, 1980.

23 Loew, Helen Z. "Modifying the Program and Providing for Change," 271-303 in June K. Phillips, ed., *Building on Experience — Building for Success*. ACTFL Foreign Language Education Series, Volume 10. Skokie, IL:National Textbook Company, 1979.

24 Maslow, Abraham H. *Towards a Psychology of Being*, Second Edition. New York:Van, Nostrand Reinhold Company, 1968.

25 Nash, Robert J., and Edward R. Ducharme. "A Future Perspective of Preparing Educators for Human Service Society: How to Restore a Sense of Social Purpose to Teacher Education." *Teachers College Record* 77(1976):441-71.

26 National Council for Accreditation of Teacher Education, *Standards for Accreditation of Teacher Education*, Washington, DC, 1977.

27 Patterson, Cecil H. *Humanistic Education*. Englewood Cliffs, NJ:Prentice-Hall, Inc., 1973.

28 Rivers, Wilga M. "Psychology and Linguistics as Bases for Language Pedagogy," 44-66 in Frank M. Grittner, ed., *Learning a Second Lan-*

guage, Seventy-ninth Yearbook of the National Society for the Study of Education, Part II. Chicago, IL:The University of Chicago Press, 1980.

29 Stevick, Earl W. *Memory, Meaning and Method (Some Psychological Perspectives on Language Learning)*. Rowley, MA:Newbury House Publishers, Inc., 1976.

30 ___ *A Way and Ways*. Rowley,MA: Newbury House Publishers, Inc., 1980.

31 Strasheim, Lorraine A. "Foreign Language Programs: Reaching Toward the Twenty-First Century." [Presentation to the President's Commission on Foreign Language and International Studies, Chicago Re-gional Hearing, 1978. Reproduction of diagram may be found in Phillips, June K. ed., *The New Imperative: Expanding the Horizons of Foreign Language Education*. ACTFL Foreign Language Education Series, Skokie, IL: National Textbook Co., 1980]

32 Strevens, Peter. *New Orientations in the Teaching of English*. New York:Oxford University Press, 1975.

33 Wing, Barbara H. "Free to Become: Preservice Education," 285-335 in Gilbert A. Jarvis, ed., *Perspective: A New Freedom*. ACTFL Foreign Language Education Series, Volume 7. Skokie, IL:National Textbook Company, 1975.

9

Language teaching/learning research: A Canadian perspective on status and directions

H.H. Stern
Jim Cummins
Ontario Institute for Studies in Education

H.H. Stern (Ph.D., University of London) is Director of the Modern Language Centre of the Ontario Institute for Studies in Education (OISE) and a Professor in the Graduate Departments of Educational Theory and Linguistics of the University of Toronto. He was head of the language department in a British grammar school; in charge of educational psychology and methodology of language teaching at the University of Hull, England; and Reader in the Language Centre, University of Essex, U.K. In 1961-1962 he served with the UNESCO Institute for Education in Hamburg. He came to Canada in 1968 where he established the Modern Language Centre. A past chairman of the Modern Language Association of Great Britain and of the Modern Language Committee of the Schools Council, he holds the Diamond Jubilee Medal of the Institute of Linguists and the Life Membership of the Ontario Modern Language Teachers Association for services to language teaching. His publications include *Languages in Primary Education; Languages and the Young School Child; Modern Languages in the Universities: A Guide; Perspectives on Second Language Teaching;* and the English translation of *Psycholinguistics: An Introduction to Research and Theory,* by Hans Hormann. He initiated, directed, and participated in several language teaching research projects and co-authored the resulting reports: *French Programs: Some Major Issues; Three Approaches to Teaching French; The Good Language Learner; Contact and Communication: An Evaluation of Student Exchanges;* and *Module Making.*

Jim Cummins (Ph.D., University of Alberta), is a Visiting Professor in the Modern Language Centre of the Ontario Institute for Studies in Education. He received his undergraduate training in psychology at the University College, Dublin, Ireland, and his doctorate in educational psychology from the University of Alberta, Canada. His publications are mainly in the areas of bilingual education and learning disabilities. In 1979 he was awarded (with J.P. Das) the International Reading Association Albert J. Harris Award for best paper on detection and remediation of reading disability. He has lectured widely on bilingual education both in Europe and North America.

Introduction

Twenty years ago John B. Carroll wrote an article entitled "Wanted: A Research Basis for Educational Policy on Foreign Language Teaching" (20). Research on foreign language teaching was of course not unknown even then. However, it was not until the end of the 1950s that research began to affect in any truly significant way the policy decisions and the method debate in foreign language education. Since then, there have been large numbers of studies that can be described as research. For example, when Frechette (51) surveyed research undertaken around 1975 and 1976 for Volume 8 of the ACTFL series, he listed over three hundred studies in the United States alone. In spite of this increase in volume, if we ask ourselves today at the beginning of the 1980s what contribution research has made, will make, could or should make, the answer would still not be unequivocal. Questions about the contribution of research to foreign language teaching continue to be raised (e.g., Stern, 128; Stern et al., 135; Tarone et al., 141). Even today we would not be remiss in reiterating Carroll's call of twenty years ago: Wanted—A Research Basis for Foreign Language Education.

In this chapter we focus on one broad area of research i.e., research on second language acquisition and second language learning. Without attempting to cover this research in any comprehensive way, we will attempt to illustrate some problems research is up against and indicate one or two directions which, in our view, research might take in this decade. In our examples, we will draw heavily on our experience of research in Canada, particularly the Modern Language Centre of the Ontario Institute for Studies in Education (OISE) in Toronto, where research has been undertaken in the area of second language and bilingual education over a period of more than ten years.

Language learning—A central issue for research

To unravel the ups and downs of language learning is a central issue for researchers and practitioners alike. As teachers we are forced to admit that our efforts at making students learn a foreign language have not exactly been a spectacular success. Again and again, we have had to ask ourselves: Why is it so hard to learn a foreign language? How is it that under certain circumstances a second and even a third language is learned without teaching and seemingly without much effort, while in other circumstances, more specifically in a school or university setting, and with the best of wills, foreign language learning is frequently abandoned in anger and frustration or is altogether ignored and avoided?

In the 1970s, for the first time in the history of FL pedagogy, sustained efforts were made to grapple directly, by means of research methods, with basic questions of second language learning, that is, not simply by extrapolation from general studies of learning or of first language acquisition. There has of course always been much debate and speculation about the effectiveness of different teaching methods, the right starting age for languages, the importance of a natural aptitude for languages, and so on. But apart from Carroll's studies on language aptitude and the work of Lambert and Gardner on attitude and motivation, which began in the 1950s, the characteristics of the second language learner and the nature of the second language learning process have hardly been investigated in any direct way and have remained a mystery. As late as 1972 Rivers pointed to "the need for us as teachers to know as much as we possibly can about the way the student learns and learns language" (113, p.73), and in the same context Stern advised that language teachers "should press for sorely needed direct research on the psychology of second language learning" (130, p.xi).

Around this time second language learning was suddenly "discovered" by a considerable number of researchers as an important and uncharted area of investigation, and the upsurge of research between 1972 and 1978 was truly amazing.

Language learning research in the early 1970s, in line with the general trend of development, strongly reacted against the pedagogy of the 1960s. Turning away from the frustrating debate on language teaching methods and the inconclusive research on these, investigators resolutely focused on learning and the learner. Their ambition was to discover the natural sequences through which second language learning would pass and, hopefully, to discover similarities in the order of language acquisition in first and second language learning. The subjects of research were frequently young children learning a second language in their social environment, learners whose language development occurred in bilingual settings, or learners who belonged to linguistic minorities or who had come to North America as immigrants or students. Consequently, it was not so much the learning of foreign languages that was the main target of research as the learning of a second language in its natural environment outside formal language instruction.

In certain ways this approach to L2 research was fortunate, in others it was unfortunate. It was fortunate in that it placed foreign language learning into a context of language learning in which the common elements of all forms of language acquisition are beginning to be recognized: foreign language learning in the school setting in the specific sense, e.g., French and German in schools or colleges in the U.S.A.; untutored or "free" second language learning by immigrants or migrant workers, e.g., Mexican migrant workers in California, Spanish Gastarbeiter in West Germany; second language learning of language minorities learning the majority language and maintaining their first language, e.g., Navahos in the United States, Ukranians in Alberta; language learning in multiple language situations across the world, e.g., the multilingualism of Nigeria, Zambia, or India; learning the standard language in situations of bidialectism, e.g., the accommodation of education to Black English in the United States or to Creole in the West Indies.

Language teaching as a profession has always been fragmented. English mother tongue educators, speech educators, teachers in bilingual education, and foreign language teachers at schools and universities with few exceptions (e.g., Perren, 105, 106) even today do not sufficiently recognize the common features of all language learning, and the research of the 1970s that has boldly stepped across the compartmentalizations of the language teaching profession has given a salutory shock to various "establishments."

On the other hand, the research approach has been unfortunate because a unified research strategy was not deliberately developed. And as the main emphasis was on "free," "natural," "undirected" second language learning, foreign language learning in a classroom setting—with a few notable exceptions—has still been rather neglected as an object of inquiry. A regrettable outcome of this development has been that language teaching has been subtly denigrated by research.

In spite of this imbalance in the research effort from the perspective of foreign language teaching, language learning research was in a lucky streak. For some years, many of the investigators working on problems of second language learning met regularly at the annual TESOL convention, and a network of fruitful collaboration evolved. An early stock-taking took place at Ann Arbor in 1975. The papers of this meeting on language learning research were published in a special issue of *Language Learning* (Brown, 12). A series of nineteen Working Papers on Bilingualism, initiated by Merrill Swain of the OISE Modern Language Centre in 1973, provided a forum for the growing research on second language learning between 1973 and 1979 (Swain and Harley, 140). *TESOL Quarterly* and the annual proceedings of the TESOL convention gave expression to the growing interest of this association in language learning research. *Language Learning,* among established journals, and several new reviews, particularly *SLANT (Second Language Acquisition Notes and Topics), Interlanguage Studies Bulletin,* and *Workpapers in TESL,* have reflected the increasing interest in this area. *Applied Linguistics, Applied Psycholinguistics,* and the *Journal of Multilingual and Multicultural Development*—all three to begin publication in Britain this year—are likely to continue to give attention to this research direction. Several books offer an excellent record of the developing thought and research preoccupations: e.g., Oller and Richards, *Focus on the Learner* (97), Richards, *Error Analysis* (108) and *Understanding Second and Foreign Language Learning: Issues and Approaches* (110), Hatch, *Second Language Acquisition: A Book of Readings* (71), McLaughlin, *Second Language Acquisition in Childhood* (86), and Gingras, *Second Language Acquisition and Foreign Language Teaching* (62).

In retrospect the 1970s can be recognized as a period in which serious attempts were made to investigate by empirical methods second language learning and bilingual development in some of its manifestations, to establish areas of research, to develop research procedures, to construct theoretical models and identify essential concepts. Advances have been made, but many controversial issues remain; and on a number of questions that are crucial to the FL teacher, we are as ignorant or uncertain today as we were ten or twenty years ago.

In taking stock and reviewing the current "state of the art" on second language learning research as it has developed during the past decade and suggesting a few directions in which we believe research should now go, we are convinced that research is an essential condition of any major advances in language teaching and learning. But research is not something that will be handed to foreign language teachers ready-made at a certain point. It is a cooperative undertaking in which teachers have an important a role to perform as the researchers themselves. It is not merely a question of disseminating research findings, important though this may be. It is much more a question of a "research attitude" adopted by all the participants in language education. Without interaction between researcher and practitioner, research on language learning cannot be expected to be very successful.

Terminology

As a general term for non-native language learning we use the term *second language* (*L2*) learning or acquisition. In contrasting native and target learning in any setting, we will use the terms *native* and *target* language (*NL* and *TL*). Where it is important to indicate that the L2 is a language geographically removed, we refer to it as a foreign language (*FL*), and where the L2 is used in the learner's environment we use the term *second language* in the more specific sense, abbreviated *SL*.

Models of second language learning

The increasing volume of research during the past decade has given rise to many models of second language learning (e.g., Bialystock, 11; Clément, 26; Cummins, 32; Gardner, 52; Krashen, 76; Naiman et al, 89; Schumann, 118, 119). The purpose and generalizability of these models varies considerably; some are designed to give expression to a specific theoretical perspective, whereas others are more taxonomic in character; most are limited in the range of second language learning situations to which they are applicable. However, at a very general level all these models are designed to bring coherence to the research findings and to provide directions for future research.

It is outside the scope of this chapter to examine the models in detail. Rather, we shall consider the recent research findings that have given rise to these models in the context of the framework outlined in Figure 1. This framework does not embody any one particular theoretical perspective and is sufficiently general to allow us to examine most of the factors that have been highlighted by other investigators.

The framework identifies three categories of variables—*social context, learning conditions, learner characteristics*—which affect the *process* and *outcomes* of second language learning. Two sets of factors directly affect the learning process. These are the characteristics of the individual learner and the immediate conditions under which the learner experiences contact with the second language. The learning conditions and learner characteristics are both influenced by the wider social context. For example, the amount of time devoted to the second language in school is likely to be a function of the importance attached to it at a societal level. The learning of French as a second

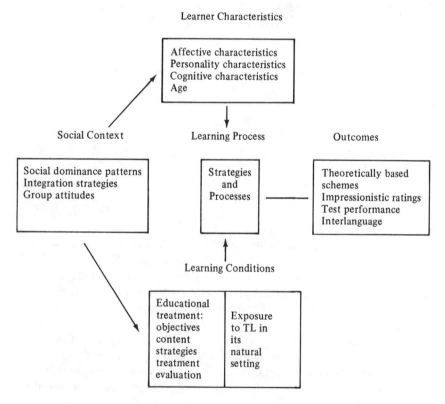

Figure 1. Framework for Examination of Second Language Learning

language in Canada is a good example. The attitudes of the individual learner are also obviously influenced by the intergroup processes in the wider social context.

The learning process can be looked upon as consisting overtly of strategies and techniques employed by the learner, and covertly of conscious and unconscious mental processes going on inside the learner. These are affected by the characteristics that the learner brings to the task as well as by the conditions under which the learner is exposed to the language. For example, certain strategies and techniques may be differentially effective in highly structured learning environments as compared to less structured environments.

Variations in second language learning outcomes have been conceptualized in a variety of ways ranging from conceptual schemes of proficiency through impressionistic ratings of proficiency to performance on formal discrete-point and integrative measures of proficiency and analysis of interlanguage patterns. These learning outcomes are examined in the next section.

Learning outcomes: Proficiency as a goal and a fact ⎯⎯⎯⎯

Beginning at the extreme right-hand end of Figure 1, the researcher, like everyone else concerned with L2 learning, is interested in learning outcomes. Teachers, administrators, curriculum developers, and test constructors must define proficiency levels as objectives or as standards by which to assess performance. For research, the objectives or standards serve as criteria against which to judge the effect of the various factors that will be considered in subsequent sections; context variables, learner variables, learning conditions, and learning processes. Research is also interested in the actual performance in the L2 as an indicator of proficiency reached by individuals or groups.

During the past decade, researchers have begun to examine the performance of language learners, not just to correct it, as had been done previously, but in order to understand its underlying mechanism. Research, therefore, has studied and described the "learner's language" as accurately and objectively as possible, and it has also tried to account for it by relating it to some of the factors indicated in the diagram.

Throughout this period, a good deal of thought went into interpretation of proficiency both as a desired outcome and as an empirical fact. Some of this thinking was contributed by course designers and test constructors, and some by researchers. Interesting conceptualizations have resulted from these different endeavors; unfortunately they do not always match up with one another, and it is not surprising to find that practitioners are somewhat confused by the discussions about proficiency in terms of behavioral or performance objectives, linguistic or communicative competence, transitional competence, interlanguage, learner's language, approximative systems, and the like. To bring together some of these different concepts into more coherent schemes of description of language proficiency appears to be one of the tasks for the 1980s. It is possible to distinguish several distinct approaches to the phenomenon of language proficiency that have characterized the past decade. These can be conceptualized in terms of a continuum ranging from theoretically based to more empirically based schemes.

Theoretically based conceptions of proficiency

Since the 1960s it has become increasingly clear that a simple classification of proficiency as the "four skills" of listening, speaking, reading, and writing is linguistically and educationally inadequate, particularly for test development. A great deal of work has been done over the past two decades to offer teachers, testers, and researchers theoretically more clearly defined, descriptively more differentiated, and practically more serviceable specifications of language proficiency (see, e.g., Carroll, 17).

One group of concepts defines proficiency as linguistic content. While until 1970 or so phonology, vocabulary, and grammar have dominated, the more recent definitions of proficiency include semantic, discourse, and sociolinguistic features. For example, Richards' analysis of proficiency (109) comprises not only grammatical well-formedness but also speech act rules, language functions, and language varieties. Proficiency is today emphatically expressed in communicative and not merely linguistic (i.e., grammatical) terms. But in defining the linguistic aspects of proficiency recent writers (e.g., Canale and Swain, 14) strongly emphasize that the stress on communication does *not* mean that the grammatical component of proficiency can be ignored. Richards rejects the idea that in all instances of language learning there is a single standard model of absolute proficiency with one unalterble set of rules. Thus if English is learned for intranational use in Africa and India, the phonological rules of British or American English may not apply to this proficiency model.

A second set of concepts is psychological or behavioral. (Figure 2). The descriptions of proficiency on this dimension cover very abstract concepts such as competence (linguistic or communicative) or more concrete descriptions of language activities in the familiar terms of the "intralingual" skills, listening, speaking, reading and writing, and the "crosslingual" or "mediating" skills of interpreting and translating; and at the most concrete level, proficiency is described through detailed inventories of language items, situations, psychological roles of the speaker, speech functions, appropriate semantic categories, and topics. The more abstract the specification of proficiency, the more widely applicable it is likely to be. The more detailed and concrete it is, the more restricted it is in its application.

For example, in the recent formulation by Canale and Swain (14) for the

Figure 2. Aspects of L2 Proficiency: Levels of Abstraction

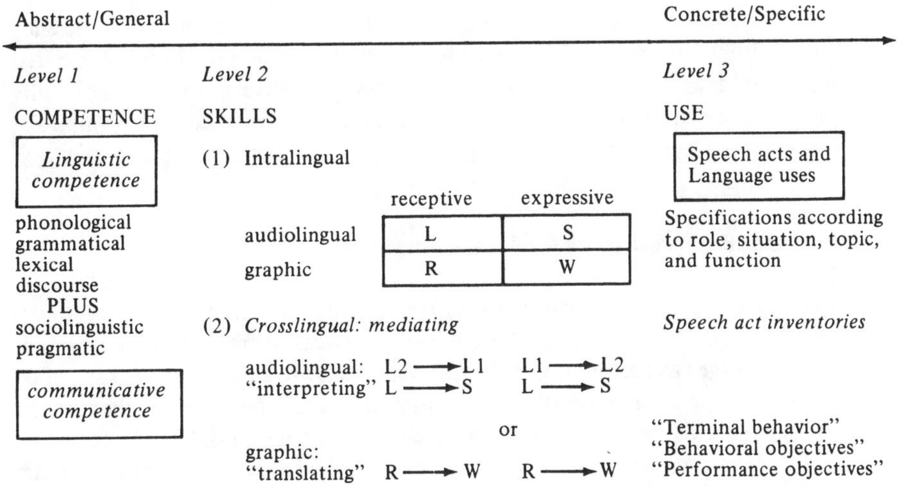

Abstract/General   Concrete/Specific

Level 1	*Level 2*	*Level 3*
COMPETENCE	SKILLS	USE

Linguistic competence	(1) Intralingual			Speech acts and Language uses
		receptive	expressive	
phonological grammatical lexical discourse	audiolingual	L	S	Specifications according to role, situation, topic, and function
	graphic	R	W	
PLUS sociolinguistic pragmatic	(2) *Crosslingual: mediating*			*Speech act inventories*
	audiolingual: L2 ⟶ L1 L1 ⟶ L2			
	"interpreting" L ⟶ S L ⟶ S			
communicative competence			or	"Terminal behavior"
	graphic:			"Behavioral objectives"
	"translating" R ⟶ W R ⟶ W			"Performance objectives"

purpose of test development, proficiency has been interpreted as communicative competence and analyzed into

1 grammatical competence
2 sociolinguistic competence
3 strategic competence, i.e., the learner's ability to compensate for problems in communication.

By contrast the Council of Europe's Threshold Level scheme for EFL (van Ek, 147) and *Niveau Seuil* (Coste et al, 31), which offers a specification of English and French language learning objectives, defined proficiency in the concrete detail of a syllabus of items useful for identifiable groups of learners, e.g., travelers temporarily in contact with the TL community.

A recent example of a definition of proficiency in curricular terms is offered by Allen (1) who has combined three elements of proficiency in a new language curriculum scheme. According to Allen, a language learner's curriculum should include: 1) a *structural* element, i.e., phonological and grammatical features of the language must be represented; 2) a *functional* element, i.e., the curriculum must advance beyond the sentence and include functional, speech act, and discourse aspects; and 3) an *instrumental* or *experimental* element, i.e., a curriculum must offer applications of the language in a real-life context where the language is used for communication. Proficiency in this scheme is therefore interpreted as structural, functional, and experiential-communicative.

A third categorization that comprises the behavioral and linguistic content categories is that of stages or levels of L2 proficiency. One such scheme, developed by Wilkins (150), involves seven levels, each of which is described in terms of listening, speaking, reading, and writing. Some Council of Europe scholars also suggested a seven-point scale ranging from "survival," "way-stage," and "threshold" to an ambilingual level (Trim, 143).

The schemes we have so far described illustrate definitions of proficiency based either on theoretical considerations or on expressions of desired outcomes. It must, however, be stressed that they have not been empirically arrived at or in most cases empirically tested. A somewhat more empirical approach has been used to develop descriptive rating scales or proficiency.

Description of proficiency levels on rating scales

Working on the assumption that proficiency ranges from zero to full bilingual proficiency, it is possible on the basis of practical knowledge of learners at different stages to define stages of proficiency that are appropriate for specified purposes. One of the best-known rating scales of this kind is that of the Foreign Service Institute and the Defense Language Institute. Such rating scales are commonly divided in terms of communicative skills into listening, speaking, reading, and writing skills; and they often fulfill a dual function. From one point of view they indicate standards expected for given purposes. For example, for certain government positions, (e.g., in the diplomatic service) standards of speaking, reading, or writing by reference to a rating scale can be specified. This is the task that the FSI rating scales have had to perform. From a more empirical point of view, rating scales can be used as descriptions or analyses of levels reached by second language learners. They can also be used by learners for self-assessment (Naiman et al, 89, Oskarsson, 99).

The difficulties in establishing sound rating scales have been perceptively analyzed by Mareschal (83) on the basis of considerable experience with establishing language norms in the Canadian public service. He points out that some rating scales of proficiency indiscriminately mix up descriptions in terms of social functions (e.g., "can meet and guide visitors") with linguistic criteria (e.g., "has a good command of the tense system").

Another problem with rating scales to which Trim (143) has drawn attention arises exactly from the double duty such scales frequently perform: as descriptions of performance levels and as objectives to be aimed at. Thus the levels of pronunciation on a 5-point proficiency rating scale can legitimately be expressed as a set of descriptors of typical learners' pronunciation in the following manner:

Level 1   often unintelligible
Level 2   usually foreign but rarely unintelligible
Level 3-4   sometimes foreign but always intelligible
Level 5   native.

However, such a scale would hardly serve as a definition of objectives in teaching pronunciation. At Level One, a teacher would not set out to make his or her students' pronunciation "often unintelligible." For an expression of expected outcomes or objectives, the proficiency levels must be expressed in positive terms of what one would wish the learner to be able to do. Nevertheless, rating scales provide very useful impressionistic descriptions of typical stages and of the development of proficiency from minimal to advanced levels, and they can usually claim to be based on practical experience with different levels of language performance.

Proficiency as measured by formal tests

Standard language proficiency tests, such as the MLA Co-operative tests or the IEA French and English tests, imply a conception of proficiency that is based on empirical data. In language proficiency testing, discrete-point tests are usually distinguised from integrative tests. The former involve separate assessment of different aspects of proficiency, usually by means of multiple-choice items. Many linguists (e.g., Oller, 91; Shuy, 122) have objected to discrete-point tests on the grounds that they assess language proficiency out of a naturally occurring context and assume that different components of language performance can be isolated from each other. Integrative tests, such as the cloze test and dictation, on the other hand, are intended to assess language proficiency in a holistic way. Language performance is not isolated from natural contexts to the same extent as in discrete-point tests.

Although there is a clear theoretical distinction between these two types of tests, Farhady (45) has recently reviewed a considerable body of data that suggests that this theoretical distinction does not have any empirical reality. In summarizing this evidence on the "disjunctive fallacy" he states:

> The preponderance of evidence presented in this paper seems to support the hypothesis that there is virtually no difference between discrete-point and integrative tests in what they measure or their results (p. 354).

What is the nature of the language proficiency measured by discrete-point and integrative tests? Oller (90, 91) has argued that "there exists a global language proficiency factor which accounts for the bulk of the reliable variance in a wide variety of language proficiency measures" (90, p. 413). Elsewhere he states that ". . . possibly all language skills are based on a rather unitary proficiency factor. . . ." Oller presents considerable evidence that this factor is strongly related to IQ and to academic achievement.

Several investigators have disputed Oller's conclusions (e.g., Cummins, 33; Palmer and Bachman, 102; Vollmer, 148). Cummins (34) suggests that it is possible to distinguish a convincing weak form and a less convincing strong form of Oller's arguments. The weak form is that there exists a dimension of language proficiency that can be assessed by a variety of reading, writing, listening, and speaking tests and that is strongly related both to general cognitive skills (Spearman's *g*) and to academic achievement. The strong form is that this dimension represents the central core (in an absolute sense) of all that is meant by proficiency in a language. The difficulty with this strong position is immediately obvious when one considers that with the exception of severely retarded and autistic children, everybody acquires basic interpersonal communicative skills in a first language regardless of IQ or academic aptitude.

For these reasons Cummins (33) suggests the term *cognitive/academic language proficiency* (CALP) in place of Oller's *global language proficiency* to refer to the dimension of language proficiency measured by most discrete-point and integrative tests, which is strongly related to overall cognitive and academic skills. He also presents evidence that measures of L1 CALP are strongly related to measures of L2 CALP and argues that L1 and L2 CALP are interdependent.

Genesee (58) has presented evidence that standardized measures of the cognitive/academic aspects of language proficiency may be only weakly related to proficiency as assessed by rating scales. He tested anglophone students in grades four, seven, and eleven in French immersion and regular French programs in Montreal on a battery of French language tests. He reported that although IQ was strongly related to the development of academic French language skills (reading, grammar, vocabulary, and so forth), it was, with one exception, unrelated to ratings of French oral productive skills at any grade level.

Palmer and Bachman (102) have also obtained evidence for the distinctness of speaking and reading traits among university level ESL learners which they suggest is contrary to Oller's unitary competence model.

In summary, the use of formal tests as criterion measures of second language proficiency may primarily assess those aspects of proficiency that overlap with general cognitive and academic skills. Other aspects of communicative or functional proficiency may not be adequately assessed by these measures. In other words, language proficiency tests as presently devised seem to be able to capture an important aspect of proficiency, the cognitive-academic component, but the interpersonal and communicative component, which should also be represented in a definition of proficiency, has so far not been adequately represented in most language tests at our disposal. Efforts are underway to include this important component in assessments of TL proficiency (see Canale and Swain, 14).

Interlanguage studies

A fourth approach to the interpretation of proficiency consists of a whole area of research that has been vigorously pursued over the past ten years or so:

interlanguage studies. Researchers are encouraged to look closely at what language learners actually do, i.e., their performance in the L2. It is the most theoretically developed and at the same time the most empirically investigated approach to the study of L2 proficiency. A few articles were seminal, particularly one by Corder (30), which suggested that one should attempt to discover the learner's "built-in syllabus," and another by Selinker (121), which described the proficiency of a second language learner as a linguistic system or "interlanguage" in its own right somewhere between the learner's native language and the target language. Selinker attempted to explain the mechanism that would account for the errors and other interlanguage phenomena. These explanations have constituted productive hypotheses for subsequent investigations on interlanguage.

Many investigators during this period have theorized about the nature, lawfulness, and changes of the interlanguage. Specific aspects of learner language development have been recorded and analyzed. The fluctuating nature of the emerging language systems has varyingly been described as "transitional competence," "approximative system," "idiosyncratic dialect," or simply as "learner language" (Corder, 28, 29).

Errors that in the language teaching theories of the 1960s were seen as signals for better pedagogical grading were recognized in the 1970s as inevitable in the development of L2 proficiency and as valuable aspects of learning: "you can't learn without goofing" (Dulay and Burt, 41). For research, errors were also an indispensible data base in the study of the learner's language. In many of these investigations, the researchers closely studied the appearance of particular grammatical features and their subsequent development in the learner's repertoire, e.g., morphemes, question forms, or the use of the auxiliary; they used the findings to answer some general questions about the nature of second language learning and indeed about the nature of language in general.

A thorough and perceptive review of much of this research was made by Hatch (70), who also tried to estimate to what extent these studies have in fact answered the questions interlanguage research set out to answer. Hatch discusses ten such questions about interlanguage research and, through a review of the most important syntax studies, attempts to estimate the present state of knowledge. Hatch's questions and answers can be summarized as follows:

Questions	*Answers*
1 "Is interlanguage real (systematic) or is it just a cover tem for random fluctuation. . . ?" (p.35)	"While there is a good deal of argument about the degree of systematicity. . ." the move from the beginning stages to fluency is not random (p.60).
2 If interlanguage is systematic, what is the system? How much variability is there?	While each learner's interlanguage may develop systematically, the system is not invariant.

3 If there is a sequence is it the same regardless of the learner's NL?

The answer to this question is not clear: there are differences of opinion about transfer or interference from the NL.

4 "Is the sequence the same for child and adult learners?" (p.35)

Yes, the same systematicity and variability are observed in child and adult learners (p.61).

5 "Is the sequence the same if the learner does/does not receive instruction?" (p.35)

No clear answer can be offered. "The literature which discusses the effect of instruction is weak. One reason is that ESL instruction, bilingual instruction, and monolingual instruction are seldom, if ever, operationally defined. We do not know what methods are involved or whether they are or are not mutually exclusive. Fairly strong claims have been made in favor of various programs. . . Fairly strong claims have been made that instruction has no effect on learning though it may have some effect on speed of learning. Hopefully, much more careful research can be done in the future" (p.61).

6 "Is the sequence the same if the learner is immersed, submersed or not mersed at all" in the L2 community? (p.35)

Children who received their education in the L2 ("immersion" or "submersion") learn more than those who receive FL instruction.

7 "If there is a sequence in second language acquisition is it the same as that described for first language acquisition?" (p.35)

No clear answer emerges. Claims and counterclaims have been made. "Similarities are there, but differences have also been shown" and explained on grounds of greater cognitive maturity and the influence of L1 on L2 (p.61).

8 If there is a sequence, can a level be defined which a learner might be expected to reach after X amount of instruction?

No. Variations in time needed must be expected. Generally, adolescents and adults learn faster *initially* (pp. 61 –62). (See p. 218 below.)

9 "If there is a sequence, is it the same as the pedagogical sequence given in language textbooks?" (p. 35)

Only approximately: "Pedagogical sequence is similar in some respects to the natural order of acquisition of structures, but pedagogical sequence has to be based on many other criteria as well" (p.62).

10 "If there is a sequence, and if that sequence appears to be similar across learners, how can we explain it?" (p.35)

Many variables—interaction with others, personal factors, instruction, etc.—are important. But we know too little to offer definitive explanations (pp. 62–66).

The main issue of the debate arising from interlanguage studies has been whether a second language learner develops L2 by a process of restructuring L1 (the Restructuring Hypothesis), or whether L2 is developed independently, rather in the manner in which a child "creates" his or her first language (the Creative Construction Hypothesis). On the basis of her review, Hatch finds no clear evidence for either theory as accounting entirely for the L2 development, a view of the learner's language which seems to be shared by Corder in the same volume (29).

Much of the research has been concerned as yet only with linguistic minutiae in the development of a second language. The hope of understanding the interlanguage of learners in its totality, the successive stages of interlanguage, the development of proficiency at different age levels and under different conditions of learning from a hypothetical zero to an advanced stage, is far from being fulfilled.

Conclusion on proficiency

In future research on proficiency in second language learning, the four approaches briefly sketched above—theoretical conceptions, rating scales, formal proficiency tests, and interlanguage research—no doubt could complement each other and serve as progressive approximations to arrive at a more definitive picture of the development of proficiency in second language learners. The conceptual schemes should serve as hypotheses of desirable alternative descriptions of possible outcomes. Rating scales could offer impressionistic, global accounts of different stages of proficiency. Formal proficiency tests may be most useful in academic learning contexts but may assess only one of several aspects of second language proficiency. Interlanguage studies could be made so as to obtain concrete data on the development of proficiency. In the study of language learning, descriptive statements of the growth of second language learning and its vicissitudes from low levels to advanced levels of proficiency are of paramount importance.

The social context in L2 acquisition

Turning now to the box on the left hand side of Figure 1, one can see clearly that students learning a second language inevitably find themselves in a certain political, cultural, and sociolinguistic milieu which exerts a major influence on their attitudes towards the target language group and on their motivation to learn the TL. Although interethnic relations have long been the concern of sociologists (e.g., Coons et al, 27; Schermerhorn, 116) it is only recently that problems of second language acquisition have begun to be systematically studied in this connection (Clément, 26; Fishman, 48; Gardner, 52; Paulston, 103; Schumann, 118; Skutnabb-Kangas & Toukomaa, 124).

Probably the most radical approach to the influence of social and psychological factors on L2 acquisition is Schumann's "acculturation" model (118). Acculturation refers to the social and psychological integration of the learner with the TL group. Schumann argues that second language acquisition is "just one aspect of acculturation and the degree to which a learner acculturates to the TL group will control the degree to which he acquires the second language" (p.34). In addition to instructional variables, individual cognitive variables such as aptitude are regarded by Schumann as "so weak in terms of the total language learning situation that no matter how much we attempt to change them we will never achieve much more success than we are achieving now" (p.47). His position illustrates the potential importance of the social context in L2 acquisition, and it has received considerable attention in the recent literature on foreign language learning (e.g., Gingras, 62), probably because of its radical implications for attempts to teach foreign languages. We feel these implications justify considering his position in some detail, although the empirical evidence relating directly to the influence of social factors is, as yet, sparse.

The social factors discussed by Schumann (118) that appear to have most relevance for L2 acquisition are social dominance patterns, integration strategies, and group attitudes. These three factors will be briefly considered in order to illustrate the basis of his position.

Social dominance patterns refer to the fact that higher status groups will tend not to learn the language of lower status groups. For example, colonial groups have seldom learned the language of the colonized. Thus, during the days of the British Empire, Britons in India and Africa did not need to learn the languages of India and Africa. Another example is the fact that until 1960, the economically dominant English Canadians in Quebec tended to acquire only minimal French skills despite the fact that French speakers represented a large majority within the province. But sociopolitical changes in Canada during the past twenty years have changed the status of French not only in Quebec but throughout Canada; and these changes have also led to an increase in the study of French as a second language. The role of social dominance factors and of language prestige can be illustrated further by contrasting the rapid expansion of French immersion programs across Canada during the past decade with the fact that Spanish and French immersion programs are still extremely rare in the United States.

Related to social dominance patterns are the *integration* strategies of assimilation, preservation, and adaptation, which a subordinate group might adopt in relation to the superordinate group. If a second language learning group *assimilates,* then it gives up its own life-style and values and adopts those of the TL group. According to Schumann, this strategy maximizes contact between the two groups and enhances acquisition of the TL. Clearly, this strategy involves a negative evaluation of the status of the L1 group in comparison to that of the TL group.

Preservation, on the other hand, involves maintenance of the group's own life-style and values and rejection of those of the TL group. Schumann suggests that the resultant social distance between the groups makes TL acquisition unlikely.

The third strategy involves *adaptation* to the life-style and values of the TL group but maintenance of the group's own values and life-style for intragroup use. According to Schumann, adaptation yields varying degrees of contact between the two groups and thus varying degrees of TL acquisition.

These strategies have recently been investigated by Taylor et al. (142) among francophones learning English in Quebec. Degree of contact with the anglophone community was the major predictor of university students' self-assessed English proficiency. However, students' perceived threat to group identity or fear of assimilation was also a significant predictor. Students who felt their identity as francophones threatened learned less English than those who did not fear assimilation. Clément (26) has also reported a negative relationship between Quebec francophones' fear of assimilation and integrative motivation for learning English. He suggests that important determinants of these two forces are the relative "ethnolinguistic vitality" of the first and second cultural groups. Ethnolinguistic vitality is defined by Giles et al. (61) as "that which makes a group likely to behave as a distinctive and active collective entity in intergroup situations" (p.308). Clément argues that "hypothetically 'integrativeness' might be related to the attractiveness or ethnolinguistic vitality of the second culture. Fear of assimilation, on the other hand, might be a negative function of the vitality of the first culture" (26, p.5).

Closely related to these integration strategies are the *attitudes* of the groups towards each other. L2 acquisition is more likely to occur when groups are positively rather than negatively disposed towards each other. Intergroup attitudes are likely to primarily reflect perceived status of the groups.

Schumann (118) discusses other social factors such as enclosure, cohesion, and intended length of residence which need not be considered here. We feel that, at the level of group processes, Schumann's emphasis on acculturation or what we would prefer to term "motivated contact," is well founded and has important implications for foreign language learning. Specifically, the acculturation concept reiterates the importance both of extensive contact with the TL and motivation on the part of the learner to internalize the TL input.

These factors undoubtedly play a major role in learning foreign languages in classrooms as well as in naturalistic environments. However, the significance of "acculturation" or "motivated contact" in accounting for *interethnic group* differences in L2 acquisition in no way implies that other types of factors may not be equally or more significant in accounting for differences in L2 acquisition between *individuals* or between groups exposed to different instructional conditions. This is clear from an examination of recent research in these areas.

Individual learner factors

Investigators have usually distinguished at least three categories of individual learner factors that are presumed to influence L2 acquisition. *Cognitive* dimensions that have been investigated include such overlapping variables as intelligence, language aptitude, L1 proficiency, and cognitive style. The *affective* variables of attitudes and motivation have continued to receive considerable attention in the literature whereas *personality* variables such as ego-permeability, extroversion/introversion, etc., have been investigated only sporadically. We shall examine recent research findings regarding the effects of each of these sets of variables in turn, starting with the affective factors since these are directly determined by the social factors considered in the previous section.

Affective factors

Much of the research and theorizing about the role of affective factors in L2 acquisition during the past 20 years has centered around the distinction between integrative and instrumental motivational orientations introduced by Gardner and Lambert (55). Second language learners who are integratively oriented are "psychologically prepared to adopt various aspects of behavior which characterize members of another linguistic cultural group" (Gardner & Lambert, 53, p.3). For learners who are instrumentally oriented, on the other hand, the main motivation for learning the language is utilitarian, such as career advancement.

In a recent critique of research on the measurement of affective variables, Oller (92) has distinguished four stages through which this research has passed. The first stage involved the relatively unelaborated claim that positive feelings towards the TL community would result in faster L2 acquisition. This view was supported by the initial research relating to the integrative-instrumental distinction which seemed to show that integrative orientations were more effective than instrumental orientations in promoting successful L2 acquisition (Gardner & Lambert, 53).

In the second stage distinguished by Oller, the possibility that L2 achievement might actually be the cause rather than the effect was raised by several investigators (e.g., Burstall et al., 13; Savignon, 115). In other words, successful L2 learners might develop positive attitudes towards the L2 group as a result of doing well, whereas unsuccessful learners might develop negative attitudes.

The third stage was characterized by inconsistent findings in regard to the effects of integrative and instrumental orientations. Oller points out that the empirical studies reported by Gardner and Lambert showed that in some settings successful learning was associated with the integrative orientation, in others with the instrumental orientation, while in others there was no contrast. Studies have also shown that the effects of the two motivational orientations vary with the setting (e.g., Burstall et al., 13; Oller et al., 93). A further difficulty was that motivational orientations were highly correlated with each other (Burstall et al., 13; Gardner, 52).

Oller (92) suggests that perhaps the most important conclusion to be drawn from this stage of research was that the relation between affective variables and learning must be dynamic and bi-directional.

The fourth stage distinguished by Oller (92) involves the attempt by Gardner (52) to resolve the apparent inconsistencies by incorporating the findings into a model where the social milieu is assumed to determine learners' attitudes that determine motivational orientation and intensity that, in turn, determine achievement. In attempting to link the social milieu to learners' motivational orientations, Gardner (52) suggests that "additive" language learning situations, where members of high status language groups add an L2 to their repertoire of skills at no cost to L1 proficiency (Lambert, 79), may give rise to an integrative orientation towards learning; on the other hand, instrumental orientations are more likely in "subtractive" situations where minority language groups tend to replace L1 by a more prestigious L2. Oller (92), however, cites Genesee's finding (59) that anglophones learning French in Montreal (an "additive" situation) were more instrumentally oriented as evidence contrary to Gardner's hypothesis.

This apparent contradiction seems to arise from the fact that the additive/subtractive distinction is too simplistic. The relationships between motivational orientation and social milieu emerge more clearly when considered in the context of the relative ethnolinguistic vitality of the two groups. Specifically, when a group's ethnolinguistic vitality is higher or as high as that of the TL group as is the case in additive situations, there is generally no instrumental necessity to acquire the TL; therefore, integrative motivation is likely to predominate and influence the L2 acquisition process. However, Genesee's findings (59) can be explained by the fact that, although the language learning situation for anglophones in Quebec is still additive in that there is no danger of replacing L1 by L2, the recent policy changes by the Quebec government have increased the vitality of French in the province to such an extent that it is now economically and socially necessary for anglophones in Quebec to learn French. Thus, it is not surprising that an instrumental orientation should predominate at the present time.

When a group's ethnolinguistic vitality is lower than that of the TL group (i.e., when the TL group is dominant) instrumental motivation is likely to be strongly in evidence because acquisition of the TL is likely to be a prerequisite for economic advancement. However, other motivational forces may also be involved. For example, the learner may also be integratively motivated and wish to assimilate with the dominant group. As pointed out by Clément (26) and by Taylor et al. (142), the instrumental motives for learning the TL may also be accompanied by a negative motivational orientation in the form of "fear of assimilation." Under these circumstances the individual is likely to institute strategies for emphasizing "psychological distinctiveness" (Giles et al., 61), and L2 acquisition will progress only to the point where instrumental needs can be fulfilled.

As this brief sketch illustrates, the relationships between the social milieu and individual motivational orientations are more complex than suggested by Gardner's (52) linking of integrative orientation with additive social milieux and instrumental orientation with subtractive milieux. It is likely that research in the coming decade will continue to explore these relationships.

However, Oller (92) points to a serious problem for future research in the area of affective influences on L2 acquisition. As a result of inconsistent findings in five studies dealing with motivational variables in L2 acquisition (6,25,93,94,96), Oller and his colleagues were led to question the validity of the self-report and questionnaire measures used to assess affective variables. Specifically, Oller (92) and Oller and Perkins (95) argue that the motivational and attitudinal measures used by Gardner and other investigators may, in reality, be tapping a language intelligence factor directly, though weakly. Oller (92) also argues that Gardner's attitudinal scales (52) are assessing very much the same dimension as the motivation index. Tucker (144) agrees with the cautions raised by Oller concerning the reliability and validity of measures of affective variables but points out that the evidence is not conclusive that these measures are in fact weak measures of language abilities.

The issues raised by Oller in relation to the measurement of affective variables could be thought of as signaling a fifth stage in the debate about the influence of affective variables on L2 acquisition. The problem of validly measuring affective variables as well as the lack of an adequate theory for predicting the relationships between the social milieu and individual affective variables represent the major obstacles to progress in this area.

Further evidence that all is not well in the study of the "affective domain" comes from a recent enquiry on the effect of bilingual exhange programs between students in French-speaking Quebec and English-speaking Ontario. In this study students were given attitude questionnaires, similar to those used by Gardner and his colleagues before and after the exchange, and they were interviewed after the exchange. While attitude measures show a slight change of attitude in a positive direction, the interviews suggest that the participants do not spontaneously produce the stereotypes of the kind included in attitude tests, but express an affective response to their immediate experience, and expressly refuse to generalize about the characteristics of anglophones and francophones (Hanna et al., 68).

Personality

Intuitively, one would expect personality variables to be related to foreign language learning. For example, teachers have suggested that the outgoing, friendly and talkative student is more successful in L2 learning (e.g., Gardner, 52; Valette, 146). However, research to date has failed to demonstrate consistent links between TL achievement and personality characteristics of the learner. The causes of this lack of consistent findings are very similar to those noted in the sphere of affective factors, namely, the complex interactions among social context, language contact conditions, and learner characteristics, combined with difficulties in validly measuring personality characteristics.

Many of the recent studies in this area have been conducted in Canada. For example, Tucker et al. (145) investigated personality traits associated with success in learning French among three groups of grade seven students in Montreal. One group ("early immersion") had been in a French immersion program since kindergarten; the second ("late immersion") had been in a regular program up to grade seven, with French as a subject of instruction for one period a day; in grade seven, however, all their instruction was in French except for English Language Arts. The third group ("regular") was in a conventional program with French SL as a subject from kindergarten through grade seven. Tucker et al. report that:

> There were important interaction effects between group membership and personality traits for the two expressive interpersonal skills—listening comprehension and oral production. In particular, success for students in the one-year late immersion program (Group 2) seems to be associated with being adventuresome and attempting to utilize French in the community. This cluster of traits seems less important as a predictor of success for students from the early immersion program who have been using French over a period of eight years (145, p. 225).

Swain and Burnaby (139) reported that "perfectionist tendencies" (as judged by teacher ratings) were strongly related to performance in French in the early grades of an immersion program. Other characteristics such as talkativeness and sociability were not related to French performance in either immersion or regular French-as-a-second-language (FSL) programs. In fact, these traits were negatively related to ability to understand French in the FSL program. Swain and Burnaby point out that these findings are contrary to the assumptions of many teachers and parents regarding the significance of the traits of sociability and talkativeness.

Genesee and Hamayan (60) report that grade 1 French immersion students who performed highly on measures of French achievement tended to be characterized by traits of "apprehensiveness." They suggest that this trait may be a positive influence on L2 learning because it derives from a concern to do well in French coupled with a fear of making mistakes.

In a study among high school students in French immersion and traditional FSL programs, Hamayan et al. (67) reported that high levels of "conformity" and "control" were associated with high French achievement in the FSL program but with low achievement in the immersion program. They interpret these results in relation to the different pedagogic emphases in the two programs. Specifically, the traits of "conformity" or "control" may be useful in the formal grammar-oriented FSL program but dysfunctional in the immersion program with its emphasis on experimentation and language use.

The traits of "inhibition" or "control" have been investigated from another perspective in the research of Guiora and his colleagues (64, 65). For example, Guiora et al. (65) reported that with the ingestion of one to one-and-one-half ounces of alcohol, foreign language pronunciation was better than in either the no alcohol or the two to three ounce conditions.

Several personality characteristics were investigated in Naiman et al. in their study of *The Good Language Learner* (89) among grades eight, ten, and twelve FSL students in Toronto, Canada. They reported that tolerance of ambiguity was a significant predictor of success in French in grade eight but not in grade ten or twelve. However, grade ten and twelve students were both significantly more tolerant of ambiguity than the grade eight students. They suggest that those students who have a high intolerance for ambiguity may have great difficulty in coping with the amount of ambiguity present in the second language classroom and therefore may drop the subject as soon as possible.

However, other personality tests administered in the Naiman study were unrelated to success in learning French. The researchers suggest that this may have been due to lack of construct validity in the tests. Specifically, they found gross discrepancies between students' results on tests of Extroversion and Sensitivity to Rejection and what students reported in interviews with the investigators. Therefore, an alternative personality measure was constructed, based upon students' responses in the interview. This variable could be described as an indication by the student of his general classroom personality, including fear of being laughed at or being embarrassed when speaking, or not putting up his hand until he was certain he knew the response, etc. It was found that this measure was a better predictor of French achievement than were any of the other personality measures given, apart from intolerance of ambiguity.

The questionable construct validity of formal personality tests is undoubtedly a factor in explaining the lack of consistent results in this area. Also, as pointed out by several investigators, personality variables are likely to interact in complex ways with type of instructional program and age of the learner.

Cognitive factors

The cognitive variable most frequently investigated in relation to foreign language learning have been aptitude and IQ, but in recent years considerable interest has focused on other cognitive variables such as cognitive style and L1 proficiency. As pointed out by Gardner (52) studies have continued to demonstrate a strong relationship between measures of foreign language aptitude (e.g., the Modern Language Aptitude Test (MLAT, 21) and L2 achievement in formal classroom settings. Gardner and Lambert (54) for example, showed that MLAT subtest scores were related in predictable ways to specific second language skills.

The superiority of the MLAT over IQ in predicting TL course grades (Carroll and Sapon, 21) may be due to the fact that the MLAT measures a wider range of L2-related abilities than IQ does. For example, abilities such as "auditory alertness" and "phonetic coding," which Carroll and Sapon claimed were tapped by the MLAT, are not included in most IQ tests but are likely to be related to L2 comprehension and production skills. However, there appears to be little difference in the power of aptitude, L1 proficiency, and verbal IQ in predicting the cognitive/academic aspects of L2 proficiency. For example, in two studies conducted with grade three Irish children learning Irish as a second language, Cummins (33) reported correlations of .77 and .58 between English (L1) and Irish reading skills, .69 and .67 between the Elemtary MLAT (EMLAT) and Irish reading, and .76 and .74 between EMLAT and English reading. In seven other studies reviewed by Cummins (33) measures of L1 and L2 cognitive/academic proficiency and verbal IQ were highly correlated with each other. The strong relationship between measures of L1 proficiency and EMLAT is consistent with recent findings reported by Carroll (18) regarding the underlying abilities measured by three of the MLAT subtests, *Phonetic Script, Spelling Clues,* and *Words in Sentences.* Carroll reports that an L1 spelling dimension accounted for most of the variance on the first two subtests whereas *Words in Sentences* was highly related to measures of knowledge of grammatical functions, self-ratings of grammatical knowledge, and verbal reasoning. Thus, given the strong relationship between these measures and TL achievement, it is not surprising that measures of L1 and L2 achievement should also relate strongly to each other.

In order to explain the consistent relationships between L1 and L2 achievement, Cummins has hypothesized that cognitive/academic language proficiency is interdependent across languages but becomes increasingly differentiated from basic interpersonal communicative skills in the L1 and L2.

According to this interpretation, measures of language aptitude such as the MLAT may be particularly appropriate for predicting the full range of L2 component skills but may be no better than measures of L1 CALP or verbal IQ for measuring the cognitive/academic component of L2 proficiency (e.g., grammatical knowledge, reading ability, vocabulary).

Two recent studies (Genesee and Hamayan, 60; Naiman et al., 89) have investigated the relationships between the cognitive style dimension of field independence/field dependence (Witkin et al., 151) and second language learning. This dimension involves the ability to dissemble simple figures from larger, more complex wholes. Naiman et al. hypothesized that the more successful second language learner is the one who can focus on those language stimuli relevant to the task at hand and disregrad the inappropriate ones. They thus predicted that the field-independent individual would be more successful in second language learning and this prediction was supported in their study involving grades eight to twelve FSL students. However, measures of aptitude or IQ were not administered and thus it is not possible to say whether this relationship is specific to field independence or part of a more general relationship between cognitive variables and TL achievement. The same caution applied to the findings of Genesee and Hamayan (60), who reported a significant relationship between French achievements and a dimension involving measures of field independence and nonverbal IQ among grade one French immersion students. The fact that field independence has been found to be positively related to L1 verbal ability (de Fazio, 36) suggests that the field independence—L2 achievement relationship may reflect a more general involvement of cognitive abilities in second language learning in a school setting.

Age

The research findings regarding age and second language learning can be interpreted in the light of the preceding discussion. If measures of L1 and L2 cognitive/academic language proficiency are interdependent, then we would expect that older learners, whose L1 CALP is more highly developed, would acquire cognitive/academic L2 skills more rapidly than younger learners. However, this would not necessarily be the case for L2 interpersonal communicative skills since, as suggested by Genesee's findings (58), these may be largely independent of cognitive/academic skills.

An examination of the considerable number of recent studies relating age to L2 learning supports the prediction made above. These studies have consistently shown a clear advantage for older learners in mastery of L2 syntax and morphology as well as in the cognitive/academic types of L2 skills measured by conventional standardized tests (Appel, 5; Burstall et al., 13; Cummins, 33; Ekstrand, 42; Ervin-Tripp, 43; Fathman, 46; Genesee 56, 57;

Skutnabb-Kangas & Toukomaa, 124; Snow & Hoefnagel-Höhle, 125). Genesee (56) for example, has reported that grade eight students in Montreal who had spent six years in a conventional FSL program followed by two years in an intensive late immersion program were performing as well on all aspects of French proficiency tested as grade eight children who had been enrolled in an early French immersion program since kindergarten. In other words, despite considerably less total accumulated hours of exposure to French, the late immersion students quickly caught up with the early immersion students in French proficiency.

Older learners do not consistently show an advantage over younger learners in aspects of L2 proficiency directly related to interpersonal communication skills such as oral fluency, phonology, and listening comprehension (Asher & Garcia, 7; Asher & Price, 8; Ekstrand, 42; Fathman, 46; Oyama, 100, 101; Seliger et al., 120; Snow & Hoefnagel-Höhle, 125). For example, Oyama reported an advantage for younger immigrant learners (six–ten years old on arrival) on both productive phonology and listening comprehension tests whereas Snow and Hoefnagel-Höhle found that older learners performed better on measures of these skills. Ekstrand reports that oral production was the only variable on which older immigrant learners did not perform significantly better than younger learners.

Krashen et al. (78) suggest that the apparent inconsistencies can be resolved by distinguishing rate of L2 acquisition from level of ultimate attainment. Specifically, "adults and older children in general initially acquire the second language faster than young children (older is better for rate of acquisition), but child second language acquirers will usually be superior in terms of ultimate attainment (younger is better in the long run)" (p. 574). Genesee (57) similarly concludes that older children and adults are more efficient L2 learners but the greater amount of time available to younger learners may give them an advantage in the long run.

In summary, there appears to be a high degree of consensus among researchers that older learners acquire at least the cognitive/academic aspects of L2 more rapidly than younger learners. This finding is contrary to the popular opinion that younger learners have an advantage all-round and that there may even be an optimal pre-pubertal age range for L2 acquisition. The immediate implication for foreign language pedagogy is that the advantage of extra time associated with an early start must be weighed against the greater efficiency of the older learner. Other factors that have not been systematically investigated in recent research should also be borne in mind. For example, complex interactions are possible between age, affective factors, instructional conditions, and aspects of L2 proficiency. It may be that older learners are less willing than younger learners to try out the L2 in the classroom and/or environment and this affective block might adversely affect their acquisition of L2 communicative skills but not their acquisition of academic L2 skills.

Different instructional conditions might also differentially exploit the strengths and weakness of older and younger learners. Thus, although the greater cognitive maturity of the older learner does appear to confer an advantage in acquiring cognitive/academic L2 skills, this is only one aspect of the issue to be considered in policy decisions. Stern (129, p. 292) has expressed this point: "On developmental grounds each age in life has probably its peculiar advantages and disadvantages for language learning. We must, without committing ourselves to a single age level, attempt to find (a) the ultimate proficiency levels that we think should be achieved in school. . . then (b) given different methodologies at our disposal, define the amount of time needed for effective language learning; and, lastly, (c) working downwards, decide in an experimental and pragmatic way, on the starting level and the approach, not forgetting educational considerations. In the sixties the mistake was made of expecting miracles merely by starting young. The miracles have not come about. Starting late as such is not the answer either."

Learning conditions

In considering learning conditions, a basic distinction to be made (Figure 1) is whether the L2 is learned in a supportive language environment in which it is used and is, therefore, "second language learning" in the specific sense, e.g. TESL, or whether it is learned in a language class in a non-supportive language environment and is "foreign language learning" in the specific sense, e.g. TEFL. If the L2 is learned in a supportive environment, the language class is likely to be only one among several language influences on the learner, the others coming from exposure to the TL in its natural setting. The millions of migrant workers in Europe, e.g. the Turkish, Spanish, or Italian *Gastarbeiter* in Germany, frequently acquire their Pidgin German entirely through exposure to the language in the natural environment and have no formal instruction whatever (72). But if the L2 is learned in an FL class in a non-supportive environment, instruction is likely to be the major or even the only source of TL input. This is precisely the condition under which most FL teachers in North America operate. Making this distinction does not mean that instruction in a supportive environment is less important than in a non-supportive environment, but the role of instruction is different in these two conditions. In this section, the neglected aspect of research, the language class, will be emphasized.

The language class or, more broadly speaking, educational treatment—objectives, content (language and culture), teaching strategies, curricula, social arrangements of the language class (e.g. individualization, Community Language Learning), and evaluation procedures—can be looked upon as the creation of different language learning environments. The educational treatment may involve fairly radical strategic actions such as putting language learners into a supportive language environment, e.g., through an exchange program, or deliberately creating a supportive language environment, e.g., an immersion program. The educational treatment interacts with the social context and particularly the language setting referred to above. Of these three factors—social context, language setting, and educational treatment—it is the educational treatment that can most readily be modified and adjusted to different social and language environments, and to individual learner factors. This gives educational treatment a special importance and makes research on it all the more imperative.

Research on undirected language learning in the natural environment

As we saw at the beginning of this chapter, language learning research in the 1970s began on a wave of reaction against research on educational treatment and against the acrimonious debate on the merits of the audiolingual vs. the cognitive approach. Turning away from these frustrating arguments researchers examined natural or free-learning of a language outside a classroom setting.

For example, the Heidelberger Forschungsprojekt "Pidgin Deutsch" (The Heidelberg Research Project on Pidgin German, 72) analyzed the "undirected *natural* acquisition of German by Spanish and Italian migrant workers." It carefully studied the interlanguage grammar of these workers and attempted to relate their language learning to the social and individual learner factors governing such undirected language learning. The investigators found that length of stay was only significant for the first two years. After that, age at time of immigration and contact with Germans during leisure and at the place of work were most significantly related to the proficiency level reached.

In an American elementary school setting, Wong Fillmore (47) has investigated social and cognitive strategies used in L2 acquisition in a one-year longitudinal study of five Spanish-speaking children learning English. She observed how these children interacted with native speakers. There were enormous differences in the extent to which the children sought out the company of English speakers and desired to identify with them. After three months of exposure to English, the most social and outgoing child, Nora, had learned more English than two of the others would learn by the end of the year. Among the *social strategies* identified by Wong Fillmore are:

1 Join a group and act as if you understand what's going on.
2 Give the impression—with a few well-chosen words—that you can speak the language.
3 Count on your friends for help.

The following *cognitive strategies* were identified:

1 Assume that what people are saying is directly relevant to the situation at hand, or to what they or you are experiencing. Metastrategy: Guess!
2 Get some expressions you understand and start talking.
3 Look for recurring parts in the formulas you know.
4 Make the most of what you've got.
5 Work on big things first; save the details for later.

Although these strategies have been identified in a naturalistic setting where the L2 learners are interacting with native speakers, they are potentially relevant for foreign language educators who are concerned with encouraging their students to communicate in the foreign language both inside and outside the classroom. The extent to which these cognitive strategies can be taught or encouraged within a conventional classroom setting is worth investigating. It should be noted that in both these investigations social contact with native speakers in the natural language environment has been an important factor in the development of proficiency.

The main theoretical concepts that aroused widespread interest since the mid-seventies were Schumann's acculturation theory (see pp. 210–12 above) and Krashen's Monitor Model with its distinction between language *learning* and *acquisition,* to be discussed shortly. Both theories by implication are negative about the contribution of language teaching. According to Schumann "language learning is not a matter of method, but is a matter of acculturation, and where acculturation cannot take place. . . we cannot expect to achieve much more than we are now achieving in our foreign language programs" (118, p. 47). With reference to the Monitor Model, it has been said that "many of the activities traditionally used in the classroom are directly involved with language learning (as distinct from language acquisition) and the Monitor Model claims that proficiency in speaking L2 cannot be obtained by explicit language learning" (Gingras, 62, p. 90).

Research on language teaching

One consequence of the lack of interest of the prevailing language learning theories in teaching has been that pedagogy has continued to change and develop without research. Individualization of instruction was introduced in FL education from the beginning of the 1970s (Altman and Politzer, 4) without any systematic research and only very few evaluative studies, (e.g., Grittner and LaLeike, 63). A number of new methods gained vogue in language teaching during the 1970s: the Suggestopedic Method, the Silent Way, Community Language Learning; but no consistent or prolonged studies that systematically analyzed these methods were undertaken. It is hardly possible to find in the literature unbiased descriptions of these innovations with a few exceptions such as Stevick (136), let alone dispassionate examinations of the effect of these methods on specified groups of students. Numerous articles have been written about aspects of teaching methodology. Many of these very legitimately represent the experience of knowledgeable practitioners, but very little has been done to substantiate the wider applicability of these experiences through systematic research.

One of the most exciting events in FL education of the 1970s has been the European attempt to develop "an overall structure for a European unit/credit scheme for foreign language learning by adults" (Trim, 143). This scheme involves the creation of an international network of flexible language learning systems. It has been brought about by voluntary cooperation of a number of noted scholars and practitioners in Britain, Germany, Netherlands, France, Sweden, and other participating countries, meeting regularly under the auspices of the Council of Europe. It has not only yielded the *Threshold Level Syllabus* of English (van Ek, 147) and the *Niveau Seuil* for French (Coste et al., 31) it has also stimulated the development of new curricula such as those for the State of Hesse in West Germany and multimedia programs in English and German. While by a broad definition this tremendous international effort can itself be regarded as research, the authors of this scheme have so far not made any move to back up these exciting developments by empirical studies. Does the Threshold Level Syllabus really meet the communicative needs of travelers? Indeed, Richterich, one of the main architects of this scheme, is quite contemptuous of any research effort when he writes:

> Some people, for instance, must use the scientific illusion, which they pass on to others, that it is useless and wrong to try to chage anything without first having carried out, with all the necessary scientific rigour, a number of fundamental and definitive studies on the motivations and needs of adults or of certain groups of adults learning a modern language. A complex, cumbersome structure is thus set up to carry out long-term studies which, once finished, are usually out of date because all sorts of events (new theories; new experiments; new facts; social, economic, or political evolution or revolution) constantly alter the hypotheses, situations and conditions of analysis (111, p.5).

Not all the experts participating in the European scheme take such a cavalier attitude to empirical research; yet this opinion is not atypical of the kinds of arguments that are often advanced against research on language teaching.

There have been a few notable exceptions to this general lack of research on the educational treatment aspect during the 1970s. Savignon's pioneer experiment on communicative language teaching (115) is too well known to need description here. Less known among foreign language teachers in the United

States may be the research on French immersion. Introduced as an innovation in Canada in the mid-1960s, French immersion was investigated systematically over a fifteen-year period. From the point of view of FL learning it is noteworthy because it is an attempt to create deliberately a TL learning environment. The research on immersion programs that emanated from the main research centers in Montreal, Toronto, and Ottawa has demonstrated the value of the cooperation between teachers, administrators, and researchers over a prolonged period in establishing a language teaching innovation: "The two principal research teams, the Language Research Group at McGill and the Bilingual Education Project at the OISE Modern Language Centre, have developed an ongoing commitment to monitor these experiments, changing the research strategy as certain questions were answered and new questions arose" (Stern, 126, p. 172). To our knowledge, nothing comparable has occurred in other innovations of the 1960s or 1970s. Anyone who would wish to study the impact of research on FL policy and curriculum development would find it rewarding to examine the literature on French immersion in Canada (e.g., 69; 80; 126; 132; 133; 134; 137).

Another language teaching innovation that was also carefully monitored by research was the British Pilot Scheme in the teaching of French in the primary schools of England and Wales. The National Foundation for Educational Research undertook a ten-year study of this experimental development of the teaching of French in junior grades of British elementary schools from 1964 to 1974 (Burstall et al., 13). It compared the progress of children who had started learning French as an FL at age eight with children who had started French at age eleven and concluded that on balance the early start was not cost-effective. The NFER study is a good example of a comprehensive long-term investigation of a language teaching innovation with interesting general findings on FL teaching and learning in a school setting. The NFER report had, however, a mixed reception. The negative tone of its main conclusion was criticized because of its important policy implications (Stern and Weinrib, 134). In retrospect, a disadvantage was that a major policy decision, namely whether or not to recommend an early start in FL education, was to be based on a single major investigation. If several groups of researchers had tackled the same question in different areas, with different populations, perhaps from different perspectives, and with different research methodologies, the ensuing debate could have given the policy maker a more diversified picture of the issues involved. It might not have made the policy decision any easier, but the strengths and limitations of research results would have become more evident.

A third example of a research approach to L2 teaching is the Schools Council Bilingual Project (SCBP) in Wales. In comparison with the immersion programs in Canada, it is characterized by a more deliberately designed teaching methodology but a less formal and less extensive approach to program evaluation. This project was designed to provide greater opportunities for communicative use of Welsh in the school context for children who were learning Welsh as a second language. The project had its origin in the Gittins Report (Central Advisory Council for Education [Wales], 23) which recommended the establishment of "bilingual schools" that would make systematic use of Welsh as a part-time medium of instruction in the infant (pre-kindergarten, kindergarten and grade one) and junior (grades two to five) schools. The report suggested that Welsh could be learned effectively if it were used during play activity and as a medium of instruction for "peripheral" subjects that constitute half the school day.

In 1968 the recommendations of the Gittins Report were implemented in the Schools Council Project on "Bilingual Education in the Primary Schools in Anglicized Areas." Sixty schools originally participated in the project, and in recent years an increasing number of primary schools in anglicized areas have adopted the SCBP approach to teaching Welsh as a second language. Although originally it was intended that up to half the school day be devoted to instruction through the medium of Welsh, in practice there has been considerable variation in the amount of time devoted to Welsh depending upon factors such as the availability of Welsh-speaking home-room teachers and willingness of teachers to devote time to Welsh. The project has been formally evaluated (Schools Council Committee for Wales, 117) and it has been reported that the project was considerably more effective in teaching Welsh than traditional Welsh-as-a-second language programs and had no detrimental effects on children's overall academic or intellectual progress.

The teaching methodology of the SCBP was influenced by the theoretical work of Dodson (38) and colleagues (39), who argued that effective L2 learning would result only when opportunities for meaningful communication were integrated with the teaching of the structure of the language itself. Dodson proposed an eight-step cycle of learning activities designed to lead the learner from pure imitation towards creative use of the L2.

A final example of an attempt in the 1970s to investigate language teaching by research methods are two major international studies on the teaching of French and English as FLs undertaken by the International Association for the Evaluation of Educational Achievement (IEA) (Carroll, 19; Lewis & Massad, 81). The IEA English and French projects developed tests in both languages that were based on an analysis of curricula at two stages of language achievement attained by FL learners in the participating countries, i.e. fourteen-year olds (Population II) and pre-university students (Population IV). The tests developed as a result of these studies therefore represent the international consensus of what proficiency to expect of language learners in regular school systems at these two levels. The tests were administered to carefully selected samples of students, e.g., to close on 30,000 students in eight countries in the French study. The test results were related to data about students, parents, teachers, and the conditions of learning that had been collected simultaneously through national, school, teacher, and student questionnaires. These two international inquiries formed part of a large international research program in which student achievement in different curriculum subjects was studied in some twenty-two countries. The questions to which these two studies sought answers were those that teachers, administrators, and some researchers in foreign language education had repeatedly raised around 1970 and in many cases are still asking in 1980. A major finding of the French study confirmed one that has also been found in the Canadian immersion projects, i.e., that time devoted to L2 is a key factor in student achievement. Like the British study, the IEA French study poured cold water on an early start in the elementary school.

While this investigation has much more to offer than can be detailed here, it remains a survey study, and as such, as Carroll, the writer of the report recognized, leaves many questions unresolved, thus requiring "conduct of further empirical studies, with more attention to the examination of selection and treatment effects over time than could be given in a survey study like the present one" (19, p. 279).

A number of investigators have become more and more convinced that language learning research must not ignore the educational treatment factor. Several attempts to describe the events of the FL classroom objectively have already been made in the course of the last decade. Adaptations of the Flanders' Interaction Analysis Technique (Flanders, 50), developed by Moskowitz (88), Wragg (152), and others, have been useful in sensitizing new teachers to the social climate of the language class.

In an Alberta study on teaching French by an audiovisual program, McEwen (84) developed a classroom observation scheme, the L2 Category System. She recognized that the events of the language class, even in very simple, structured programs, are not uni-dimensional. McEwen's scheme allowed for three dimensions and demanded a threefold analysis in terms of content, thought processes, and verbal functions. In applying this system she recorded as many as twenty-seven events per minute. Other investigators have tried to focus on particular aspects in the language class. For example, Allwright (3) and Chaudron (24), investigating error correction, have noted the frequent misunderstandings between teachers and students that occur when teachers correct errors.

A comprehensive scheme for FL classes is one recently developed by Fanselow (44) called FOCUS: 'Foci for Observing Communication Used in Settings'. His scheme distinguishes five features: source, medium, use, content, and pedagogical purpose. Fanselow's intention is to describe and conceptualize what "teachers actually do." Another approach has been to apply to language classes a scheme of linguistic analysis developed in Britain by Sinclair and Coulthard (123) that analyzes a lesson in terms of discourse functions and moves. Basing French language classroom observation on a scheme derived partly from Fanselow and partly from Sinclair and Coulthard, an observational study, undertaken in the OISE Modern Language Centre, tried to analyze the differences between learning French in a conventional (Core), class and in an immersion class. The differences can be illustrated by this example from the unpublished report.

The Core class teacher restricts language use to a minimal level due to the students' basic level of competence. Sentence structure is simple, functional, without digressions. Questions are brief, frequently followed by a single-word response and exact repetition. The Immersion teacher on the other hand expands, elaborates, and digresses using language in a natural and expanded manner. The following interactions exemplify these traits:

Immersion:

T	*Pos. Eval'n*	Oui, c'est très bien.
	Disciplinary Directive	Je répète, James, que pour que l'enregistremente soit utile, on évite de faire des bruits par—comme tu es en train d'en faire. Tu n'as pas touché à ton cahier.
	Pos. Eval'n.	Oui, Anne. Anne a absolument raison.
	Comment	Andréa a répété la dernière phrase qui était copiée au tableau. C'est "Soudain le feu est passé au vert" et Andréa a continué en disant "Le feu est passé au vert quand le vieux monsieur a lâché le poteau il a —"
	Implicit Correction	Ah, c'est pas. . .
S	*Response*	Oh—"aussitôt qu'il a lâché le poteau"
T	*Accept*	Oui, c'est ça.

Core:

T	*Spec. Info.*	Qu'est-ce que c'est? Jason. *(picture cue)*
S	*Response*	Matin.
T	*Explicit Correction*	*Le* matin.
S	*Repetition*	Le matin.
T	*Accept*	Oui.
	Spec. Info.	Et ça? Danny. *(picture cue)*
S	*Response*	L'après-midi.
T	*Accept*	Uh huh (nodding).

What investigators, e.g., Allwright (2), are moving towards but have not yet discovered are comprehensive and theoretically sound models for investigating language instruction models that would be helpful in the description and analysis of all kinds of L2 teaching. As Naiman et al (89) noted:

> ...the absence of an empirical scheme analyzing language teaching was felt to be a disadvantage and led to ad hoc inquiries on relevant aspects of teaching. Research should therefore be conducted into the identification and classification of teaching techniques and into the effectiveness of alternative techniques for different kinds of students (p. 101).

The observation schemes that have so far been developed appear to lack criteria by which to capture the essential and specific characteristics of L2 teaching and learning. These could perhaps be discovered if we related L2 teaching more deliberately to the process of L2 learning.

Language learning process

Theoretical considerations

From the perspective of L2 teaching, it is rewarding to relate the theoretical conceptualizations of the 1970s on L2 learning to interpretations of language learning developed in language pedagogy. This is not far-fetched. FL teachers inevitably make fundamental assumptions about language learning. The controversies about language teaching, it can be argued, reflect the main difficulties encountered by learners; and different pedagogical approaches, curricula, and teaching strategies represent attempts to overcome them. The concepts of language learning research are in many instances theoretical reformulations of issues that have also been concerns of language teachers.

Language pedagogy between 1900 and 1980 and language learning research between 1950 and 1980 have tried to come to grips with four major language learning problems:

1 The first is that of the disparity between the inevitable dominance in the mind of the learner of the L1 and other languages previously learned, and the inadequacy of the learner's knowledge of the second language: *The L1-L2 connection.*

2 The second is the problem of choice between deliberate, "conscious," or relatively cognitive ways of learning an L2 and the more "subconscious," automatic, or more intuitive ways of learning an L2: the *explicit-implicit option.*

3 The third issue is the learner's problem of how to cope with the dilemma presented by the fact that it is impossible for an individual to pay attention to linguistic forms, the language as a code, and simultaneously to communicate in that code: The *code-communication dilemma.*
4 A final problem is how best to represent the "macro" process of the learning of a language as a developmental sequence from a hypothetical beginning to a hypothetical end: *Language learning as a developmental process.*

The L1-L2 connection

The one-hundred year old debate in FL pedagogy between the "traditional" or "grammar-translation" method and the "direct" method centers around the L1-L2 connection. Should the L2 learner be encouraged to exploit his L1 knowledge and learn the L2 crosslingually through his L1, or should he keep his L2 learning completely separate and learn the L2 entirely within and through the L2, *intralingually*? As a psycholinguistic theory of L2 learning this conflict reappeared in 1954 in Ervin and Osgood's differentiation (Osgood and Sebeok, 98) between coordinate (intralingual) and compound (crosslingual) bilingualism. Around 1960 contrastive analysis was a re-affirmation of the importance of L1 in the learning of an L2. The rejection by some researchers of the contrastive hypothesis (e.g., Dulay and Burt, 40) from around 1970 represents a shift towards accounting for L2 learning in intralingual rather than crosslingual terms. On the other hand, Schumann's acculturation theory in the same decade was concerned again with the learner's attempt at resolving the problem of moving from his L1 as an existing reference system to the TL as a new reference system.

Selinker's concept of "interlanguage" (121) or other similar concepts that recognized the systematic nature of the learner's language assumed that the learner to a certain extent develops his own L2 system on the basis of his L1. What remained controversial was, as was noted above, whether the interlanguage is predominantly a reconstruction of the L2 on an L1 basis (the Restructuring Hypothesis) or whether the interlanguage is "created" by the learner independently of L1 influences, (the Creative Construction Hypothesis). The advocates of the Creative Construction Hypothesis looked for inherent principles of L2 development and for parallelism between L1 learning in early childhood and L2 learning. Thus, the Restructuring Hypothesis assumes the learner's L1 as a basis for L2; it is in that sense a crosslingual theory of L2 learning. The Creative Construction theory by contrast offers an intralingual interpretation of L2 learning. When Corder makes a case for an interlanguage continuum "intermediate between the restructuring and the recreation hypothesis" (29, p. 90), this view of the language learning process parallels a pedagogic compromise between an intralingual (e.g., direct method) and a crosslingual (e.g., translation) teaching strategy. Neither in learning research nor in FL pedagogy has this issue been resolved and in both areas it demands further investigation.

The explicit-implicit option

A second issue is whether the language learner should treat the language task intellectually and systematically as a mental problem, or whether he should avoid thinking about the language and absorb it more intuitively. As a choice of teaching methodologies, it crystallized between 1965 and 1970 (e.g., Carroll, 15) in the debate on the relative merits of the cognitive or the audiolingual approach. It was the subject of numerous studies and discussions. Carton (22) around the same time advocated the concept of *inferencing:* "A language pedagogy that utilizes inferencing removes language study from the domain of mere skills to a domain that is more closely akin to the regions of complex intellectual process" (pp. 57-58). In short, Carton opted for an explicit rather than an implicit strategy of teaching.

In recent research on language learning this question reappeared as the Monitor theory, developed by Krashen (76) who together with some colleagues, carried out a series of theoretical and experimental studies between 1972 and the present. These studies explored the explicit-implicit distinction as different ways of language learning.

Setting out from the distinction between language *learning* (explicit) and language *acquisition* (implicit), Krashen views language *learning* as a conscious process, acquisition as more subconscious. To learn a language (consciously) the learner must know the rules of the language. Given these conditions he can 'monitor' his linguistic output. Developing the construct of a "Monitor," Krashen has argued that the Monitor acts as a kind of editor. It comes into play particularly in reading and writing in the L2 because under these conditions there is time to go over and check the linguistic output. In some communication the Monitor would tend to interfere with fluency. Some language learners overuse the Monitor and become inhibited, others are overconfident and underuse it. For the development of L2 proficiency, the acquisition process in Krashen's view is more important than learning. In other words, proficiency develops more through use in communication than through conscious study and the slow control of the language by the Monitor.

McLaughlin (85) has questioned the Monitor theory and particularly the distinction between conscious "learning" and subconscious "acquisition," preferring instead the more behavioral and less mentalistic distinction between "controlled" and "automatic" processing. In our view, the entire discussion is inadequately related to the psychology of learning, where conscious and deliberate learning has for decades been contrasted with such concepts as social learning, latent learning, and blind learning, without considering these distinctions dichotomous. Drawing attention to the same distinction between learning with or without understanding, the eminent psychologist Hilgard wrote long ago in *Theories of Learning* (73):

> What is the place of understanding and insight? Some things are learned more readily if we know what we are about. We are better off as travelers if we can understand a timetable or a road-map. We are helpless with differential equations unless we understand the symbols and the rules for their manipulation. But we can form vowels satisfactorily without knowing how we place our tongues, and we can read without being aware of our eye movements. Some things we appear to acquire blindly and automatically; some things we struggle hard to understand, and can finally master only as we understand them (p. 8).

Unlike Krashen, Hilgard avoids a rigid choice between learning and acquisition when he writes: "Because all learning is to some extent cognitively controlled, the distinction between blind learning and learning with understanding becomes on of degree" (p. 343).

How to relate deliberate and more automatic learning to each other in L2 learning has remained another unresolved issue in pedagogy as much as in language learning research.

The code-communication dilemma

The third issue, the code-communication dilemma, has become a major focus of interest in recent years. Classroom language teaching is mainly concerned with code, and is therefore "formal," or as Dodson (37) calls it, "medium-oriented," whereas language use in the natural language environment is "communicative" or, again in Dodson's terms, "message-oriented." Both the formal and communicative teaching and learning strategies have in fact always been known, but in the past it was taken for granted that a language is learned in the classroom through study and practice. The use of communication as a deliberate teaching strategy is a relatively recent development. (e.g., Allwright, 2; Stern, 127). The Canadian immersion programs or the Welsh Bilingual Project, for example, have demonstrated that even in a quasi-FL+ situation, a communicative strategy can be an effective means of language teaching. It creates in a school setting the "field" conditions of language learning through communication.

The interplay between formal learning of the language as a code and the learning of the language through use in communication aroused most wide-spread attention in the late 1970s, but the relative contribution of formal and communicative strategies to effective language learning is another question that has largely remained unresolved (d'Anglejan, 35; Stern, 127).

Language learning as a developmental process

As a developmental process, L 2 learning can be viewed in an idealized way as a progression from zero proficiency to 100 percent, full, or native-like proficiency, and it can be thought of as divided into stages. The problems that arise in the real world are that the progression is hardly ever a regular one, that it often is arrested at some point well below the ideal end point, and that learners not infrequently regress.

Any language curriculum implicitly makes assumptions about the entire L2 developmental process. For example, when Halliday et al. (66) and Mackey (82) insisted on grading and sequencing the language input, the assumption was that it would facilitate learning. A recent conception of the learner's language development is offered by Trim's justification of the Council of Europe Unit/Credit Scheme of a curriculum for adult language learners (143). He writes:

> The idea of language development as a straight-line process does not stand up to closer inspection. We are not all marching at different speeds along the same road towards a common goal (p. 7). We abandon the aim of leading the learner step-by-step along a path from the beginning to the end of the subject. Instead, we set out to identify a number of coherent but restricted goals relevant to the communicative needs of the learner (p. 9).

The question, of course, is whether adult learners in fact fit this very challenging non-linear interpretation of the progression in a new language. Research on the developmental sequence does not yet have the answer to this question. But the issue has started to be investigated through interlanguage studies (see pp. 206–9).

The foregoing discussion shows that the parameters of language learning research—perhaps unintentionally—have been close to the problems that have been for many years areas of controversy in language pedagogy. Consequently, such research can be expected to be highly relevant to the concerns of FL teachers.

The claim has been advanced (Stern, 131) that good language teaching and learning must involve the development of strategies that meet these four basic issues of language learning. So far this claim has never been put to the test in any systematic way. The empirical research on the FL learning process has only dealt with particular aspects.

Empirical studies

Various approaches have been tried to study the L2 learning process directly; among them: observation of language learners in action, interviews with language learners, introspections about learners' cognitive or affective learning experiences, and experimental studies.

In the early 1970s Joan Rubin (114) the well-known sociolinguist, began to pursue the idea of investigating language learning by studying the "strategies" of successful language learners. She observed language classes directly or on videotape, listened to tapes of students discussing their own strategies, observed herself in language learning situations, and elicited observations from second language teachers. On this basis she established a provisional list of learning strategies. She defined strategies as techniques or devices that a learner may use to acquire L2 knowledge, Rubin suggests that the good language learner is 1) a willing and accurate guesser, 2) has a strong drive to communicate, 3) is often uninhibited about his weaknesses in the L2 and ready to risk making mistakes, 4) is willing to attend to form, 5) practices, 6) monitors his speech and compares it to the native standard, and 7) attends to meaning in its social context.

The OISE Modern Language Centre also undertook studies of language learning strategies and processes. The first approach, similar to Rubin's attempts to examine the strategies of good language learners based on a list developed by Stern (131). In one of these enquiries, the investigators Naiman et al., (89) probed the learning strategies of some thirty outstanding adult language learners through intensive retrospective interviews. The successful learners who were asked to recall the ups and downs of their language learning careers expressed a consensus among some of the strategies to be employed: a combination of formal self-instruction with the attempt to immerse themselves in a communicative setting. This study found that "...good language learners take advantage of potentially useful learning situations and if necessary create them. They develop learning techniques and strategies appropriate to their individual needs" (p. 25).

In another study (Wesche, 149) Canadian civil servants learning French were videotaped in their classes and the videotapes were later analyzed for behavioral clues characterizing successful language learning. The subjects were also interviewed. The observational data suggested that "realistic, communicative use of the second language, talking about the language (perhaps reflecting both an analytical and interest component), the number of different kinds of learning activities pursued, and an element of persistence are characteristic of those students who most rapidly improve their L2 fluency in this intensive training situation" (p. 422). The interviews brought to light a diversity of practice activities, insight, interest in ways of learning and remembering, and personal involvement. Wesche found that her findings had much in common with a theoretical information processing model that had been presented by Carroll (16) in Volume 6 of the ACTFL Series.

A classroom observation study at the high school level, on the other hand, in the Good Language Learner Project of the OISE Modern Language Centre did not reveal anything of value about learning strategies, probably because the highly structured setting of the conventional classroom did not offer students opportunities for displaying noticeable strategies. But interviews with the same high-school students were somewhat more revealing: the great variety of opinions about classroom language learning gave support to the idea of individualization. Moreover, the students' answers suggested that they had distinct likes and dislikes about different classroom activities, and that therefore their criticisms "could be more constructively used if students were induced to reflect about their learning situation so as to identify reasons for their negative or positive reactions towards specific learning tasks and activities" (89, p. 81).

A productive approach to the study of language learning in progress is a research method developed by Hosenfeld, which has become familiar to readers of ACTFL Series through an account that Hosenfeld gave of this method in Volume 7. Briefly, she invites students individually to perform typical language learning exercises in textbooks and simultaneously to think aloud as they complete the exercise. Through these introspections, Hosenfeld has been able to discover in concrete and vivid detail how students tackle learning tasks. A recent study (Hosenfeld, 74) is a useful check on a well-known sequential classification of drills as mechanical, meaningful, and communicative (Paulston & Selekman, 104). In this study Hosenfeld was able to show that a student in an individualized program, bypassing all the drills offered by the text, immediately applied the fairly advanced grammatical explanations to examples drawn from her own life experience. In other words, she moved straight from a grammatical explanation to an imagined communicative situation. This simple interview method of enquiry does reveal a student's learning strategy, and shows the assumptions that teachers or textbook writers had made about the learning process did not necessarily agree with the procedures actually employed by the learner.

A valuable and as yet insufficiently explored source for studying language learning is to invite sophisticated language learners to record their experiences. Among a few such records that are available, mention should be made of a language learning diary which Wilga Rivers (112) kept during a six-weeks' stay in Latin America. Such records lend themselves to an analysis in terms of strategies or learning difficulties. An insightful analysis of the experiences and enormous difficulties in learning Danish was made by Terence Moore (87), an English psychologist who was appointed to the Chair of Clinical Psychology at the University of Aarhus in Denmark. He divides his account into the problems of decoding and comprehension and encoding and expression, and he further illustrates the frustrations resulting from feeling restricted in communication events such as listening to lectures, participating in small group meetings and face-to-face conversations, and in taking part in casual talk with academic colleagues. As a clinical psychologist, he was led by his experiences to empathize with patients who suffer from language handicaps.

A third approach that has been tried during the past few years in order to come to grips with understanding the L2 learning process is one developed by Bialystok and consisting of specific experimental tasks within a theoretical framework. Bialystok (11) developed a model of L2 learning that was broadly based on the language learning models referred to on page 199; it incorporated aspects of Krashen's Monitor, the distinction between formal and communicative strategies, as well as the explicit and implicit categorizations described above. The Bialystok model has the merit of being designed to account for all language output, comprehension as well as production, and it relates to learning in a formal (classroom) as well as to an informal or natural setting.

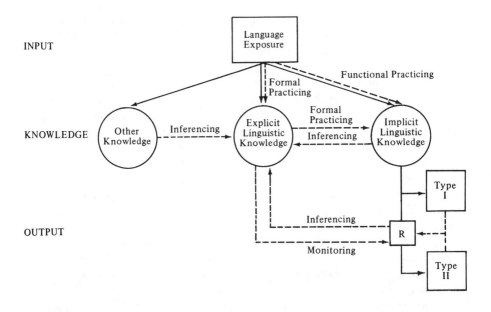

Figure 3. Model of Second Language Learning
(Bialystok, 1978).

_____ Processes
_ _ _ _ _ _ _ Strategies

This model is on three levels, labeled *input, knowledge,* and *output.* At the input level we are outside the learner and take note of the sources of language which impinge on him. At the knowledge level we are, so to speak, inside the "black box" in which we visualize three stores: the first, "Other Knowledge," consists of the learner's L1 and all the information he has gathered about languages and the world in general. The second and the third stores are those that contain the TL knowledge. Some of this knowledge that is consciously held consists of grammar rules, vocabulary knowledge, and so on: the Explicit L2 Knowledge Store. The Implicit Knowledge Store contains intuitively known items in the new language. The system comes into action through processes that activate all three knowledge stores. A small number of strategies that the learner may or may not employ link the input, knowledge, and output levels with one another: formal or functional (communicative) practice, monitoring, and inferencing. The output of this system is of two types: Type I is immediate and spontaneous, e.g., talking to people, or listening to a radio broadcast. The Type II output is slower and more deliberate, e.g., doing a written classroom exercise with an emphasis on rules, a written test, or reading a text—all tasks that make it possible to go over one's performance and check and correct it. It is in Type II output that the Monitor can come into play.

With this framework Bialystok has devised a number of ingenious experiments in which the input is deliberately modified, and the use of different strategies is then studied. For example, in one set of experiments Bialystok (10) studied the inferencing strategy by examining the effect of different cues on the comprehension of a reading passage in a foreign language: what difference does it make if we provide a picture, a summary of the gist of the passage, or a glossary of words used in the passage (dictionary), or if, instead of these aids, we give a short lesson on "how to inference"? The results of this study suggested that the deliberate provision of different kinds of contextual help (pictures, dictionary, and lesson) help learners in different ways: a thematic picture aids in global understanding, a glossary provides both global assistance and assists the reader at the detailed word level. A lesson in inferencing in this instance proved less effective than the more specific aids of a picture or dictionary.

In another experiment (9) grades ten to twelve high school students and a group of adults learning French had to listen to correct and incorrect sentences in French, e.g., *Maman a donné un petit pain à Paul et el a mangé le; Il s'est dépêché mais l'autobus était déjà parti.* In one of the experiments the subjects had only to listen to each sentence and indicate if it was correct or contained a grammatical error. In a second experiment, subjects had to determine which part of speech was in error. In the third experiment, they were given a list of nine rules (e.g., the object pronoun comes directly before the verb) and they had to identify the rule that was broken. This study was undertaken to examine the distinction between implicit intuitive knowledge and the more explicit knowledge of the language. As a result of this study, Bialystok was led to the pedagogical conclusion that "the learner's intuition (his implicit knowledge store) must be developed and encouraged, and efficient strategies for consulting explicit knowledge must be trained... Concentration on only the formal aspect of the language and rule formation not only precludes important aspects of the language but ignores as well the learner's great intuitive source" (9, p. 101).

Conclusion on the learning process

As a result of the type of investigations of which we have given a few examples, the knowledge of learning strategies and processes has been advanced to a certain extent during the past decade. However, the overall picture of L2 learning is still not very clear. At a global level the researcher cannot yet give authoritative guidance to the curriculum developer about the right way of planning a language curriculum because the developmental process of L2 learning is not well understood. We still do not know in any definitive way what differences exist between the learning processes in the child or the adult learning a second language. Nor do we know with any degree of assurance what helps some learners to reach a high level and what causes others to fail or to become arrested at a low level of language. Even a highly sophisticated language learner like Wilga Rivers (112), in spite of her vast and unrivalled knowledge of language teaching and learning, as a language learner is not immune from the frustrating minor difficulties that would also inhibit the learning efforts of a far less sophisticated learner. The studies undertaken by Hosenfeld and Bialystok are a beginning in developing a fund of empirical data on L2 learning.

The logical next step of research would be to attempt, on the basis of the theoretical and empirical findings now at our disposal, to construct a comprehensive model of the language learning process and to test it by means of the kinds of empirical methods which have been developed. The aim of such research remains, as before, to better understand L2 learning under different conditions, at different age or maturity levels, and at different levels of proficiency. The pragmatic test of such research would be that it could help in an improved design of curricula and that it would offer help to learners with difficulties in acquiring a second language.

Conclusion: Research directions

This review of second language learning research has not attempted to cover every aspect. For example, we have said little about human relations in language learning, and the important question of remembering and forgetting has not even been mentioned. However, enough has probably been covered to show that significant advances have been made in theory and in empirical research to provide a basis for a somewhat better understanding of second language learning and for undertaking the necessary further studies. A considerable number of areas of ignorance and uncertainty have been identified.

One of the main characteristics of research in the 1970s has been that it has dichotomized L2 acquisition in a 'natural' setting and L2 learning in instructional settings. The main research emphasis has been on natural acquisition processes while learning from instruction has received far less attention.

Given that language learning may have as its source of input the natural language environment or organized instruction, a timely resolution for the 1980s would be to include in future language learning research a systematic program of study on aspects of L2 teaching in association with research on L2 learning. Such research would of course not ignore the influence of the social context and the language situation, which may or may not be supportive. But because only the educational treatment can be controlled, it should play a more important role in language learning research than it has done in recent years.

A research program that would continue to consider the many aspects indicated in Figure 1 could not be carried out in a short time, by a single researcher, or even by a single institution. It is a long-term undertaking that would demand specialization as well as cooperation among several research centers and could not be done without the participation of informed practitioners. While some researchers may wish to focus on specific but important aspects of L2 learning, L2 forgetting, the affective component, or personality, and others will continue to work on undirected learning in the language setting, we feel it would be appropriate at this state of development to include a systematic research program of studies on L2 teaching.

Research on L2 teaching of course does not mean either research on global "methods" as it was understood in the 1960s or on this or that technique out of context. For example, the President's Commission Report (107) emphasizes the value of drama in FL teaching. This could of course be one such aspect to inquire into. But it would be naive to investigate this technique in isolation and without considering in what kinds of situations, for what kinds of students, at what stage in a program, and to what extent this technique is to be employed as well as how it relates to other language learning activities. Consequently thought will have to be given in the first instance to a general model of FL instruction enabling us to view particular studies in a theoretical framework. The model we have used to discuss learning is an example of a framework within which educational treatment could be considered.

Within the context of a general model, research on aspects of L2 teaching can be thought of as requiring four approaches, which in many instances could give rise to more restricted specific studies contributing to a better understanding of the aspect in question and ultimately to better L2 teaching.

1 A first approach consists of *theoretical enquiries* into concepts, ideas, and problems in a historical perspective and in relation to relevant disciplines. The theoretical study should identify the major issues to investigate. We have attempted to indicate what they might be. Thus the teaching-learning strategies referred to on pp. 228–32 have hardly yet been systematically investigated. Taking the crosslingual-intralingual dimension as an example, the role of L1 in L2 instruction is still unresolved in spite of a century of debate about translation and the direct method. As House (75) has pointed out, the role of translation in language pedagogy has never been given a theoretically adequate analysis. This, then, would be an argument for theoretical and historical studies on translation in language teaching. The same would apply to the other strategies referred to and to other aspects of language pedagogy.

2 *Descriptive studies,* including surveys, observational data, questionnaire and interview findings constitute a second approach. They are needed in order to find out how educational practice in a variety of contexts concretely deals with the issue in question. If we want to know about the use of translation and other crosslingual techniques in L2 instruction, investigations are needed to discover how at different levels of instruction, in different language learning situations, crosslingual or intralingual techniques are used. Such descriptive studies should lead to information about current experience with this aspect of language teaching, and they would indicate the questions and problems that arise for teachers and students.

3 On the basis of the fact-finding studies in a theoretically defined framework, a third group of studies can be envisaged. These would be relatively *small-scale experimental studies* of the kind illustrated by the work of Bialystok, Hosenfeld, and others. In this way, particular teaching techniques, e.g., translation, role playing, inferencing and so on, can be more systematically explored in a laboratory or small-scale classroom setting.

4 If these small-scale studies are promising, variations in teaching strategies can be deliberately introduced under controlled conditions into larger-scale and *longer-term teaching studies* in which teachers in various language learning circumstances (e.g., urban/rural, adult/child, beginners/advanced), in different systems, and in various languages would be invited to cooperate. Such cooperative ventures would put the experimental conditions to the test in the regular circumstances of foreign or second language instruction in different social contexts and different language settings, and enable researchers to formulate generalizations of a more substantial kind than has previously been possible.

These four research approaches must be regarded as overlapping and cyclic. As new facts or problems come to the surface, the enquiry process can be repeated so that a research approach is implanted into the process of development and innovation of language instruction, and a substantial body of theory, research, and documentation on actual practice is gradually built up.

Concluding comment

We do not wish to suggest that, for FL teaching, research on teaching and learning of the kind that has been discussed here is more important than, say, basic research on the languages, literatures, and cultures, or more important than curriculum development, or more important than creativeness in pedagogical practice. However, the research component has been neglected in the past and it has not been given sufficient emphasis in the President's Commission Report (107). We would therefore urge that in responsible L2 policy development for the 1980s—as was recognized by J.B. Carroll twenty or even thirty years ago, at an earlier stage of development—a strong research component be acknowledged as vitally important.

References, Language teaching/learning research: A Canadian perspective on status and directions

1 Allen, J. Patrick. *A Three-Level Curriculum Model for Second Language Education.* [Keynote address presented at the Spring Conference of the Ontario Modern Language Teachers' Association, Toronto, Ontario, April 1980.] [Mimeo.]

2 Allwright, Richard L. "Language Learning through Communication Practice." *ELT Documents* 3(1976): 2–14.

3 _____ "Problems in the Study of the Language Teacher's Treatment of Learner Error," 96–109 in M. K. Burt and H. C. Dulay, eds., *New Directions in Second Language Learning, Teaching, and Bilingual Education.* Washington: TESOL, 1975.

4 Altman, Howard B., and Robert L. Politzer, eds. *Individualizing Foreign Language Instruction: Proceedings of the Stanford Conference, May 6–8, 1971.* Rowley, MA: Newbury House, 1971.

5 Appel, René. *The Acquisition of Dutch by Turkish and Moroccan Children in Two Different School Models.* [Unpublished research report, Institute for Developmental Psychology, Utrecht, 1979.]

6 Asakawa, Yoshio, and John W. Oller, Jr. "Attitudes and Attained Proficiency in EFL: A Sociolinguistic Study of Japanese Learners at the Secondary Level." *SPEAQ Journal* 1(1977):71–80.

7 Asher, James J., and R. Garcia. "The Optimal Age to Learn a Foreign Language." *Modern Language Journal* 53(1969):334–41.

8 _____ and B. Price. "The Learning Strategy of the Total Physical Response: Some Age Differences." *Child Development* 38(1967):1219–27.

9 Bialystok, Ellen. "Explicit and Implicit Judgements of L2 Grammaticality." *Language Learning* 29(1979): 81–103.

10 _____ "Inferencing: Testing the 'Hypothesis-Testing' Hypothesis." [Unpublished manuscript, 1980.]

11 _____ "A Theoretical Model of Second Language Learning." *Lan-*

guage Learning 28:1(1978):69–83.

12 Brown, H. Douglas, ed., *Papers in Second Language Acquisition.* Special Issue, *Language Learning* 4 (1976).

13 Burstall, Clare, Monika Jamieson, Susan Cohen, and Margaret Hargreaves. *Primary French in the Balance.* Windsor, England: NFER Publishing Company, 1974.

14 Canale, Michael, and Merrill Swain. "Theoretical Bases of Communicative Approaches to Second Language Teaching and Testing." *Applied Linguistics* 1(1980):1–47.

15 Carroll, John B. "The Contributions of Psychological Theory and Educational Research to the Teaching of Foreign Languages," 93–106 in A. Valdman, ed., *Trends in Language Teaching.* New York: McGraw-Hill Book Company, 1966.

16 _____ "Learning Theory for the Classroom Teacher," 113–49 in Gilbert A. Jarvis, ed., *The Challenge of Communication.* ACTFL Foreign Language Education Series, v. 6. Skokie, IL:National Textbook Company, 1974.

17 _____ "The Psychology of Language Testing," 46–69 in Alan Davies, ed., *Language Testing Symposium: A Psycholinguistic Approach.* London: Oxford University Press, 1968.

18 _____ "Psychometric Approaches to the Study of Language Abilities," 13–31 in C. J. Fillmore, D. Kempler, W. S. Y. Wang, eds., *Individual Differences in Language Ability and Language Behavior.* New York: Academic Press, 1979.

19 _____ *The Teaching of French as a Foreign Language in Eight Countries.* New York: John Wiley, 1975.

20 _____ "Wanted: A Research Basis for Educational Policy on Foreign Language Teaching." *Harvard Educational Review* 30:(1960)128–40.

21 _____ and Stanley M. Sapon. *Modern Language Aptitude Test* (MLAT). New York: The Psychological Corporation, 1959.

22 Carton, Aaron S. "Inferencing: A Process in Using and Learning Language," 45–58 in Paul Pimsleur and Terence Quinn, eds., *The Psychology of Second Language Learning.* Cambridge, England: Cambridge University Press, 1971.

23 Central Advisory Council for Education (Wales). *Primary Education in Wales.* London, England: HMSO, 1967.

24 Chaudron, Craig. "A Descriptive Model of Discourse in the Corrective Treatment of Learners' Errors." *Language Learning* 27(1977):29–46.

25 Chihara, Tetsuro, and John W. Oller, Jr. "Attitudes and Attained Proficiency in EFL: A Sociolinguistic Study of Adult Japanese Learners." *Language Learning* 28(1978): 55–68.

26 Clément, Richard. *Ethnicity, Contact and Communicative Competence in a Second Language.* [Paper presented at the International Conference on Social Psychology and Language, University of Bristol, July 1979.]

27 Coons, W. H., D. M. Taylor and M. A. Tremblay, eds., *The Individual, Language and Society in Canada.* Ottawa, Ontario: The Canada Council, 1977.

28 Corder, S. Pit. "Error Analysis, Interlanguage and Second Language Acquisition," 60–78 in Valerie Kinsella, ed., *Language Teaching and Linguistics: Surveys.* Cambridge, England: Cambridge University Press, 1978.

29 _____ "Language-Learner Language," 71–93 in J. C. Richards, ed., *Understanding Second and Foreign Language Learning: Issues and Approaches.* Rowley, MA: Newbury House, 1978.

30 _____ "The Significance of Learners' Errors." *IRAL* 5(1967):161–70. Also in Jack C. Richards, ed., *Error Analysis: Perspectives on Second Language Acquisition.* London, England: Longman, 1974.

31 Coste, Daniel, Janine Courtillon, Victor Ferenczi, Michel Martins-Baltar, Eliane Papo, and Eddy Roulet. *Un Niveau-seuil.* Strasbourg, France: Council of Europe, 1976.

32 Cummins, James. "Linguistic Interdependence and the Educational Development of Bilingual Children." *Review of Educational Research* 49 (1979):222-51.

33 _____ "Cognitive/Academic Language Proficiency, Linguistic Interdependence, the Optimal Age Question and Some Other Matters." *Working Papers on Bilingualism* 19(1979).

34 _____ "The Cross-Lingual Dimensions of Language Proficiency: Implications for Bilingual Education and the Optimal Age Question." *TESOL Quarterly* 14(1980), in press.

35 d'Anglejan, Alison. "Language Learning In and Out of Classrooms," 218-37 in Jack C. Richards, ed., *Understanding Second and Foreign Language Learning: Issues and Approaches.* Rowley, MA: Newbury House, 1978.

36 de Fazio, N. "Field Articulation Differences in Language Abilities." *Journal of Personality and Social Psychology* 25(1973):351-56.

37 Dodson, Carl J. "The Independent Evaluator's Report." In Schools Council Committee for Wales, *Bilingual Education in Wales, 5-11.* London, England: Evans/Methuan, 1978.

38 _____ *Language Teaching and the Bilingual Method.* London, England: Pitman, 1967.

39 _____ Ewen Price, and Ina Tudno Williams. *Towards Bilingualism.* Cardiff, Wales: University of Wales Press, 1968.

40 Dulay, Heidi C., and Marina K. Burt. "Errors and Strategies in Child Language Acquisition." *TESOL Quarterly* 8(1974):129-36.

41 _____ and Marina K. Burt. "You Can't Learn without Goofing: An Analysis of Children's Second Language 'Errors,'" 95-123 in Jack C. Richards, ed., *Error Analysis: Perspectives on Second Language Acquisition.* London, England: Longman, 1974.

42 Ekstrand, Lars Henric. *Bilingual and Bicultural Adaptation.* [Doctoral Dissertation, University of Stockholm, 1978].

43 Ervin-Tripp, Susan. "Is Second Language Learning Like the First?" *TESOL Quarterly* 8(1974):111-27.

44 Fanselow, John F. "Beyond Rashomon—Conceptualizing and Describing the Teaching Act." *TESOL Quarterly* 11(1977):17-39.

45 Farhady, Hossein. "The Disjunctive Fallacy Between Discrete-Point and Integrative Tests." *TESOL Quarterly* 13(1979):347-58.

46 Fathman, Anne. "The Relationship Between Age and Second Language Productive Ability." *Language Learning* 25(1975):245-53.

47 Fillmore, Lily Wong. "Individual Differences in Second Language Acquisition," 203-28 in Charles J. Fillmore, Daniel Kempler, and William S.-Y. Wang, eds., *Individual Differences in Language Ability and Language Behavior.* New York: Academic Press, 1979.

48 Fishman, Joshua A. "The Social Science Perspective." *Bilingual Education: Current Perspectives.* Arlington, VA: Center for Applied Linguistics, 1977.

49 Flanders, Ned A. *Analyzing Teaching Behavior.* Reading, MA: Addison-Wesley, 1970.

50 _____ "Teacher Influence in the Classroom," 103-16 in Edmund J. Amidon and John B. Hough, eds., *Interaction Analysis: Theory, Research, and Application.* Reading, MA: Addison-Wesley, 1967.

51 Frechette, Ernest A. "Directions of Research in the 1970s," 351-95 in Gilbert A. Jarvis, ed., *An Integrative Approach to Foreign Language Teaching: Choosing Among the Options.* ACTFL Foreign Language Education Series, vol. 8. Skokie, IL:

National Textbook Company, 1976.

52 Gardner, Robert C. "Social Psychological Aspects of Second Language Acquisition," in H. Giles and R. St. Clair, eds., *Language and Social Psychology*. Oxford, England: Basil Blackwell, 1978.

53 _____ and Wallace E. Lambert. *Attitudes and Motivation in Second Language Learning*. Rowley, MA: Newbury House, 1972.

54 _____ and Wallace E. Lambert. "Language Aptitude, Intelligence, and Second-Language Achievement." *Journal of Educational Psychology* 56(1965):191–99.

55 _____ and Wallace E. Lambert. "Motivational Variables in Second Language Learning." *Canadian Journal of Psychology* 13(1959): 266–72.

56 Genesee, Fred. "A Comparison of Early and Late Immersion." Montreal, Quebec: McGill University, 1979. [Mimeo.]

57 _____ "Is There an Optimal Age for Starting Second Language Instruction?" *McGill Journal of Education* 13(1978):145–54.

58 _____ "The Role of Intelligence in Second Language Learning." *Language Learning* 26(1976):267–80.

59 _____ "Second Language Learning and Language Attitudes." *Working Papers on Bilingualism* 16(1978): 19–42.

60 _____ and Else Hamayan. Individual Differences in Young Second Language Learners. [Unpublished research report, McGill University, 1979.]

61 Giles, Howard, Richard Y. Bourhis, and Donald M. Taylor. "Towards a Theory of Language in Ethnic Group Relations," 307–48 in Howard Giles, ed., *Language, Ethnicity, and Intergroup Relations*. London, England: Academic Press, 1977.

62 Gingras, Rosario C., ed. *Second Language Acquisition and Foreign Language Teaching*. Arlington, VA:

Center for Applied Linguistics, 1978.

63 Grittner, Frank M., and F. H. LaLeike. *Individualized Foreign Language Instruction*. Skokie, IL: National Textbook Company, 1973.

64 Guiora, A. Z. "Construct Validity and Transpositional Research: Toward an Empirical Study of Psychoanalytic Concepts." *Comprehensive Psychiatry* 13(1972):139–50.

65 _____ Beit-Hallahani, R. C. L. Brannon, C. Y. Dull, and T. Scovel. "The Effects of Experimentally Induced Changes in Ego States on Pronunciation Ability in a Second Language: An Exploratory Study." *Comprehensive Psychiatry* 13(1972): 421–28.

66 Halliday, Michael A. K., Angus McIntosh, and Peter Strevens. *The Linguistic Sciences and Language Teaching*. London, England: Longmans, Green and Co., Ltd., 1964.

67 Hamayan, Else, Fred Genesee, and G. Richard Tucker. "Affective Factors and Language Exposure in Second Language Learning." *Language Learning* 27(1977):225–41.

68 Hanna, Gila, Anthony H. Smith, Leslie D. McLean, and H. H. Stern. *Contact and Communication: An Evaluation of Bilingual Student Exchange Programs*. Toronto, Ontario: The Ontario Institute for Studies in Education, 1980.

69 Harley, Birgit, ed. "Alternative Programs for Teaching French as a Second Language in the Schools of the Carleton and Ottawa School Boards." *Canadian Modern Language* 33: 2(1976).

70 Hatch, Evelyn. "Acquisition of Syntax in a Second Language," 34–70 in Jack C. Richards, ed., *Understanding Second and Foreign Language Learning: Issues and Approaches*. Rowley, MA: Newbury House, 1978.

71 _____, ed. *Second Language Acquisition: A Book of Readings*. Rowley, MA: Newbury House, 1978.

72 Heidelberger Forschungsprojekt "Pidgin-Deutsch". 'The Acquisition of German Syntax by Foreign Migrant Workers," 1-22 in David Sankoff, ed., *Linguistic Variation: Models and Methods*. New York: Academic Press, 1979.

73 Hilgard, Ernest R. *Theories of Learning*. New York: Appleton-Century-Crofts, 1948.

74 Hosenfeld, Carol. "Cora's View of Learning Grammar." *Canadian Modern Language Review* 35(1979): 602-7.

75 House, Juliane. *A Model for Translation Quality Assessment*. Tübingen, Germany: Verlag Gunter Narr, 1977.

76 Krashen, Stephen D. "The Monitor Model for Second Language Acquisition," 1-26 in Rosario Gingras, ed., *Second Language Acquisition and Foreign Language Teaching*. Arlington, VA: Center for Applied Linguistics, 1978.

77 _____ "A Response to McLaughlin, 'The Monitor Model: Some Methodological Considerations.'" *Language Learning* 29:1(1979):151-67.

78 _____ Michael A. Long, and Robin C. Scarcella. "Age, Rate and Eventual Attainment in Second Language Acquisition." *TESOL Quarterly* 13(1979):573-82.

79 Lambert, Wallace E. "Culture and Language as Factors in Learning and Education," 55-83 in A. Wolfgang, ed., *Education of Immigrant Students*. Toronto, Ontario: The Ontario Institute for Studies in Education, 1975.

80 _____ and G. Richard Tucker. *Bilingual Education of Children: The St. Lambert Experiment*. Rowley, MA:Newbury House, 1972.

81 Lewis, E. Glyn, and Caroline E. Massad. *English as a Foreign Language in Ten Countries*. New York: Wiley, 1975.

82 Mackey, William Francis. *Language Teaching Analysis*. London, England: Longman, 1965.

83 Mareschal, Roger. "Normes linguistiques: Détermination, description, contenu, utilité." *Canadian Modern Language Review* 33(1977):620-31.

84 McEwan, Nelly Z. *An Exploratory Study of the Multidimensional Nature of Teacher-Student Verbal Interaction in Second Language Classrooms*. [Unpublished Doctoral Dissertation, University of Alberta, 1976.]

85 McLaughlin, Barry. "The Monitor Model: Some Methodological Considerations." *Language Learning* 28:2(1978):309-32,

86 _____ *Second-Language Acquisition in Childhood*. New York: John Wiley and Sons, 1978.

87 Moore, Terence. "An Experimental Language Handicap (personal account)." *Bulletin of the British Psychological Society* 30(1977):107-10.

88 Moskowitz, Gertrude. "The FLINT System," in A. Simon and E. G. Boyer, eds., *Mirrors for Behavior*, 1. Philadelphia: Research for Better Schools, 1967.

89 Naiman, Neil, Maria Fröhlich, H. H. Stern, and A. Todesco. *The Good Language Learner*. Toronto, Ontario: The Ontario Institute for Studies in Education, 1978.

90 Oller, John W., Jr. "The Language Factor in the Evaluation of Bilingual Education," 410-422 in James E. Alatis, ed., *Georgetown University Round Table on Languages and Linguistics, 1978*. Washington, D.C.: Georgetown University Press, 1978.

91 _____ *Language Tests at School: A Pragmatic Approach*. New York: Longman, 1979.

92 _____ "Research on the Measurement of Affective Variables: Some Remaining Questions," in R. Andersen, ed. *New Dimensions in Research on the Acquisition and Use of a Second Language*. Rowley, MA: Newbury House, in press.

93 _____ L. Baca, and F. Vigil. "Attitudes and Attained Proficiency in ESL: A Sociolinguistic Study of Mexican Americans in the Southwest." *TESOL Quarterly* 11(1978): 173-83.

173–83.

94 _____ Alan Judson, and P. Liu. "Attitudes and Attained Proficiency in ESL: A Sociolinguistic Study of Native Speakers of Chinese in the United States." *Language Learning* 27(1977):1–27.

95 _____ and Kyle Perkins. *Language in Education—Testing the Tests.* Rowley, MA: Newbury House, 1978.

96 _____ Kyle Perkins, and Mitsuhisa Murakami. "Seven Types of Learner Variables in Relation to ESL Learning," 233–40 in J. W. Oller and Kyle Perkins, eds., *Research in Language Testing.* Rowley, MA: Newbury House, 1980.

97 _____ and Jack C. Richards, eds., *Focus on the Learner: Pragmatic Perspectives for the Language Teacher.* Rowley, MA: Newbury House, 1973.

98 Osgood, Charles E., and Thomas A. Sebeok, eds. *Psycholinguistics: A Survey of Theory and Research (with A Survey of Psycholinguistic Research, 1954–1964).* Bloomington, IN: Indiana University Press, 1967 [First published as a monograph in 1954].

99 Oskarsson, M. *Approaches to Self-Assessment in Foreign Language Learning.* Strasbourg, France: CCC/Council of Europe, 1978.

100 Oyama, S. "A Sensitive Period for the Acquisition of a Non-Native Phonological System." *Journal of Psycholinguistic Research* 5(1976): 261–85.

101 _____ "The Sensitive Period and the Comprehension of Speech." *Working Papers on Bilingualism* 16(1978):1–18.

102 Palmer, A. S., and L. K. Bachman. *Basic Concerns in Test Validation.* [Paper presented at the Fifteenth Regional Seminar of the SEAMEO Regional Language Centre, April 1980.]

103 Paulston, Christina Bratt. "Ethnic Relations and Bilingual Education: Accounting for Contradictory Data," 235–62 in James E. Alatis and Kristie Twaddell, eds., *English as a Second Language in Bilingual Education.* Washington, DC: TESOL, 1976.

104 _____ and H. R. Selekman. "Interaction Activities in the Foreign Classroom, or How to Grow a Tulip-Rose." *Foreign Language Annals* 9(1976):248–54.

105 Perren, George E., ed. *Foreign Languages in Education.* National Congress on Languages in Education Papers and Reports 1(1978). London, England: CILT, 1979.

106 _____, ed. *The Mother Tongue and Other Languages in Education.* National Congress on Languages in Education Papers and Reports 2(1978). London, England: CILT, 1979.

107 The President's Commission on Foreign Language and International Studies. *Strength Through Wisdom: A Critique of U.S. Capability.* November 1979.

108 Richards, Jack C. *Error Analysis: Perspectives on Second Language Acquisition.* London, England: Longman, 1974.

109 _____ "Models of Language Use and Language Learning," 94–116 in Jack C. Richards, ed., *Understanding Second and Foreign Language Learning: Issues and Approaches.* Rowley, MA: Newbury House, 1978.

110 _____, ed. *Understanding Second and Foreign Language Learning: Issues and Approaches.* Rowley, MA: Newbury House, 1978.

111 Richterich, René. "The Analysis of Language Needs: Illusion-Pretext-Necessity," 4–6 in *A European Unit/Credit System for Modern Language Learning by Adults.* Strasbourg, France: Council of Europe, 1978.

112 Rivers, Wilga M. "Learning a Sixth Language: An Adult Learner's Daily Diary." *Canadian Mod-*

ern Language Review 36(1979): 67–82.

113 _____ *Speaking in Many Tongues: Essays in Foreign Language Teaching.* Rowley, MA: Newbury House, 1972. (2nd ed., 1976).

114 Rubin, Joan. "What the 'Good Language Learner' Can Teach Us." *TESOL Quarterly* 9(1975):41–51.

115 Savignon, Sandra J. *Communicative Competence: An Experiment in Foreign Language Teaching.* Philadelphia, PA: Center for Curriculum Development, 1972.

116 Schermerhorn, R. A. *Comparative Ethnic Relations: A Framework for Theory and Research.* New York: Random House, 1970.

117 Schools Council Committee for Wales. *Bilingual Education in Wales, 5–11.* London, England: Evans/Methuen, 1978.

118 Schumann, John H. "The Acculturation Model for Second-Language Acquisition," 27–50 in Rosario C. Gingras, ed., *Second Language Acquisition and Foreign Language Teaching.* Arlington, VA: Center for Applied Linguistics, 1978.

119 _____ "Social Distance as a Factor in Second Language Acquisition." *Language Learning* 26(1976): 135–43.

120 Seliger, Herbert W., Stephen D. Krashen and P. Ladefoged. "Maturational Constraints in the Acquisition of Second Language Accent." *Language Sciences* 36(1975): 20–22.

121 Selinker, Larry. "Interlanguage." *IRAL* 10(1972):219–31.

122 Shuy, Roger W. "On the Relevance of Recent Developments in Sociolinguistics to the Study of Language Learning and Early Education." *NABE Journal* 4(1977):51–71.

123 Sinclair, John McH., and R. M. Coulthard. *Towards an Analysis of Discourse.* London, England: Oxford University Press, 1975.

124 Skutnabb-Kangas, T., and P. Toukomaa. *Teaching Migrant Children's Mothertongue and Learning the Language of the Host Country in the Context of the Socio-cultural Situation of the Migrant Family.* Helsinki, Finland: The Finnish National Commission for UNESCO, 1976.

125 Snow, Catherine E., and M. Hoefnagel-Höhle. "The Critical Period for Language Acquisition: Evidence from Second Language Learning." *Child Development* 49 (1978):1114–28.

126 Stern, H. H. "Bilingual Schooling and Foreign Language Education: Some Implications of Canadian Experiments in French Immersion," 165–88 in James E. Alatis, ed., *International Dimensions of Bilingual Education,* Georgetown University Round Table 1978. Washington, DC: Georgetown University Press, 1978.

127 _____ "The Formal-Functional Distinction in Language Pedagogy: A Conceptual Clarification." *Proceedings of the Fifth International Congress of Applied Linguistics,* Montreal 1978, forthcoming.

128 _____ "Language Research and the Classroom Practitioner." *The Canadian Modern Language Review* 34(1978):680–87.

129 _____ "Optimal Age: Myth or Reality?" *The Canadian Modern Language Review* 32(1976):283–94.

130 _____ Preface to Wilga M. Rivers' *Speaking in Many Tongues: Essays in Foreign-Language Teaching.* Rowley, MA: Newbury House, 1972.

131 _____ "What can we Learn from the Good Language Learner?" *The Canadian Modern Language Review* 31(1975)304–18; also 54–71 in Kenneth Croft, ed., *Readings on English as a Second Language for Teachers and Teacher Trainees.* Cambridge, MA: Winthrop Publishers, Second Edition, 1980.

132 _____ Merrill Swain, and Leslie D. McLean. *French Programs—Some Major Issues.* Toronto: Ontario Ministry of Education, 1976.

133 _____ Merrill Swain, Leslie D. McLean, Ronald J. Friedman, Birgit Harley, and Sharon Lapkin. *Three Approaches to Teaching French.* Toronto: Ontario Ministry of Education, 1976.

134 _____ and Alice Weinrib. "Foreign Languages for Younger Children: Trends and Assessments." *Language Teaching and Linguistics: Abstracts* 10(1977):5–26. Also 152–72 in Valerie Kinsella, ed., *Language Teaching and Linguistics: Surveys.* London, England: Cambridge University Press, 1978.

135 _____ Marjorie B. Wesche, and Birgit Harley. "The Impact of the Language Sciences on Second-Language Education," 397–475 in Patrick Suppes, ed., *Impact of Research on Education.* Washington, DC: National Academy of Education, 1978.

136 Stevick, Earl W. *Memory, Meaning and Method—Some Psychological Perspectives on Language Learning.* Rowley, MA: Newbury House, 1976.

137 Swain, Merrill. "Bilingual Education for the English-Speaking Canadian," 141–54 in James E. Alatis, ed., *International Dimensions of Bilingual Education,* Georgetown University Round Table. Washington, DC: Georgetown University Press, 1978.

138 _____ "French Immersion: Early, Late or Partial." *The Canadian Modern Language Review* 34 (1978):577–85.

139 _____ and Barbara Burnaby. "Personality, Characteristics and Second Language Learning in Young Children: A Pilot Study." *Working Papers on Bilingualism* 11(1976):115–28.

140 _____ and Birgit Harley. "Editorial." *Working Papers on Bilingualism* 19(1979):i–ii.

141 Tarone, Elaine, Merrill Swain, and Anne Fathman. "Some Limitations to the Classroom Applications of Current Second Language Acquisition Research." *TESOL Quarterly* 10(1976):19–32.

142 Taylor, Donald M., R. Meynard, and E. Rheult. "Threat to Ethnic Identity and Second-Language Learning," 99–118 in H. Giles, ed., *Language, Ethnicity, and Intergroup Relations.* London, England: Academic Press, 1977.

143 Trim, John L. M. *Some Possible Lines of Development of an Overall Structure for a European Unit/Credit Scheme for Foreign Language Learning by Adults.* Strasbourg, France: Council of Europe, 1978.

144 Tucker, G. Richard. "Comments on J. W. Oller, Jr. Research on the Measurement of Affective Variables: Some Remaining Questions," in R. Andersen, ed., *New Dimensions in Research on the Acquisition and Use of a Second Language.* Rowley, MA: Newbury House, forthcoming.

145 _____ Else Hamayan, and Fred Genesee. "Affective, Cognitive and Social Factors in Second-Language Acquisition." *Canadian Modern Language Review* 32(1976):214–26.

146 Valette, Rebecca M. "Some Reflections on Second-Language Learning in Young Children." *Language Learning* 14(1964):91–98.

147 van Ek, Jan A. *Systems Development in Adult Language Learning: The Threshold Level in a European Unit/Credit System for Modern Language Learning by Adults.* Strasbourg, France: Council of Europe, 1975.

148 Vollmer, H. J. "Why are We Interested in General Language Proficiency?" To appear in *Lingua et Signa,* Volume 1. Bern, Frankfurt, Las Vegas: Peter Lang Verlag, 1980.

149 Wesche, M. Bingham. "Learning Behaviours of Successful A Adult Students on Intensive Language Training." *Canadian Modern Language Review* 35(1979):415–30.

150 Wilkins, David. "Proposal for Level Definitions," 71–78 (Appendix C) in John L. M. Trim, ed., *Some Possible Lines of Development of an Overall Structure for a European Unit/Credit Scheme Foreign Language Learning by Adults.* Strasbourg, France: Council of Europe, 1978.

151 Witkin, C. A. Moore, D. R. Goodenough, and F. W. Cox. "Field-Dependent and Field-Independent Cognitive Styles and Their Educational Implications." *Review of Educational Research* 47(1977): 1–64.

152 Wragg, E. C. "Interaction Analysis in the Foreign Language Classroom." *Modern Language Journal* 54(1970):116–20.

10

The National Assessment of Educational Progress, foreign language education, and the future

Wayne H. Martin

National Assessment of Educational Progress

Introduction

National Assessment of Educational Progress, conducted by the Education Commission of the States under a grant from the U.S. Department of Education, was designed in the 1960s to monitor the nation's educational progress; it was designed to be an ongoing, long-term program with no specified end date. Although it has collected data since the spring of 1969, National Assessment has collected no data concerning foreign languages to date. The questions raised in this chapter deal with whether such an omission should continue, and, if not, what might be done.

As America enters the 1980s, many challenges face it—especially in the field of education. National Assessment is well aware of this, and its governing body, the National Assessment Policy Committee, is actively seeking to conduct an "assessment of the Assessment" to determine what modifications or adjustments need to be made to ensure its continued usefulness in the 1980s. The American Council of the Teaching of Foreign Languages might have suggestions and be a participant in these discussions.

Wayne H. Martin (University of Connecticut) is Director of Public Information for the National Assessment of Educational Progress. He has taught graduate courses in statistics and measurement and has conducted formative and summative evaluations for curriculum projects while with the Education Research Council of America. He has also had experience as associate director of a needs assessment program in New England for teacher education.

Section 1: History and description of National Assessment

Upon becoming Commissioner of Education, Francis Keppel was concerned that that the Office of Education was not being true to its original responsibility for the monitoring of the nation's educational progress. Accordingly, he initiated a series of events that led to the establishment of the National Assessment of Educational Progress. Between 1963 and 1969, the Exploratory Committee on Assessing the Progress of Education (ECAPE), chaired by Dr. Ralph Tyler, and its successor, the Committee on Assessing the Progress of Education (CAPE), chaired by Dr. George Brain, established the basic framework of an assessment program that would serve the needs of the education community, keep the public informed of the nation's educational progress, and provide the federal government with the data it desired. The fact that it took six years to accomplish this is indicative of the political and technical problems that faced both committees.

The resulting assessment program had to represent a balance between the concerns of educational policy makers and technical experts; between federal, state, and local government and educational agencies; and between the public and the education profession. Educators saw the assessment program as a potential attack upon them by the "elitist" leaders of the private foundations and Ivy League schools; they also saw it as a potential educational accountability tool that could threaten their autonomy and livelihood. State and local leaders saw it as further federal encroachment in the area of education—an area that was constitutionally their responsibility. Scholars feared that the assessment program would lead to an emphasis upon easily measured aspects of an individual's education at the expense of other learning areas and experiences. All of these groups plus the public suddenly saw the specter of national curricula and/or national performance standards being promulgated by the federal government. Federal officials saw the potential for a program that could serve everyone's interests and needs—everyone's but their own. They also recognized the potential for establishing an overly ambitious program that could seriously disrupt the delicate relationship between the federal government and state and local authorities in the areas of education. As a result of the voiced concerns and potential abuses, the program established by ECAPE and CAPE:

- was not limited to the traditional "3 Rs" or reading, writing, and arithmetic but covered ten learning areas (cited below) and allowed for the the addition of other learning areas in the future
- did not place its emphasis on the performance of individuals, schools, school districts, or states, but instead emphasized the performance of groups
- was not a mandatory but a voluntary, cooperative program
- would set up neither national criteria or standards for performance nor national core or standardized curricula but it would measure the attain-

ment of consensus goals or objectives (established by scholars, educators, and concerned lay people) in each of ten learning areas
- was not to be governed and/or controlled by the federal government but would represent a joint venture between the education community (which would have program and policy control) and the federal government (which would have funding control, fiscal responsibility, and program and policy input).

The assessment plan developed by ECAPE and implemented by CAPE was designed to determine what young Americans (at the ages of 9, 13, 17, and 26 to 35) know and can do in the following ten learning areas: Art, Career and Occupational Development, Citizenship, Literature, Mathematics, Music, Reading, Science, Social Studies, and Writing. More specifically the assessment program was to measure the knowledge, skills, and attitudes possessed by young Americans at key points in the education system (at the end of primary, intermediate, secondary, and formal postsecondary education) and to measure changes (growth or decline) in their educational attainments over time.

Under the auspices of the Committee on Assessing the Progress of Education, the assessment program began data collection with the assessment of seventeen-year-olds in the spring of 1969. The assessment program was placed under the governance and administration of the Education Commission of the States (ECS) on July 1, 1969. The Commission, an interstate compact of fifty states, American Samoa, Puerto Rico, and the Virgin Islands, has had responsibility for the program since then and will retain this responsibility under the terms of its current grant with the federal government through December 31, 1983.

At the point that ECS became responsible for the assessment program, it formally became the National Assessment of Educational Progress (NAEP) and the federal government assumed financial responsibility. Previously, the assessment had been funded largely through private foundation funds (the Carnegie Corporation, the Fund for the Advancement of Education, and the Ford Foundation). National Assessment was initially funded by the United States Office of Education (USOE) as a grant. In 1973 the National Center for Education Statistics (NCES) assumed federal administrative responsibility for the program and funded it by a sole-source contract. As a part of the Education Amendments Act of 1978, a statutory basis for the National Assessment was explicity established and federal administrative responsibility for the program was transferred from NCES to the National Institute of Education (NIE).

As a part of its governance and administration efforts, the Education Commission of the States established a policy committee for the assessment program. The National Assessment Policy Committee, whose members represent state and local education associations and the business community, provides direction and policy decisions. The Policy Committee has formally adopted the following goals for National Assessment:

To detect the current status and report changes in the educational attainments of young Americans. This represents National Assessment's original purpose as the program was developed by ECAPE and CAPE. It is the overarching goal for the program upon which all other goals are built.

To report long-term trends in the educational attainments of young Americans. This recognizes the ongoing, long-range nature of the assessment program and the unique information it will provide. Assuming that the continuity and integrity of National Assessment will be preserved, it will be possible to examine long-term trends as well as short-term changes and current status. The potential wealth of such information is truly awesome; its analogue, the U.S. Census Bureau, is only beginning to tap fully the wealth of data it now possesses.

To report assessment findings in the context of other data on educational and social conditions. This goal recognizes that while the assessment program must remain true to its original purposes and not adopt an experimental research design, its data are best utilized by examining them in terms of other educational and social data. It will be possible to accomplish this through additional analyses that link assessment data to other data bases and through minor alterations of data collection variables and techniques. This will ultimately result in greater policy relatedness of assessment data and in greater utility of the data for various levels of educational planners and decision makers.

To make the National Assessment data base available for research on educational issues, while protecting the privacy of both state and local units. This goal recognizes the assessment's commitments both to open access to its data base and to honoring the pledges of anonymity made to respondents and state and local education agencies who have voluntarily participated in the assessment program. The present staff and policy committee members encourage the concept of secondary analyses of assessment data and attempt to facilitate such projects whenever and wherever possible. Only through greater utilization of assessment data (by both staff and external researchers) will National Assessment's full potential be realized.

To disseminate findings to the general public, the federal government, and to other priority audiences. This goal reflects the lessons that the present staff have learned over the years. To be useful, data and findings must be widely disseminated and suited to the desired audiences. Reports developed only for the research community do not suffice. This initially resulted in underutilization of the data and a view of the assessment program as a statistical maze. The current dissemination efforts, which gear materials to the specific audiences being served, have been quite successful and have helped raise the general acceptance and visibility of the assessment program to its present status.

To advance assessment technology through an ongoing program of research and operation studies. This goal acknowledges the program's commitment both to greater efficiency (in terms of cost and data collection efforts), to continued refinement of measurement techniques, and to the development of new data collection and analysis techniques that enhance the usefulness of assessment results. The development of the primary trait scoring system for writing is an example of staff efforts in refining and evolving measurement techniques. Development of a four-year master sample and subsequent lowering of both sampling costs and burden on participating schools within that four-year period is an example of improved efficiency.

To disseminate assessment methods and materials, and to assist those who wish to apply them at national, state, and local levels. The final goal reflects National Assessment's obligation to share its methods and materials with various education agencies. The program's release to state and local education agencies and the research community of materials developed for its regular assessment areas and probes (Basic Life Skills, Health, Energy, and Consumerism assessments) have proven to be immensely helpful. NAEP staff have also developed an excellent assistance program; to date, thirty-nine states have applied portions of the assessment model, methods, and/or materials to their own programs.

The goals adopted by the National Assessment Policy Committee reflect the stage to which the program has now evolved. The goals acknowledge the potential of the assessment program, recognize the strides it has made thus far, and provide future direction. However, the goals are not considered to be immutable. Both the present staff and policy committee members realize that the goals must evolve as the assessment program continues to function.

During the eleven years that it has been collecting data, National Assessment has conducted and reported the initial assessment for nine-, thirteen-, and seventeen-year-olds in each of the ten learning areas originally selected for assessment. It has developed, conducted, and reported the first measurement of change in six learning areas and the second measurement of change in science. By the end of 1980, National Assessment will have reported the second assessment of writing and will be preparing to report the results of the first measurement of change in art, music, and literature as well as the second measurement of change in reading. Although the assessment of young adults (ages 26 to 35) was initially seen as part of each year's work, this assessment was placed on a periodic basis after the fifth year of data collection (1973–1974 school year) due to budgetary constraints.

National Assessment also recognizes that special needs for data not included in the ongoing assessment frequently arise. To address such needs, the program has added special purpose "probes." A probe is designed to be a small-scale assessment of a specific topic and is usually administered to only one age group. It is designed to provide a "snapshot" of the topic and not to measure change.

National Assessment has administered probes in basic life skills (1977) and consumerism (1978) for seventeen-year-olds and in health and energy (1977) for adults. In addition, the assessment program administered, analyzed, and reported the assessment of functional literacy of seventeen-year-old students under contract to the Right-to-Read Program. Probes provide National Assessment with the flexibility to address timely educational topics without disrupting its ongoing task of monitoring the nation's educational progress.

Section 2: Methodology of National Assessment   _____

Objectives Development. One distinguishing feature of National Assessment is that it is objective referenced. The project employs the consensus approach for objectives development, review, and redevelopment, and for item development and review. A particular objective or item must be judged as important for students to know or be able to do; this judgment is made by scholars in that learning area, educators responsible for transmitting that learning area to students, and concerned laypeople. The use of consensus should help prevent fads from appearing in the objectives, while the review and redevelopment of objectives prior to each assessment of a learning area ensures that new approaches and emphases are included. The objectives for each learning area are printed and made available to anyone interested.

Item Development. The items or exercises to be used for the assessment are developed specifically for National Assessment. They are objective referenced and written by a variety of item writers who are, for the most part, educators or learning specialists in the area being assessed. They are reviewed by individuals representative of the same major groups used in the development of the objectives, that is, scholars, educators, and laypeople. Reviewers are asked to evaluate items on the basis of stereotyping of or offensiveness to racial, ethnic, religious, political, social, and regional groups and organizations.

Although National Assessment uses multiple-choice items (and these predominate in some of the learning areas), many open-ended or free response items are also used. These range from items requiring a few words as answer to those requiring a long essay. The assessment materials are considered "consumable," and respondents are required to do all writing on them. This has allowed for the development of detailed scoring analyses for many of the open-ended items. During item development, writers attempt to produce formats that provide the most direct and practical measure of the objective to be assessed. Individual interviews, the manipulation of apparatus to solve a problem, and observations of the respondent's problem-solving techniques have been used to supplement the usual paper and pencil measures. To determine the effect of hand-held calculators on students' capabilities to compute, the recent mathematics assessment provided calculators for some respondents to use.

Items are tried out on small groups of students in order to eliminate specific problems of wording. Item analyses are used in an effort to locate problems, but items are *not* subjected to the usual item analytic procedures designed to maximize item discrimination and to secure item difficulties as close to 50 percent as possible. National Assessment tries to develop sets of items with a wide range of item difficulties. This is done because we want to know what young Americans of a given age know and can do—and we want to know this about most individuals, typical individuals, and the ablest individuals at that age.

Data Collection. National Assessment employs a multistage sample design that is stratified by region of the country, size of community, and socioeconomic level. This yields a representative national sample of public and private schools for each year's assessment. Participation in the assessment is voluntary for the schools selected for each year's assessment sample. Over 90 percent of the selected schools have participated in the assessment thus far. To reduce its impact upon school districts, NAEP draws a four-year master sample of schools. This allows the project to guarantee the vast majority of school districts that, if they are selected for participation in the sample, it will only be once during a four-year period. It is necessary, however, for National Assessment to include a portion of the school districts within the nation's twelve largest standard metropolitan sampling areas in each year's project to guarantee a valid sample, though these districts can be assured that a particular school within their system will be selected only once in a four-year period. A national probability sample of households is used for the adult assessment. The probability that any individual, either in or out of school, would be assessed more than once is extremely small.

National Assessment does not develop or use scores for individual respondents. It determines instead how each age level performs on specific items and, within an age level, how groups of individuals (based on demographic and sociological variables) perform. As a result it is not necessary for each repondent to take every item. The items are divided into booklets or packages, and each in-school respondent takes only one package. (Out-of-school respondents are allowed to take up to four assessment packages.) Since the samples for different packages are statistically equivalent, group comparisons can be made across packages. This allows NAEP to assess performance on far more items in a learning area than would normally be feasible. It also provides broader coverage of the objectives for each learning area.

In order to guarantee uniformity of data collection, the assessment is administered by specially trained personnel. Permanent district supervisors stationed all over the country have the responsibility for handling local assessments for NAEP. They do a portion of the assessment administrations themselves and hire and train local persons for the remainder. Thus, a school district is asked only to provide the students selected in the sample and space for the test administration. A student may choose not to participate. Most assessment materials are administered to groups of sixteen to twenty students using a paced tape technique. The administrator plays a recorded set of directions, with each question (including distractors of multiple choice questions) read aloud on the tape. The tape provides silence for a period of time sufficient to answer each question. This technique ensures uniform presentation of directions and provides respondents with reading problems an opportunity to hear the item as they are reading it. A paced tape is not used for either the reading assessments or for individually administered items. A maximum of fifty minutes is required from an individual student. These techniques guarantee a minimum of disruption to a school.

Approximately 1,500 schools participate in each year's assessment. The sample size for every assessment package administered at an in-school age is between 2,200 and 2,600 respondents. The sample size for young adults varies from 1,450 to 2,200 respondents for each group of four assessment packages. Depending upon the number of packages being assessed at each age, the total sample size for an assessment year has been between 70,000 and 100,000 individuals.

Student names are not recorded on the tests. They are used only for selection of the local sample. Thus, students are guaranteed anonymity. In addition, no reports are developed for school districts or for states. The sample design does not permit making inferences about any geographic unit smaller than a region. The United States is divided into four regions for sampling purposes.

Reporting. Results are reported for the nation, the four regions of the country, sex, race, size and type of community, and level of parental education for each age group. No comparisons are made of individual students, schools, school districts, or states.

The project reports results on all items and, in addition, releases the entire text of approximately half of the items. This allows for a detailed understanding of the assessment's purposes and construction and for greater flexibility in interpretation or further analysis. The unpublished items are kept secure and used in subsequent assessments of the learning area to measure change over time. Although the project does not interpret the assessment data, National Assessment learned from its first few reports that numbers and statistics alone are not sufficient for results to be widely used by the public, policy makers, or practitioners in the field. To meet the needs of these constituents, a variety of reports for each assessment is prepared, including selective reports (dealing with subsets of items) and an overview.

Technical reports are prepared for the research and evaluation units of state and local education agencies and the educational research community. In addition, a brochure that provides a nontechnical summary of the assessment is prepared. National Assessment involves representatives from various professional organizations in the development and review of objectives and items, the review of analysis and reporting plans, and the actual review of assessment results. The comments and reactions of practitioners are often included in special interpretation chapters of project reports. The early concerns about influences from a national program seem to have changed enough so that the interpretations developed by the various professional groups independent of NAEP are welcomed by the education community.

Services. The items released in National Assessment reports are made available to state and local education agencies and the research community for use in other assessment or evaluation projects. To facilitate the use of NAEP materials and methods, National Assessment has staff who provide service to state and local education agencies, federal agencies and panels, professional organizations, the education departments of foreign governments, international education organizations, the educational research community, and the general research community. The project also sponsors an annual conference on large-scale assessment that provides a forum for the discussion of policy and technical issues facing assessment/evaluation projects and for the sharing of ideas and technology.

National Assessment conducts regional meetings with a variety of its constituents (at the state, local, federal, and national levels) to review future plans, to consider possible new directions for the project and additional learning areas for assessment, and to critique current assessment procedures and policies. Mail surveys are also conducted to gather input from constituents. This input is shared with the project's two advisory committes (the Analysis Advisory Committee and the Exercise Development Advisory Committee) and the National Assessment Policy Committee, the governing body responsible for the establishment of policies and guidelines for the project.

Section 3: National Assessment and foreign languages ——

To date, National Assessment has conducted no assessments in the area of foreign languages. This has been the result of both history and historical decisions. When National Assessment was being designed in the 1960s, the goal was to establish a program that would measure the nation's educational progress in learning areas that spanned the school system. All ten of the learning areas initially selected for assessment met this criteria, from art to writing. In addition, the learning areas affected *all* students, not just a subset of students. Although the mathematics and science course offerings at the secondary level are often elective, there is a commonly recognized set of knowledge, skills, understandings, and concepts that all high school students should possess in these areas. This is true whether a student stopped taking science and mathematics courses once they were no longer required or is currently enrolled in advanced courses.

Unfortunately, foreign language education did not meet these criteria. Traditionally, foreign language instruction in this country has been limited to the secondary and/or post-secondary level—though some school systems also include it at the intermediate (junior high or middle school) level. Further, there is not a recognized set of knowledge, skills, understandings, and concepts in the field of foreign language that one wishes *all* students to posses. Foreign language education has been historically perceived as an elective for the advanced or college-bound student. Somehow, the public perception of foreign language education has elements of elitism and "snobbery" attached to it; at best, it is often seen as a "curricular frill" for gifted students.

Fortunately, this anachronistic view of foreign languages is gradually being replaced by a more realistic view of the role foreign languages play in the educational system. There has been a gradual recognition that America must educate her students to deal with the world and its problems—and that those problems do not end at America's shores. American society's gradual move to the metric system of measurement is one concrete indication of this move. The objectives developed for National Assessment's next survey of citizenship and social studies similarly indicate this move; these new objectives reflect the theme of global interdependence. The recent report from the President's Commission on Foreign Language and International Studies is perhaps the most concrete indication that this view is being changed.

What could be done by National Assessment to begin to gain a baseline of information about foreign language education? A simple starting point would be to collect information about the current status of foreign languages. Given that National Assessment uses a national sample of schools to collect its data and that every principal involved in the sample responds to a short question-naire, it would take very little to add a question about whether the school offers programs in foreign languages and what estimated percentage of students participate in such programs. If more detailed information were desired, it would be possible to develop a supplemental principal's question-naire for use in the field. Indeed, such questionnaires have been used by National Assessment to collect additional information about reading, art, music, and mathematics programs. The data derived from such a survey could then be used document the current status of foreign language programs.

Similarly, it would be possible to add a short question pertaining to foreign languages to the traditional background questions asked of students. Again, it would be possible to expand this from a single question to a series of questions pertaining to the student's perceptions of and attitudes toward foreign language instruction. For example, given the theme of global interdependence, a logical case could be made for why such a question should be included in the next assessments of citizenship and social studies. During the second assess-ment of mathematics (1977–1978 school year) and the third assessment of writing (1978–1979 school year), National Assessment developed fairly de-tailed background questions about course-takings, attitudes, and other ele-ments of these two learning areas. Similar work could be done in the area of foreign languages.

Finally, it would be possible to develop a regular assessment in the area of foreign languages. Given that foreign languages are still usually not taught at the elementary level across the country, such an assessment would probably best be designed as a "probe" limited to the two older in-school age groups (thirteen- and seventeen-year-olds) or simply to seventeen-year-olds. Or it would be possible to develop a special sample for use with a survey of foreign languages. For example, a special study was conducted (in conjunction with

National Assessment) to look at the achievement and participation of women in mathematics. To accomplish this study, thirteen-year-olds and high school seniors (rather than seventeen-year-olds) were surveyed. Because there was concern about gaining an adequate sample of students enrolled in advanced mathematics classes, such students were purposely oversampled in the twelfth grade. Thus it was possible to take a detailed look at males and females enrolled in such courses while at the same time using sample-weighting procedures to provide an accurate view of *all* twelfth-grade students. Similarly, the foreign language education community might determine that it wished to survey high-school freshmen and seniors rather than thirteen- and seventeen-year-olds.

Given National Assessment's expertise in working with scholars, educators, and concerned laypeople to develop objectives and exercises in other learning areas, the foreign language area would not seem to pose an insurmountable obstacle. And given the assessment's experience in devising ways to measure both musical and artistic performance, it should be able to develop measurement techniques in the foreign languages that go beyond traditional paper-and-pencil measures. National Assessment has a commitment to remain on the frontiers of educational measurement, and this commitment should allow it to work successfully with the foreign language education community to develop an assessment that would be a source of pride to all.

Editor's Note: As of this writing, the National Assessment program is in danger of curtailment due to the fiscal constraints growing out of attempts to balance the federal budget. If funding is drastically cut, National Assessment could be limited to its three R's mandate, a move that could preclude a future foreign language assessment as recommended by the report of the President's Commission on Foreign Language and International Studies. It behooves language educators and those in other fields to follow these developments as they continue to affect the broader educational domain.

Index to persons cited

Index to topics and institutions cited

263

XYZ

NTC PROFESSIONAL MATERIALS

ACTFL Review

Published annually in conjunction with the American Council on the Teaching of Foreign Languages

Foreign Language Proficiency in the Classroom and Beyond, *ed. James*, Vol. 16 (1984)

Teaching for Proficiency, the Organizing Principle, *ed. Higgs*, Vol. 15 (1983)

Practical Applications of Research in Foreign Language Teaching, *ed. James*, Vol. 14 (1982)

Curriculum, Competence, and the Foreign Language Teacher, *ed. Higgs*, Vol. 13 (1981)

Action for the '80s: A Political, Professional, and Public Program for Foreign Language Education, *ed. Phillips*, Vol. 12 (1980)

The New Imperative: Expanding the Horizons of Foreign Language Education, *ed. Phillips*, Vol. 11 (1979)

Building on Experience—Building for Success, *ed. Phillips*, Vol. 10 (1978)

The Language Connection: From the Classroom to the World, *ed. Phillips*, Vol. 9 (1977)

An Integrative Approach to Foreign Language Teaching: Choosing Among the Options, *eds. Jarvis and Omaggio*, Vol. 8 (1976)

Perspective: A New Freedom, *ed. Jarvis*, Vol. 7 (1975)

The Challenge of Communication, *ed. Jarvis*, Vol. 6 (1974)

Foreign Language Education: A Reappraisal, *eds. Lange and James*, Vol. 4 (1972)

Foreign Language Education: An Overview, *ed. Birkmaier*, Vol. 1 (1969)

Professional Resources

Complete Guide to Exploratory Foreign Language Programs, *Kennedy and de Lorenzo*

Award-Winning Foreign Language Programs: Prescriptions for Success, *Sims and Hammond*

Living in Latin America: A Case Study in Cross-Cultural Communication, *Gorden*

Teaching Culture: Strategies for Intercultural Communication, *Seelye*

Individualized Foreign Language Instruction, *Grittner and LaLeike*

Oral Communication Testing, *Linder*

Transcription and Transliteration, *Wellisch*

ABC's of Languages and Linguistics

 For further information or a current catalog, write:
National Textbook Company
4255 West Touhy Avenue
Lincolnwood, Illinois 60646-1975 U.S.A.